SERIAL KILLERS

ABOUT THE AUTHOR

William Harmening is a recognized expert in the area of criminal behavior and is the author of "Criminal Triad Theory," a widely-accepted psychosocial theory of criminality being taught in colleges and universities across the country. He serves as an adjunct faculty member at Washington University in St. Louis, Missouri, where he teaches undergraduate courses in forensic psychology and criminology. In addition to his teaching duties, he is also a 33-year law enforcement officer who has commanded statewide units in Chicago, Illinois tasked with investigating such crimes as securities fraud and child exploitation/pornography. He is a licensed polygraph examiner and a certified forensic hypnotist, providing both services to law enforcement agencies throughout Illinois, Missouri, and Indiana. He has spoken internationally on the subject of criminal behavior and has appeared on national television multiple times. This is his eighth book.

SERIAL KILLERS

The Psychosocial Development of Humanity's Worst Offenders

By

WILLIAM M. HARMENING, M.A.

*Adjunct Professor of Psychology
Benedictine University
Springfield, Illinois*

*Adler School of Professional Psychology
Chicago, Illinois*

CHARLES C THOMAS • PUBLISHER, LTD.
Springfield • Illinois • U.S.A.

Published and Distributed Throughout the World by

CHARLES C THOMAS • PUBLISHER, LTD.
2600 South First Street
Springfield, Illinois 62704

This book is protected by copyright. No part of
it may be reproduced in any manner without written
permission from the publisher. All rights reserved.

© 2014 by CHARLES C THOMAS   PUBLISHER, LTD.

ISBN 978-0-398-08788-3 (paper)
ISBN 978-0-398-08114-0 (ebook)

Library of Congress Catalog Card Number: 2014020428

With THOMAS BOOKS *careful attention is given to all details of manufacturing and design. It is the Publisher's desire to present books that are satisfactory as to their physical qualities and artistic possibilities and appropriate for their particular use.* THOMAS BOOKS *will be true to those laws of quality that assure a good name and good will.*

Printed in the United States of America
MM-R-3

Library of Congress Cataloging-in-Publication Data

Harmening, William M.
  Serial killers : the psychosocial development of humanity's worst offenders / by William M. Harmening, M.A., Adjunct Professor of Psychology, Benedictine University, Springfield, Illinois, Adler School of Professioal Psychology, Chicago, Illinois.
      pages cm
  Includes bibliographical references and index.
  ISBN 978-0-398-08788-3 (pbk.) -- ISBN 978-0-398-08114-0 (ebook)
  1. Serial murderers–Psychology. 2. Murderers–Psychology. 3. Personality development. 4. Homicide–Psychological aspects. I. Title.

HV6515.H357 2014
364.152'32019–dc23

2014020428

PREFACE

Whether it be Jack the Ripper in nineteenth-century England or Ted Bundy in 1970s America, the public has always been strangely fascinated by the criminal offender type we know as the *serial killer*. They are the subject of endless movies and books; the police and media assign them colorful monikers like comic book antiheroes; women agree to marry them while they await execution or live out their days in prison; and for the few who have never been caught, such as the infamous *Zodiac,* we continue to speculate and develop new theories about their identity decades after their crimes have ended.

But what is it that causes such evilness in an individual? What is it that compels a person to take an innocent life, not once but multiple times, and for no apparent reason beyond their own perverse psychological gratification? In the pages that follow we will explore this question by looking at the psychosocial determinants of criminal behavior, including serial murder. The role of such internal processes as *attachment, moral development,* and *identity formation* in the development of a person's predisposition to various forms of social deviance, including physical and sexual aggression, is reviewed. This information is then applied to actual serial killers in an effort to construct a psychosocial profile of each and to attempt to pinpoint the various developmental factors that contributed to their eventual criminality. Finally, early intervention strategies are explored that can potentially redirect a child's developmental trajectory away from crime and deviance, and toward a more adaptive and socially-acceptable behavioral repertoire.

CONTENTS

	Page
Preface	v

Chapter

1. INTRODUCTION 3
   Peering into the Mind of Evil

2. WHERE IT ALL BEGINS 23
   The Role of Attachment in Infancy

3. LEARNING TO FEEL 51
   The Role of Moral Development in Early to Middle Childhood

4. WHO AM I? 86
   The Role of Identity Formation During Adolescence (Part I)

5. CLOSING THE GAP 121
   The Role of Identity Formation During Adolescence (Part II)

6. CRIMINAL BEGINNINGS 135
   A Killer Is Born

7. DAVID BERKOWITZ: THE SON OF SAM 155
   An Ego-Directed Killer, Subtype: Deficient Sexual Self

8. CHARLES MANSON 174
   An Ego-Directed Killer, Subtype: Deficient Social Self

9. ERIC RUDOLPH: GOD'S CRUSADER 188
   An Ego-Directed Killer, Subtype: Hyper-Ideological Self

10. THEODORE "TED" BUNDY: THE FACE OF EVIL 199
    An Opportunistic Killer

11. EDMUND KEMPER: THE CO-ED KILLER 215
    A Symbolic Killer

12. THE ZODIAC KILLER 226
    A Lingering Mystery

13. INTERVENTION STRATEGIES 236
    Changing a Killer's Course Before They Kill

Bibliography 261
Index 267

SERIAL KILLERS

Chapter 1

INTRODUCTION
Peering into the Mind of Evil

INTRODUCTION

There are only three types of serial killers. During the last four decades, a number of typology schemes have been offered, many based on the apparent motive of the killer. But these types of schemes say little about the offender, at least little that can be used to identify such an individual in their preoffending stage of development. They tell us much about the killer's actions but say little about why those actions were viewed as a viable option in the first place. For example, it's easy to speculate that rage caused a killer to act as they did. But to truly understand this class of evildoers, we must first explore why they felt the level of rage they did, and further, why any amount of rage would lead them to kill multiple people. Also, while the emotion of rage has on many occasions led people to kill in the heat of the moment, the type of rage that leads one to commit multiple premeditated murders does not happen at a moment in time, but rather, develops over the course of a person's early psychosocial development. So once again, it is not enough to say that the person's rage caused them to kill, and that their rage was brought on by the victim's rejection of their sexual advances, for example. The fact is, for every serial killer who kills for reasons of rage, there are hundreds of thousands of people who experience that same rage and make the decision not to kill, or to commit any crime at all. So the question becomes, what is it in a serial killer's development that creates such a deadly pattern of behavior? That question will be the focus of our inquiry.

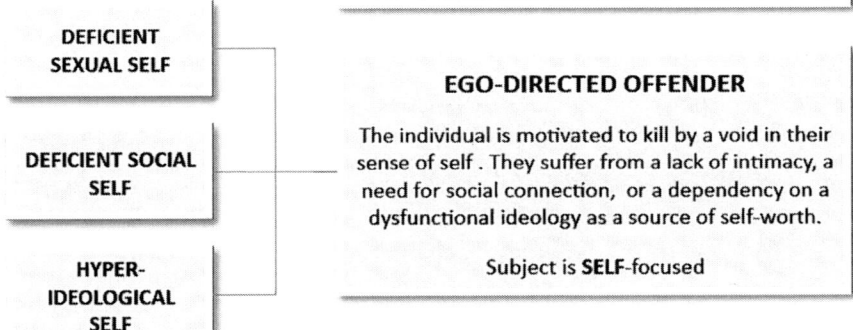

Figure 1.1. Serial killer types.

What are the three types of serial killer? As shown in Figure 1.1, the first is the *opportunistic* killer, or the person who simply kills for the enjoyment of the act, or for some material or psychological gain. The second is the *symbolic* killer, or the person whose victims serve as surrogates for someone else, such as an abusive parent. And the third type is the *ego-directed* killer, or the person whose heinous acts serve the purpose, at least in the short term, of filling some perceived void in their sense of self. Under this type we will discuss three subtypes: the *deficient sexual-self, deficient social-self,* and the *hyper ideological-self.* Another way of looking at this simple scheme is to say that the motivations empowering serial killings are either *other-focused* (symbolic), *act-focused* (opportunistic), or *self-focused* (ego-directed). Which type it is will determine the type of victims they select, the level of cruelty they may dole out, the extent to which rehabilitation is a possibility, and in the event that they have eluded identification and capture, the probability they will eventually cease their deadly routine. In the chapters to follow we will explore each of these serial killer types, including their psychosocial development, as well as their methods and the characteristics of the crime scenes they leave behind. While the foregoing is not intended as a *profiling* system per se, we will explore ways in which a thorough understanding of the serial killer's psychological functioning and development can lead to information and clues that will potentially benefit the investigation of an unknown serial offender.

Misconceptions

Many misconceptions have arisen over the years about serial killers, many the result of Hollywood's creative license. But still others, perhaps the majority, have been the product of an academic community's efforts to explain this purely psychological phenomenon from a sociological or criminological perspective, a truly difficult task, if not impossible. In doing so, they tend to look at serial killing at a point in time, typically the period of the killer's known offenses, rather than over the entire course of their psychosocial development, extending all the way back to their first year of life. As we shall see in the chapters to follow, the etiological factors giving rise to serial killing occur years before the serial killer ever takes their first victim. It is critical to our understanding of this phenomenon that we not let these misconceptions cloud our inquiry:

1. *Serial killers are motivated by the desire to gain power and control over their victims.* This is true only in the case of opportunistic killers, and not even all of them. Symbolic killers tend to seek power and control over the haunting remnants of a dysfunctional development. For them, their heinous acts are intended to quiet the demons that remain after years of parental abuse, neglect, or abandonment. The victims they select are simply a means to an end. And ego-directed killers seek power and control over their own sense of personal failure or emptiness. For them, the experience of their victims is secondary to their own. As we shall see, some ego-directed killers have little contact with their victims, killing them from a distance, or, in the case of Ted Kaczynski, a.k.a. the *Unabomber,* without ever laying eyes on them at

all. Obviously, gaining some level of power and control over his victims was not part of his motivation. He was motivated by a delusional ideology that was grounded in mental illness.

2. *Serial killers are psychopaths.* Hollywood has done a good job over the years portraying serial killers as psychopathic murderers who lurk in the shadows waiting for their unsuspecting victims to enter their kill zone. But nothing could be further from the truth. Psychopaths, by definition, suffer a disconnect from reality and a complete lack of moral awareness. While this is certainly true of some serial killers, most have been found through psychological evaluations of competency to be completely sane and fully connected to reality. Leon Festinger (1957), in his famous study of *cognitive dissonance,* found that completely normal people are quite capable of committing horrific acts, and then justifying those acts in ways that absolve them of any shame or guilt. Such is the case with certain serial killers. While their crimes, and the ways they justify those crimes, can certainly be said to be dysfunctional and outside the norms of acceptable behavior, in all other ways, many of them appear to be quite sane.

3. *There is a sexual component to all serial killing.* While it is true that certain serial killers are sexually motivated, many others are not. Many serial killings have no sexual component. David Berkowitz, the "Son of Sam" killer, shot his victims through the windows of their cars and then ran into the darkness without even taking the time to determine if his victims were dead. And Doctor Michael Swango, the "Dr. of Death," killed by injecting a deadly dose of various drugs into his patients. Again, there was no sexual component to his crimes. Also, it is important to distinguish between those who are sexually motivated and those who are motivated by deficits and dysfunctions related to *sexuality,* a much different thing. Those who are sexually motivated are primarily opportunistic offenders who rape, torture, and kill for sexual gratification. This gratification becomes a craving that must be satisfied. In contrast, the killer who is motivated by deficits in their sense of sexuality, the ego-directed killer, does not necessarily crave gratification, but rather, a need to feel differently about themselves in some significant way. They may rape and kill as a way of destroying what they can't have, or perhaps as a way of feeling a sense of power and control by controlling someone else with the ultimate power, the power over life and death. Either way, sexual gratification, which may not

even be possible, is less of a motivation than the need to fill some deficiency or void in their sense of self.

4. *Serial killers are beyond rehabilitation.* It would certainly seem that this is anything but a misconception. Many, if not most serial killers likely are beyond rehabilitation, but this has never been one of the goals of our postconviction efforts with these offenders, nor arguably should it be. And for those who have never been caught, such as California's "Zodiac Killer," we simply don't know if something changed their behavior and thinking to such an extent that it led them to permanently desist from their criminal ways. In other words, we don't know if they somehow rehabilitated themselves. In the chapters to follow, we will argue that in theory anyway, certain types of serial killers, specifically ego-directed and some symbolic offenders, are in fact capable of rehabilitation, and why. This is not to suggest that those efforts should ever be made, but to effectively answer this question could perhaps benefit our understanding of their development, and more importantly, allow us to more effectively target intervention efforts at an early age.

5. *We can profile serial killers based on the crime scenes they leave behind.* Very few serial killers have ever been found to be incompetent to stand trial due to mental illness. Most are as sane as anyone walking the street. With the ability to plan and anticipate, it is very easy for a serial killer to clean, manipulate, or even create a crime scene with the intent of leading investigators down the wrong path. Those who come from a psychological perspective will argue that even when a serial killer takes these types of steps, what they do in the process is still a significant reflection of their personality, and thus a potential clue. And so it is, but the traditional FBI style of profiling tends to assume that the crime scene is in its natural state. It is a profiling technique that has never really been developed beyond that limited capability. And with even serial killers being educated in our modern day by the endless supply of reality-based television shows, those among them who wish to protect their prospects for future victims will undoubtedly take steps to use their crime scenes to gain an advantage over the police. So we must be careful making any definitive judgments about an unknown offender from the characteristics of the crime scene alone. This is not to say the crime scene is not an important piece of psychological evidence, in addition to its obvious potential for physical evidence.

It absolutely is. Like all aspects of profiling, however, we must always be ready to adjust our beliefs and assumptions and not be limited by preconceived ideas and expectations.

6. *We should define serial killers by the number of victims attributable to them.* Much energy has been expended over the years, especially in the academic community, on the question of how we define and categorize serial offenders. There is still debate over the issue of exactly how many people a person must kill before we bestow upon them the infamous moniker, "serial killer." Currently, the most widely held consensus on this issue is that a person must kill a minimum of three people. Others argue for just two, and out there somewhere are those who undoubtedly are arguing for a higher number. But the whole issue of numbers does little to further our understanding of the developmental factors that can lead to a propensity to engage in such deviance. The numbers may be relevant, however, to our understanding of self-deterrence, even among serial killers. However, when we look at these offenders from a personality perspective, we focus on the personality and not the number of crimes. In fact, as we shall see in the discourse to follow, there are undoubtedly those with a developed propensity to engage in such deviance who never choose to cross that line.

A Word about Mental Illness

Very few serial killers meet the legal standard for *insanity*. In fact, very few meet even the mental health industry's diagnostic criteria for mental illness. In cases where the offender is clearly mentally ill, there really isn't much to be learned about serial offending. Perhaps there is much to learn from these people about mental illness, but to include them in our serial killer typology schemes is of little value, and only muddies the waters of any etiological study. If an offender truly is being instructed to kill by alien voices or dogs, then in our pursuit of the *why* of their crimes, we will likely end up no further than alien voices or dogs. In those cases, our focus need not be on their crimes or how they came to make such choices, but rather, and necessarily so, on the auditory hallucinations that compelled their deadly behavior, a pursuit better left to the world of neurology and psychiatry.

So for purposes of this text, we will not be addressing the issue of mental illness, or those who kill for reasons related to extreme psychosis. They and their unfortunate victims are a product of Man's complex yet fragile neurological system, and while developmental factors may have contributed to their syndrome, it is likely those factors are not directly linked to their offenses, as they are in the case of those serial offenders who will be the focus of this text. Put another way, there is no reason to believe that if any of these individuals were suddenly cured of their insanity, they would still commit their deadly crimes.

A Word about Organized Crime

Those who study and write about the phenomenon of serial killing eventually come to a point where they attempt to fit into their etiological model those who kill multiple people for gang- or mob-related reasons. After all, if we base our definition of serial killing in part on the number of victims, then many mobsters and gang members meet the criteria. But those who attempt to understand these typologies in the same context as the classic serial killer quickly run into problems. The problem is that very few measurable differences can oftentimes be found between these individuals and the nonoffending public. Their crimes don't result from a deviant need to kill, as in the case of the classic serial killer, but rather from issues related to group affiliation. Their crimes can thus best be explained in sociological terms rather than psychological. And while there are certainly psychological factors that can in part account for deviant group affiliation, it is really a much different issue than the psychosocial development of the serial killer's personality. For this reason, individuals who commit these types of murders are not included in our typology scheme or etiological model.

TYPOLOGY SCHEMES

Any study of the serial killer's mind requires that we first classify these offenders in a way that allows for the study and understanding of causative factors. There have been many classification schemes offered by members of the criminal justice and academic communities. All are different in many respects, and all are open to criticism. There has never been consensus on a single typology scheme to guide our research and understanding. We will look here at the two predominant schemes currently being employed.

The FBI Scheme: Organized versus Disorganized

According to the FBI Crime Classification Manual (Douglas, 2006), serial killing is defined as follows:

> The term "serial killings" means a series of three or more killings, not less than one of which was committed within the United States, having common characteristics such as to suggest the reasonable possibility that the crimes were committed by the same actor or actors.

The FBI categorizes serial killers as either *organized* or *disorganized*, with characteristics of both coming together in the *mixed* killer. Their system is intended to have utility in the investigation of unidentified serial killers by allowing investigators to look for similarities between their active crime scenes and those of serial offenders previously apprehended and incarcerated. The system was developed when members of the FBI's Behavioral Sciences unit interviewed 36 incarcerated serial killers during the early 1980s and catalogued all the known facts and variables they were able to ascertain. From their data, two predominant serial killer typologies emerged, and the belief that a killer's methods and crimes scene can in most cases point to which type of serial killer the case investigators should be looking for.

The organized killer, whom we can describe as *psychopathic*, is one who is well aware of the deviant nature of their acts. They typically plan out their crimes, select specific types of victims, and take significant steps to avoid detection. These killers will clean or manipulate their crime scenes, seldom leaving the bodies in the locations where they are killed, and may even plant evidence designed to lead investigators in the wrong direction. They are methodical killers who tend to follow the reporting of their crimes in the news media. Some have even attempted to get close to investigators working their cases, either socially or in some professional capacity. While some have done this for reasons of self-preservation, attempting to track the investigators' moves as closely as possible, others have done so simply to satisfy a perverse need for power and status.

In contrast, the disorganized killer, whom we can describe as *psychotic*, is oftentimes one who suffers from some type of mental illness. They may lack the ability to fully comprehend the criminality of their actions, and may even commit their crimes at the direction of some

Characteristics of the Organized Offender	Characteristics of the Disorganized Offender
• IQ above average, 105-120 range • socially adequate lives with partner or dates frequently • stable father figure • family physical abuse, harsh • geographically/occupationally mobile • follows the news media • may be college educated • good hygiene/housekeeping skills • does not usually keep a hiding place • diurnal (daytime) habits • drives a flashy car • needs to return to crime scene to see what police have done • usually contacts police to play games • a police groupie or wanabee • doesn't experiment with self-help • kills at one site, disposes at another • may dismember body • attacks using seduction • into restraints • keeps personal, holds a conversation • leaves a controlled crime scene • leaves little physical evidence • responds best to direct interview	• IQ below average, 80-95 range • socially inadequate • lives alone, usually does not date • absent or unstable father • family emotional abuse, inconsistent • lives and/or works near crime scene • minimal interest in news media • usually a high school dropout • poor hygiene/housekeeping skills • keeps a secret hiding place in the home • nocturnal (nighttime) habits • drives a clunky car or pickup truck • needs to return to crime scene for reliving memories • may contact victim's family to play games • no interest in police work • experiments with self-help programs • kills at one site, considers mission over • usually leaves body intact • attacks in a "blitz" pattern • depersonalizes victim • leaves a chaotic crime scene • leaves physical evidence • responds best to counseling interview

Figure 1.2. Organized versus disorganized serial killers.

imagined voice, character, alien, or animal. The disorganized killer tends not to seek out their victims in a methodical way but is more opportunistic, taking advantage of the opportunity to kill when it presents itself. They typically leave their victims right where they kill them, and are unconcerned about the crime scene they leave behind. Disorganized killers may leave a great amount of evidence behind, including the weapon they used. For this reason, these types of killers are much less likely than their organized counterparts to continue their killing sprees for extended periods of time.

Figure 1.2 illustrates a number of the differences found between the organized and disorganized typologies.

Criticisms: A number of valid criticisms have been leveled against the FBI's classification scheme. Canter et al. (2004) tested the validity of the FBI's dichotomy. They analyzed the patterns of co-occurrence of 39 different features identified from the crime scenes of 100 murders committed by 100 different serial offenders in America. These features, all related to the behavior of the killers, included such things as facial disfigurement, gagging, ligature strangulation, and rape. The researchers did a statistical analysis to determine the co-occurrence of each of these features with each of the others. If the FBI's dichotomy of organized vs. disorganized were valid, then two distinct subsets should emerge from such an analysis. In this case, no such dichotomy was found. Rather, they found a subset of features the FBI considers part of the organized typology being present in all serial killings. They also found that features related to the disorganized typology were rare and not co-occurring as a distinct subtype.

The researchers in this study concluded that methodological problems in the FBI's data collection process resulted in a dichotomy that lacks any validity. The greatest weakness of the FBI's method was the unstructured way they conducted their interviews of the 36 serial offenders, as well as a lack of random sampling. The agents involved developed their interviews in an *ad hoc* manner, depending on the particular offender being interviewed. They then simply divided their sample into two groups based on characteristics they felt would discriminate between them. Canter et al. (2004) believes these methodological flaws resulted in flawed data that was then used to develop their dichotomy.

O'Connor (2012) has pointed out a number of other weaknesses in the FBI's dichotomy, including the fact that the amount of evidence left behind at a crime scene, the basis for the FBI's typologies, ignores the context of the situation. The FBI scheme also has an inherent bias in favor of disorganized for crimes motivated by hate, anger, or domestic strife, as well as those committed while the killer was heavily influenced by alcohol or drugs. O'Connor points out that contrary to the FBI's scheme, *psychotic* is not the polar opposite of *psychopathic,* and thus, any dichotomy based on characteristics that correlate with these two conditions is flawed. And finally, the FBI's scheme tends to overlook signature characteristics of the crime, or the *why,* in favor of modus operandi characteristics, or the *how* of the offense.

Holmes and Holmes

One of the more popular and widely researched typology schemes is that of Ronald M. and Stephen T. Holmes (1998). Building upon an earlier work (Holmes and DeBurger, 1988), and using data from 110 serial murders, including interviews, their typology scheme provides four distinct serial killer types—*visionary, missionary, hedonistic, power and control*—with the hedonistic killer further divided into two subtypes, the *lust* and *thrill* killer.

Under this model, serial killers can be further categorized as either *act-focused* or *process-focused.* For the former, or those who kill quickly, the act of killing is all about the act itself. Their reasons for killing are external to the specific victims they choose. They kill for what they perceive to be a higher purpose. Their victims are little more than a necessary means to a desired end. This category includes the following typologies:

• *The Visionary Killer*—This individual typically suffers from some type of mental illness, most commonly schizophrenia. They carry out their killings at the behest of some voice or vision, usually that of an angel, demon, or alien. Oftentimes the underlying theme of their killng is the battle between good and evil. Visionary killers don't seek a connection, however morbid, with their victims. For the most part, their victims are just nameless and faceless individuals who must be killed in order to achieve their delusional goal. They are thus focused on the *why* of their killing rather than on the *how*.

• *The Missionary Killer*—These killers take it on as their personal mission to rid society of a particular group of people for some reason. Like the visionary killer, they see a higher purpose in their acts, and any connection with their victims is of little consequence. An example is the healthcare worker, perhaps even a physician, who kills terminally ill patients, either because they believe these patients are a burden on society, and thus better to terminate their lives, or because they see virtue in relieving them of their pain and suffering. Other missionary killers may attempt to eradicate prostitutes from the streets of their city, or perhaps even an entire ethnic group. They may also kill a certain type of individual in the belief that others will be blamed, and some type of needed social conflict will result.

In contrast to the above typologies, for the process-focused killer, killing is all about the victim, and their interactions with them in the process of carrying out their crimes. They are less focused on *why* they are killing, and more on *how* they are going to do it. Those who torture or sexually assault their victims, as well as those who practice necrophilia and cannibalism, would all be considered process-focused killers. They have no higher purpose in mind for their crimes beyond the simple desire to kill. Rather than their victims being a means to some desired end, the victims themselves are the killer's end.

- *The Hedonistic Killer*–These killers commit their heinous acts for the pure thrill of killing. Holmes and Holms have argued that this typology accounts for the majority of known serial killers. They further divide this category into two subtypes: *lust* and *thrill* killers. The lust killer is one who derives sexual gratification from and in relation to the killing. Oftentimes these killers will engage in postmortem sex acts. Closely related to this subtype is the serial killer who kills simply for the thrill of killing. These individuals oftentimes torture their victims, and while they may, and oftentimes do sexually assault their victims, their primary motivation is not sexual gratification, but rather the intense excitement they feel when they kill.
- *The Power and Control Killer*–This type of killer is motivated by the power and control they have over their victims. These individuals are slow killers, and may even keep their victims alive for extended periods, torturing, raping, and psychologically tormenting them. They are excited by feelings of omnipotence and the knowledge that they have complete control over whether their victims live or die. For them, a victim pleading for their life and showing extreme fear will only feed their excitement. It is when a victim finally gives up and accepts their inevitable fate that this type of killer begins to lose this feeling of power and control. This typically is when the killing takes place.

Criticisms: Like the FBI's typology scheme, Holmes and Holmes's scheme has met with criticism. Canter and Wentink (2004) point out a number of major concerns related to their model. First, they question the reliability and validity of their data collection. Like the FBI, the data used in the construction of their typologies came from interviews–in their case, interviews conducted earlier by Holmes and DeBurger (1985)–and their interview methodology was never disclosed. They also point out a lack of empirical testing of their model and the fact that Holmes and Holmes provides no empirically-validated criteria for assigning serial killers to a particular typology. Instead, they base their classification on offense and crime scene characteristics that are very subjectively interpreted. In fact, when their classification scheme was tested using the same methodology used to test the FBI's dichotomy (Cantor et al., 2004), only limited support was found for their model, and then only for the lust, thrill, and missionary typologies.

Another major shortcoming of this model is that is assumes all serial killers are either mentally-ill, mission-oriented, or they kill because they enjoy the process of killing. Where do we place a serial killer who does not enjoy the act of killing, who is not mentally ill, and whose only purpose in killing is to quiet some internal rage that has resulted from a life of abuse? An example is Aileen Wuornos, a female serial killer put to death in 2002 for the murders of seven men in Florida during 1989–90. Another example is the individual who kills for the purpose of filling some void or emptiness in their sense of self. An example is David Berkowitz, the *Son of Sam* killer, currently serving multiple life sentences for murdering six people in New York City during 1976–77. As we shall see in the chapters to follow, there simply is no room in Holmes and Holmes's classification scheme for people like Wuornos or Berkowitz, or others who do not fit the classic profile of a mentally-ill or bloodthirsty killer.

Creating Typologies

Creating typologies should be for the purpose of furthering our study and understanding of the serial killer phenomenon. There is a two fold goal in developing this understanding as much as possible. First is to facilitate the identification and apprehension of unknown serial offenders, or what has come to be widely known in our pop culture as *criminal profiling*. It is difficult to watch television on any given night without seeing some portrayal of the profiling process. Americans have always had a strange fascination with serial killers, and profiling, however baseless its dramatization by Hollywood, only feeds that fascination. But it is a technique that has only minimal efficacy for law enforcement authorities, and it remains far from being developed to the level of a scientific discipline. The typologies discussed above were developed for this purpose. They were constructed using all the data their authors were able to gather relating to the motives and methods of known adult serial killers. This type of typology then becomes a template investigators can hopefully lay atop a crime scene to better focus their investigative efforts in the right direction.

Our second goal, and certainly the more important of the two, is to be able to identify potential serial killers in their preoffending years and engage them with some type of intervention. This too is a type of profiling–what we might call personality profiling–but much different from criminal profiling. Obviously, things such as crime scenes and MOs are of little value to this discipline. Here we are most interested in the psychosocial development of serial offenders, and commonalities and correlates in that regard. We may certainly be able to identify correlations between crime scene characteristics and certain aspects of development, but what we will be identifying is not a small population of potential suspects, but a very large population of those with a propensity to commit such an act, the vast majority of whom have and never will engage in criminal conduct for reasons related to their social circumstances and psychological needs. So any typology scheme developed for this purpose must make the connection between the behavioral characteristics of known serial offenders and what we know about childhood and adolescent psychosocial development.

CRIMINAL PROFILING

If you ask any particular group of criminal justice students what they hope to do with their degrees, a good many of them will express their desire to become criminal profilers. But few have a real understanding of the technique, especially its limitations and past failures. The truth is profiling alone has never resulted in the capture of a single serial killer in America. In many high profile cases, the FBI has created profiles based on their model that turned out to be terribly wrong once the killer was identified. A good example is the case of John Muhammad and Lee Boyd Malvo, the Beltway Snipers. During a three-week period in 2002, Muhammad and Malvo shot and killed ten people in the Washington, D.C. metro area. As Baltimore Sun reporter Elsbeth Bothe (2002) pointed out, essentially every profiler who weighed in on the case got it wrong. No one had concluded prior to their arrest that African-Americans were the killers, as they turned out to be, and neither did they conclude that one or both of them might be juveniles, as Malvo was at the time.

There have also been instances of false positives, cases in which a suspect was publicly identified by the FBI based on a profile, only to discover later they were wrong. Such was the case with Richard Jewel, who was working as a security guard at Centennial Park in Atlanta, Georgia during the 1996 Olympics when a bomb exploded, killing one and injuring over a hundred others. Resulting mostly from their belief that Jewel fit the profile of a *lone bomber,* the FBI identified him as a person of interest almost immediately (Sack, 2007). Sadly, Jewel was probably responsible for saving lives that day by spotting the green knapsack containing the bomb and quickly evacuating people from the area. Years later the real bomber, serial killer Eric Robert Rudolph, would plead guilty to the Olympic bombing. For Richard Jewel and his family, however, the damage had already been done.

The use of profiling to assist in the investigation of serial killers has certainly been overplayed, not just by Hollywood, but by the very agency that brought it to the forefront of public awareness, the FBI. The truth is that the use of profiling has long been left behind by other, more effective investigative techniques and technologies, including DNA and the analysis of trace evidence, the widespread use of video security cameras, and good old fashion police work—knocking on doors, tracking down leads, and thinking in creative ways to locate evidence of the killer's trail. There is also value in employing the techniques of *geographic profiling,* a different type of profiling used to analyze the location of crime scenes, abduction points, and body dump sites in an effort to determine where the killer finds his victims, where he might strike next, and perhaps even the general area where he lives.

For all of its limitations, criminal profiling is likely here to stay. Hopefully, as the amount of available data on serial killers increases, the technique will become more refined as a way of identifying within a narrowly-defined population an unknown serial killer. It is therefore of benefit here to review this investigative technique.

Crime Phases

Every serial homicide occurs across four phases, each of which includes behaviors reflective of the killer's personality. In any particular case, the goal of the criminal profiler is to gather as much evidence and information as possible relating to each of these four phases. From this data, and correlations found between these and the characteristics of known serial killers, a particular personality type emerges. McCrary (2004) describes these phases as follows:

• *Antecedent*–This is the period before the murder takes place. What is the killer doing in the period before the murder, and what circumstances have taken place in his or her life to stimulate their need to once again kill? For example, let's assume we have a series of murders in a particular city, all involving women abducted in public parking lots at various times of the day, including the evening, and all sexually assaulted and mutilated prior to death. From this we can begin to develop antecedents. We can assume the individual is likely unemployed. We can assume they are fantasizing prior to selecting a victim about sexual mutilation. We can assume they are planning exactly where and how they will kill their next victim, and that they are randomly driving about in a selected geographic area in search of a victim.

• *Method and manner*–This involves the killer's *modus operandi,* or their usual method of selecting, taking, and ultimately murdering a victim. In our previous example, we will likely have much evidence relating to this phase of the killing. Some of the possible inputs might include:

- Only middle-aged Caucasian women are selected.
- The victims are all abducted from public parking lots.
- There is no sign of struggle at the location of the victims' cars.
- There is no sign of struggle and limited physical evidence at the location of the body.
- Victims are all sexually assaulted (anal penetration).
- Victims all suffered genital mutilation prior to death.
- Victims all suffered facial disfigurement
- No semen evidence is found

There are potentially hundreds of inputs that can be included in the construction of a profile. But just with the few included here in our hypothetical example, a particular personality type is starting to emerge. We can make some basic untested assumptions at this point. First, the individual is likely using a firearm to abduct his victims since there is no sign of struggle at the abduction points. The killer is motivated most by the desire to torture. It is significant that the only type of sexual assault is anal penetration. This coupled with the presence of genital mutilation is significant. There is a reason the killer does not engage in vaginal penetration, and this reason is no doubt connected to why he engages in genital mutilation while the victim is still alive. Facial disfigurement is always a significant piece of evidence. And finally, the lack of semen evidence indicates either the use of a condom or a failure to ejaculate.

• *Body disposal*–Even how a killer disposes of their victims' bodies is reflective of their personality. In our above example, the fact that there is limited physical evidence at the locations where the bodies are found, including the victims' clothing, indicates that the crimes took place somewhere other than where the bodies are discovered. The bodies are all found next to rural roads in ditches. There are no apparent efforts to cover or conceal the bodies. All are found approximately 20 miles from their abduction points. This may indicate a concern on the part of the killer about leaving behind evidence and being detected. It may also point to significant amount of preplanning. Both of these inputs are important to understanding the mind and motivation of our killer.

• *Post-offense behavior*–This phase of the crime includes any identifiable postoffense behavior by the killer. For example, let's assume it is known that our hypothetical killer confesses his crimes over the telephone to a local priest or pastor after each killing. He voices his sense of guilt for what he has done, and tells the clergyman that he is possessed by a demon. This is a very complex set of behaviors that may indicate a number of things. It may indicate that the person truly does feel remorse for what he has done. He may truly believe he is demon-possessed, but it may also be a delusional belief (i.e., schizophrenia) if he actually hears the voice of the purported demon directing his actions.

Examples of this type of behavior have certainly happened in the past. Some killers have contacted newspapers, taunted the police, and a few have even contacted family members of their victims. All of these behaviors are highly significant in constructing a profile of the killer. For example, taunting the police may feed their craving for power and control over the situation. Contacting family members may allow them to relive the excitement of causing their victim pain and suffering, or it may allow them to feel some morbid connection to their victim. And contacting the newspaper may indicate a need for *ego-stroking* through notoriety.

Constructing the Profile

In the U.S., the process of constructing an offender profile typically follows the FBI model (Douglas et al., 1986). The process begins with the *assimilation phase*. During this phase, the primary task of the profiler is to gather and assimilate all available evidence relating to the crime(s). This may include witness accounts, crime scene photos, crime lab reports, autopsy reports, and photos, everything that is known about the victim(s), and all reports filed by responding police officers or assigned investigators. The profiler, typically a law enforcement officer, is given complete access to the investigation.

Next is the *classification stage*. During this stage, the profiler takes all the available inputs they have gathered and classifies the killer as either organized or disorganized. As we previously discussed, the FBI model defines the organized killer as one who plans their crimes and takes steps to avoid detection. In contrast, the disorganized killer is impulsive, opportunistic, and is unconcerned about the evidence they leave behind. They may engage in postmortem sexual activity, and are more likely to suffer from mental illness.

Following the classification of the unknown offender, the profiler attempts to reconstruct the *behavioral sequence* of the crime. This includes their likely behavior before, during, and after the offense. Additionally, during this phase, the profiler attempts to identify *signatures* of the killer from an analysis of the crime scene. Signatures are behaviors carried out by the killer in each and every case, and are typically done to satisfy some psychological desire or need. For example, the killer may take one particular article of clothing from each and every victim, or mutilate the same part of each victim's corpse. It is a behavior that is consistently demonstrated in each murder they commit, and becomes sort of psychological fingerprint that can both link crimes and assist in identifying the killer.

The final step in the process is to generate the actual profile. By analyzing the killer's likely antecedents, their methods and M.O., and by reconstructing their behavioral sequence before, during, and after their crimes, the profiler is able to hopefully correlate the data with data obtained previously from known serial offenders. The profiler attempts to paint a psycho-demographic picture of the offender, including their personality characteristics, family background, employment status, race and age, education, and the likelihood of more killings. They also attempt to profile the killer's possible motivations, as well as the likelihood of mental illness. Obviously, the goal in developing this profile is for the police to be able to use the information to focus their investigation in the right direction and onto the right suspect pool.

CHAPTER SUMMARY

No other type of criminal activity has received more media attention over the years than serial homicide. This focus, from newspapers and books, to Hollywood movies and heavy metal music, has been fueled in part by the strange fascination the general public seems to have with serial killers. They are among the antiheroes of American society, people with absolutely no morally-redeeming qualities, but who, through the powerful imagery of their evil personas, have caused the line between hero and villain to become blurred for many. While they sit in our jails and prisons awaiting trial, sentencing, or even execution, most enjoy a steady stream of fan mail and marriage proposals.

The serial killer phenomenon also along the way caught the interest of academia. Many researchers have tried to better understand the serial killer's methods and motives. For some, the holy grail of their efforts is to develop a more effective way of identifying and apprehending active serial offenders. While for others, their research is aimed at identifying potential serial offenders in their preoffending stages of development and intervening in ways that will facilitate change in their developmental course away from juvenile delinquency and adult criminality.

Many have attempted to classify serial killers. Typology schemes have been created based on offender motivations (e.g., lust, thrill, power and control), as well as on the characteristics of the crime scenes they leave behind (e.g., organized, disorganized). Essentially all typology schemes have been criticized heavily. The biggest problem researchers face is the limited size of the population of serial killers available for study. Many have been executed, and others simply refuse to be interviewed. And the ones who do submit to interviews many times have their own selfish interests in mind in what they say and how they answer questions. So the integrity of the data obtained from incarcerated serial killers, regardless of the study or the method of the data collection, is almost always questionable.

One of the intended uses of serial killer typologies is to facilitate the identification and apprehension of unknown offenders through the process of offender profiling. What profilers attempt to do is to collect as much data as possible about known and incarcerated serial killers, and to then look for ways to classify those killers into qualitatively different groups based on their methods, motives, and behaviors before, during, and after their crimes. Once they have created these classifications, or *typologies,* then they attempt to construct profiles of unknown serial offenders by comparing the characteristics of their crimes to the characteristics of these typologies. It is hoped that as correlations are found, then a picture of the unknown offender will begin to emerge and allow investigators to more tightly focus their investigation.

And finally, this book makes use of its own typology scheme, one based on a series of psychosocial developmental variables. Using this scheme, serial killers can be typed as *opportunistic, symbolic,* or *ego-directed.* And while the proposed scheme may have some utility in terms of identifying and apprehending an unknown serial offender, its primary purpose is to facilitate the identification of potential serial killers in their preoffending stages of development during childhood and adolescence. The obvious goal is to be able to intervene in the lives of at-risk children in an effort to redirect their developmental course away from criminality. Studying the serial killer, society's worst and most evil offender, allows us to begin at the end point of a killer's developmental trajectory, and then work backwards from there to identify the variables that led to such a deadly outcome.

Chapter 2

WHERE IT ALL BEGINS
The Role of Attachment in Infancy

INTRODUCTION

We will conduct our study of the serial killer's mind in the context of *Criminal Triad Theory* (Harmening, 2010). CTT is a theory of criminal behavior that takes a negative approach to understanding why people engage in deviant behavior by first understanding the internal psychosocial mechanisms that allow law-abiding individuals to self-deter from such behavior. The theory describes the interaction of three psychosocial developmental processes–*attachment, moral development,* and *identity-formation*–that occur between and during infancy and adolescence. These processes, when allowed to progress normally, ultimately lead to the development of a child's internal deterrence system. Any disruption in the child's developmental course can potentially lead to the development of a *criminal personality type,* or a "propensity" to engage in deviant behavior when the opportunity presents itself. At its most extreme, this deviant personality may manifest itself in the form of serial offending.

THE CRIMINAL TRIAD

Criminal Triad Theory is essentially a synthesis of existing psychological theories. It incorporates the work of Erik Erikson, Lawrence Kohlberg, and Mary Ainsworth, among others, in a unique new way that provides a picture of the internal human deterrence system. It is this same system that at the minimal end of the deviance spectrum deters a young child from lying to their mother, and at the more extreme end, an adult from killing multiple people. Its development is a complex process that begins on day one of a child's life, and reaches its apex during adolescence when the pressures of identity-formation have their maximum impact on the young person's behavior.

Each of the three developmental processes—attachment, moral development, and identity-formation—has a corresponding internal deterrence mechanism that is present and active if the child's developmental course has been nonproblematic. Combined, they lead to an integrated internal deterrence system that acts to deflect any deviant temptations, and provides redundancy in the event one or two of its component parts fail. The criminal personality type ("CPT") then is one lacking a fully developed internal deterrence system. The person either has no deterrence mechanism(s) to serve in a backup capacity, or their developmental course has left them with none at all. As a theoretical construct then, the CPT can be described as an individual lacking any two or all three of these internal deterrence mechanisms. The internal deterrence system is illustrated in Figure 2.1.

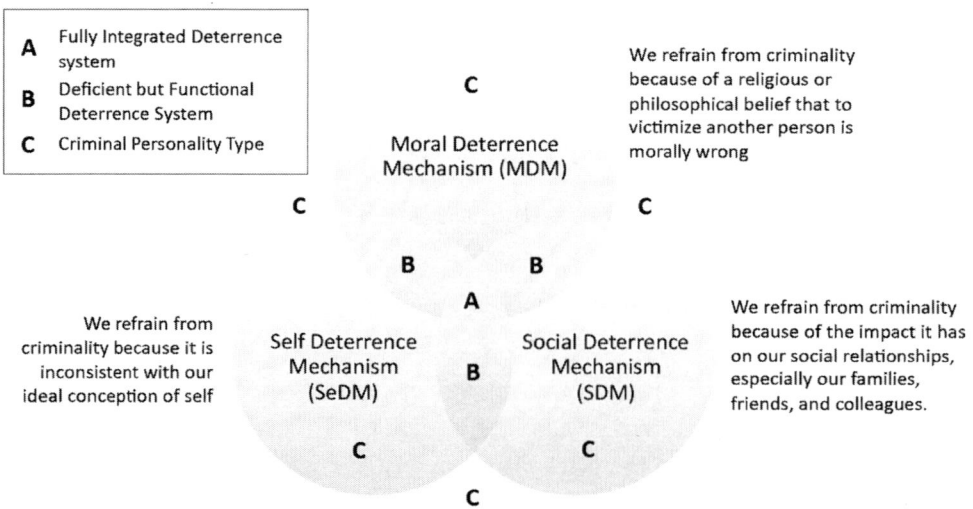

Figure 2.1. The internal deterrence system.

The internal deterrence system is the result of many developmental factors, but primarily the parent-child relationship. This relationship begins a developmental process that leads to the child becoming socially-competent, morally aware, and able to internalize a sense of self-efficacy. Each of these personal characteristics serves as the foundation for, and is representative of, its corresponding deterrence mechanism. Conversely, a child who is exposed to abusive, neglectful, or authoritarian parenting is at risk of entering adolescence without the social competence needed to develop friendly and intimate relationships, or the sense of personal-efficacy to develop a healthy concept of self. Each of these circumstances contributes to an underdeveloped sense of morality and a lack of understanding and awareness of social norms and expectations.

Figure 2.2 illustrates the Criminal Triad, including its three component parts, each of their subcomponent parts, and the three corresponding deterrence mechanisms that result from these developmental processes. As we move forward in this chapter we will discuss each of these processes separately.

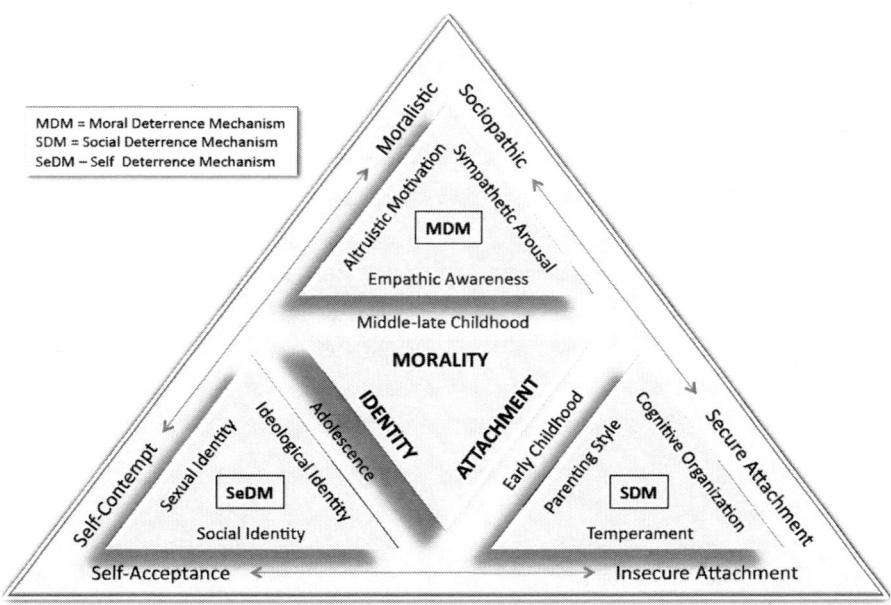

Figure 2.2. The Criminal Triad.

THE ATTACHMENT PROCESS

First, we must define exactly what *attachment* is. For this we can turn to the pioneering work of two particular theorists, John Bowlby (1988) and Mary Ainsworth (1978). Together they have given us a comprehensive theory of the attachment process that is considered seminal. For them, attachment is the emotional bond a child develops with one or more caregivers that results from an intrinsic need to feel safe and secure. The attachment figure, usually the parent, is a base of operations from which the child experiences the world in the early years of life. Evolutionists would argue that a child's need to attach is a product of natural selection, and that in prehistoric and dangerous times, it was the child who felt a need to seek safety under the protective watch of a parent who survived more successfully and passed on their genetic code.

But as Bowlby and Ainsworth have shown us, the attachment process is a more complex dynamic than simply a child's need to feel safe. How well a child attaches to an attachment figure has lifelong implications. Eventually it will impact their ability to establish childhood friendships, their academic performance, their development of a healthy identity, their ability to develop and maintain intimate relationships, and yes, even their ability to self-deter from socially-deviant behavior. Many consider it the most important developmental process a child will experience, with the success of all future development dependent upon the child's ability to form a healthy and secure attachment.

Bowlby published his full theory in a trilogy titled *Attachment and Loss* (1969, 1973, 1980). He viewed the attachment process as happening instinctively in children. Rather than a display of love and affection, Bowlby viewed attachment as a survival mechanism in which the child seeks proximity to the attachment figure in times of stress. It is during these times of stress when the child's attachment behavioral system is activated to elicit the protective care of the attachment figure. This behavioral system may involve a number of behaviors, to include crying, clinging, various facial expressions, and outstretched arms. Bowlby believed this behavioral system is activated by two emotions. The first is alarm, caused by a fear of some stimulus in the child's sensory field, such as an approaching stranger. The second is anxiety, the child's fear of being separated from the protective care of the attachment figure. In either case, the child's attachment system is activated in an effort to diminish the perceived danger.

Both of these responses can be clearly seen in the everyday behavior of small children. When a mother attempts to hand her young child off to an admiring stranger–a stranger at least to the child–the child repels the outstretched hands of the person and seeks safety by clinging to the mother as tightly as possible. For another mother, each time she attempts to drop her child off at the daycare center the child lets out a panicky cry when she turns to leave. In both cases the children are activating their attachment behavioral systems; one out of fear, the other anxiety. Both are normal responses. In the first scenario, the child will eventually adapt to the stranger's presence and loosen their grip on mom, and may even interact with the stranger in a positive way. In the second scenario, the child will rather quickly get beyond its separation anxiety and join the other kids in play. A healthy attachment will not preclude the child from experiencing fear or anxiety when its proximity to the attachment figure is threatened, or in the presence of a stranger, but it does greatly lesson the intensity by leading the child to develop an internal working model of the world as a safe and secure place where the comfort and protection provided by the primary attachment figure can be found in others as well, such as daycare staff and friendly strangers.

For the child who has not developed a healthy attachment, the fear and anxiety experienced in these situations is intense and exaggerated, and does not recede quickly or easily. They do not possess an internal working model of a safe and secure world, but instead are plagued by a chronic sense of fear that in later years can develop into everything from despair and paranoia, to interpersonal hostility. As Bowlby points out, and as we shall see later in this chapter, the quality of a child's attachment in infancy will significantly influence all later stages of development.

As part of her research on attachment, and more specifically the various attachment patterns displayed by children, Mary Ainsworth conducted an observational study that has become one of the most celebrated studies in modern psychology. In her *strange situations experiment,* Ainsworth (1978) observed the behavior of infant children while their caregivers and various strangers entered and departed the room in a particular sequence. She was specifically looking for the level of fear and anxiety they displayed at various points in the sequence, consistent with Bowlby's theory.

The sequence began with the child and parent in the room together, with the child being allowed to freely explore the various toys and objects scattered about. Then a stranger entered, first engaging the parent, and then engaging the child in a friendly manner while the parent quietly slipped out of the room. After a short period of time, the parent returned to the room. Following this, a second separation sequence was executed involving the stranger. Ainsworth noted individual differences in a number of behaviors, including the extent to which the child would venture away from the parent and explore the room, the child's reaction to the stranger's presence and engagement, the child's reaction to the parent's departure from the room, and the child's reaction upon being reunited with the parent.

From her observations, Ainsworth was able to identify three distinct attachment patterns in the children. Each of these patterns, Ainsworth believed, is directly related to the quality of the parent-child dynamic, and each has important implications for later development.

• *Secure attachment:* The child who was found to be securely attached to their mother demonstrated a high degree of autonomy during the study. They were quick to venture about the room and explore once they felt safe in the new surroundings, and they had little difficulty engaging the stranger with the mother present. They were mildly distressed when the mother left the room, and happy to see her when she returned. After quickly re-engaging the mother, the child would again venture out to explore the room. It was also found that the child would not interact with the stranger with the mother absent.

Ainsworth considered this attachment pattern to be most closely related to a healthy parent-child relationship. The child feels safe to venture out from the mother because they see her as a secure base to return to in times of need or distress. Because of the mother's effective and consistent parenting style, the child develops a sense of confidence that their needs will be met, and is therefore able to engage the stranger with little fear and confront the mother's absence with only moderate and temporary distress. The child has developed a sense of trust in the world, and is now able to seek autonomy from the parents to begin the developmental task of forming a healthy self-image.

- *Anxious-ambivalent insecure attachment:* The child Ainsworth placed in this category was anxious about venturing away from the mother to explore the room. The child also refused to engage the stranger even with the mother present, and showed fear when the stranger was in close proximity. When the mother departed the room the child became severely distressed. Upon her return the child appeared ambivalent or even resentful toward the mother, while again maintaining close proximity or even clinging to her. Some of the children showing this attachment pattern even hit or pushed the mother away upon her return and refused to be comforted. The mothers of these children too were inconsistent in their behavior, at times showing no sensitivity to their child's distress, and at others, discouraging such behavior while making no effort to comfort the child.

Ainsworth believed these children lack a sense of trust in the world, and a confidence that their needs will be met on a consistent basis. Because of this lack of trust, and the chronic sense of fear that results, they maintain a close proximity to the mother and fail to develop a sense of autonomy. Separation anxiety is routinely experienced by these children. They seek physical closeness to the parent, but not emotional closeness. The parents of these children are engaged, but on their own terms, and thus the parent-child dynamic may be motivated as much by the needs of the parent as it is by the needs of the child. Unlike the securely attached child, these children have difficulty forming a sense of self because of their inability to separate from the parents, instead remaining dependent to the detriment of their own emotional developmental.

- *Anxious-avoidant insecure attachment:* The child showing this attachment pattern tended to ignore the mother, and showed no considerable distress when she departed the room, and little or no emotion upon her return. At times, this child would even run from the mother when she re-entered the room and attempted to pick the child up. The child ignored the presence of the stranger, and showed no significant level of fear either with the mother present or absent. The child also showed little interest in exploring the room. As expected, the child's lack of attention was reciprocated by the mother, who was inconsistent in her responsiveness, and at times even neglectful.

Emotionally speaking, this child is essentially on its own. According to Ainsworth, this pattern of behavior represents a parenting style that is disengaged and insensitive to the needs of the child. The child eventually comes to believe that it has little influence on the mother, and that communicating its needs to the mother in the manner children typically do is futile. The quality of the parent-child bond is very low or nonexistent. The child experiences chronic self-doubt, which a few years later will lead to feelings of inferiority and identity problems. With little or no feedback from a disengaged parent, the child is at a disadvantage in developing a sense of self-worth since it requires that they experience some degree of success and achievement. This happens when the parents set achievable goals and expectations for the child, and when they provide positive feedback when those goals and expectations are successfully met. With the disengaged parent, this critical feedback is absent.

Dr. Mary Main (1990), a researcher at the University of California, Berkeley, expanded Ainsworth's model by adding a fourth attachment pattern based on her analysis of Ainsworth's results. The *disorganized-disoriented insecure attachment* is a pattern of behavior that is entirely inconsistent, and at times incoherent and confused. These children act in abnormal ways, both in terms of affect and conduct. They may attempt to avoid or resist the mother, and may even appear frightened when the mother approaches. The mothers of these children also behave in inconsistent and confusing ways. They display inappropriate affect, high levels of negativity, and interact with the child in ways the child may perceive as frightening and intrusive.

Obviously, it is a serious concern when this type of attachment pattern is displayed. There is a complete lack of emotional bonding between parent and child, and such a pattern may even indicate abuse within the home. It is typically the case with this attachment style that the child is actually frightened of the mother. It is seen in households where there is a high level of drug and alcohol abuse, intimate partner abuse, or both. It is also seen in lower socioeconomic households with parents who suffer significant cognitive deficits, and who have very minimal parenting skills. Many of these families will eventually become involved, either voluntarily or by court order, with their particular state's child and family services department. The implications of this attachment pattern for later psychosocial development are obvious. It is almost guaranteed that without intervention there will be significant deficits in essentially every area of the child's life, including interpersonal relationships, academic performance, moral development, and the development of an identity during adolescence.

Before we talk specifically about the relationship between infant attachment and later criminality, including serial murder, we must first identify and discuss the three essential component parts that come together either to facilitate or encumber the attachment process: *neurocognitive organization, temperament,* and *parenting style.* A deficit in any one of them can and oftentimes does negatively impact the parent-child relationship and impede the development of the type of emotional bond so critical to development.

Neurocognitive Organization

From the moment of birth, a child is adapting to its environment. It does so physically, psychologically, and neurologically. The brain of a newborn baby is truly a work in progress. What begins as a mass of undifferentiated neural circuitry in a very short time develops into a highly specialized system of neural pathways that guides and mediates our every movement, emotion, and cognition. The brain develops and organizes itself through two particular processes that must take place for normal development to occur—*dendritic spreading* and *myelination.* It is through these two processes, both initiated and propelled forward by the individual's biological constitution and experience, that the brain becomes the command center for all behavior and emotion.

The brain, and for that matter the entire central nervous system (CNS), is composed of a special type of cell called a *neuron.* Neurons carry the electrical impulses necessary for the various components of the CNS to communicate with each other. The cellular infrastructure upon which these impulses travel is created by millions of neurons attaching to one another through long tentacles that protrude outward from the cell bodies. These tentacles, called *dendrites,* connect one neuron to many others, and allow many neurons to form a neural pathway that will specialize for a particular function such as vision, walking, speech, or even playing the piano. Without these pathways developing to a significant degree, the individual would exist with the intellectual, sensory, and motor capacity of a newborn baby.

Early on in development, during approximately the first four years of life, the infant brain actually overdevelops these neural connections as a protective measure. If damage occurs in an area that specializes for a particular function, there will be plenty of unused neural pathways that will come to the rescue and compensate for the loss. Eventually though, once the brain has organized itself to a significant degree, these unused pathways will start to recede. The unused neurons will then be used for some function other than their genetically-determined purpose, or they will begin to die off. This overproduction of dendritic connections, and their eventual decline, explains why it is so much easier for a young child to recover from a traumatic brain injury than an adult.

The other major process that must occur in the developing brain is *myelination.* If you were to magnify a neuron, you would see a long axon running between the cell body and to the dendrites of other neurons. You would also see that this axon is covered by a layer white matter called the Myelin Sheath. The purpose of the Myelin sheath is to act as a conductor of the electrical impulses that travel the length of the axon. It further insulates the axon and prevents the electrical impulses from escaping the cell body. The simple act of reaching for an object on a table illustrates the activity of the neural pathway leading from the motor cortex of the brain to the nerve endings that stimulate the muscles of the arm, hand, and fingers as they reach and grasp the object. This simple action is made possible by the myelinated axons of the millions of neurons that make up this particular neural pathway. Once a decision is made to reach and grasp, electrical impulses travel down the pathway from one neuron to the next. Without the necessary myelination, this action would not be possible. It is precisely why young infants lack the coordination to walk, catch a ball, or do simple things like grasp objects. They simply have not yet developed the necessary neural pathways or myelination to allow for such activities. Even in adults, long after these processes are complete, problems can occur. Demyelination, or the deterioration of the myelin sheath, can result in many different types of problems, including such diseases as *multiple sclerosis, Alexander's disease,* and *Guillain-Barre Syndrome.*

To understand the role of neurocognitive organization in the attachment process, we must first understand the concept of *critical periods.* Critical periods are windows of opportunity during which neurological development is maximally influenced by experience. This in turn has a critical impact on future behavior. For example, there is a critical period during the first year of life for language development.

The neurological centers for language development, located primarily in the brain's left hemisphere, will experience a sudden developmental surge during this window of opportunity. This surge, however, requires environmental stimulation in the form of human interaction, both verbal and nonverbal. If this stimulation is not present during the critical period, the language centers of the brain will not develop normally. This has been shown in reported cases of feral children, and children held in captivity with little human contact. These children, because they have missed their critical period for language development, never fully develop this ability to the extent most children do.

So is there a critical period for the development of an attachment to a caregiver? It would appear so, and that this critical period occurs in an infant sometime between six and 24 months (Bowlby, 1969). By this time, the child has acquired *object permanence,* or the ability to know that something or someone still exists even when the object is outside the child's visual field. Further, the child can now attend to, and show a preference for a particular caregiver. Infants are born with a preference for faces over objects, but it requires environmental support to allow the brain to organize itself to the extent that the child can discern one face from another. Once this ability is in place, the child then begins to show a preference for a familiar face, in particular that of the primary caregiver.

Therefore, the first critical cog in the attachment wheel is the necessary degree of neurocognitive organization to sensitize the child to the influence of experience during the critical period. Similar to its role in the development of language, this experience is absolutely critical to the development of a healthy attachment to a primary attachment figure. It has been found that children not regularly stimulated during the critical period by a consistent caregiver, such as those reared in orphanages or raised by neglectful parents, are at a much greater risk of developing maladaptive patterns of behavior later in life. Experience therefore has a twofold purpose. First, it is through environmental stimulation (i.e., experience) that the brain develops and organizes itself to the point of initiating a critical period for attachment. And second, it is the influence of experience, specifically attachment-related experience, during the critical period that causes the attachment bond to form.

Temperament

While neurocognitive factors certainly prepare the infant for the attachment bond to form during the critical period, two other factors work together to shape the quality of the attachment: the child's biologically-determined *temperament,* and the parents' ability to adjust to that temperament in order to foster a nurturing relationship. It is this ongoing socioemotional dance between parent and child that determines the quality of the experience that ultimately will serve as the foundation for the attachment bond. If the underlying experience is frustrating, fearful, or contemptuous for either parent or child, chances are the quality of the attachment will suffer.

A child's temperament can be described as their general mood and demeanor, or put another way, their emotional response pattern to changing stimuli. Some children are chronically happy, while others are persistently fussy or emotionally subdued. Some children easily adapt to new situations, while others become easily frustrated at even the slightest change to their routine. Some children have little difficulty at bedtime, while others loudly protest and cry themselves to sleep nightly. All children seem to consistently display a particular temperament. It is their temperament that oftentimes becomes the primary descriptor the parents use to describe their child—*she's such an easy child . . . he was a difficult baby.*

Two important researchers in the area of temperament, Alexander Thomas and Stella Chess (1977), have described nine different dimensions of temperament in children. These dimensions provide a framework for identifying and understanding individual differences in temperament among different children. The findings were based on their own observations of children and their families during the course of their research. The nine dimensions are as follows:

• *Threshold of Responsiveness.* This is the amount of stimulation required to elicit an emotional response in the child. At one end are children who are emotionally flat, and who require a great deal of stimulation. At the opposite end of the spectrum are children who respond emotionally with minimal stimulation. The former child may willingly share toys during periods of play, and move on to another if a playmate takes the one they happen to be playing with. The loss of the toy is simply not enough stimulation to elicit much of an emotional reaction. The latter child, in contrast, may scream loudly each time another child even touches the toy they are playing with.

• *Activity Level.* This is the amount of physical activity the child engages in. At the low end of the spectrum are children who like quiet, nonphysical activities. These are children who sit quietly in their seats or strollers, quite preoccupied with whatever object they happen to have in their hands at the time. Meals and bedtime are nonstressful events for the parents of these children. Their demeanor is mostly calm and content. At the other end of the spectrum are those children who are constantly fidgeting and moving about. These children never seem content, and require a great deal of supervision by the parents. For these families, meals and bedtime are anything but calm. These children tend to fight against the constraints of a highchair or crib, and have a difficult time self-regulating their activity level.

• *Intensity.* This is an indicator of the level of emotional responsiveness in a child. One child may respond to a particular stimulus with a noticeable, but appropriate level of anger, quickly self-regulating and calming themselves down. Another may respond with extreme emotionality: screaming, kicking, crying, and demonstrating little ability to self-regulate their emotional outburst. In either case, their level of intensity is a product of their temperament.

• *Rhythmicity.* This is a measure of the predictability of a child's eating, sleeping, and bowel and bladder patterns. A child with high rhythmicity is one who tends to get hungry and tired at roughly the same times each day. Their bowel and bladder activity also can easily be predicted and timed, making toilet training easier on the parents. Conversely, the child with low rhythmicity is very unpredictable. They may fall asleep at varying times, and their eating habits may be very irregular. Similarly, their bowel and bladder activity may be unpredictable and inconsistent, making toilet training more difficult and stressful for the parents.

• *Adaptability.* This is an indicator of how well a child responds to change. The child with a higher level of adaptability remains calm and open to new circumstances. New rules are adhered to with little protest, and new activities in the child's life, such as daycare or kindergarten, are initially stressful but not overly traumatic. The child quickly adapts and becomes comfortable. Conversely, the child with a low level of adaptability becomes overly stressed with any amount of change.

Things such as daycare and kindergarten are traumatic events, and even changes within the family, such as new rules or living conditions are difficult for the child. Routine activities such as getting a haircut or changing clothes are met with emotional outbursts. The child simply cannot handle even moderate amounts of novel or changing stimuli. This characteristic is often seen in children diagnosed with Attention Deficit and Hyperactivity Disorder (ADHD). These children are easily overloaded with sensory information and tend to respond with higher than normal levels of frustration, anger, and even aggression.

• *Mood.* This is the primary expression of the child's temperament. It is their typical demeanor throughout the day, even absent any new or changing stimuli. Some are happy and content, while others are sad and withdrawn. Still others are cranky and easily agitated. Parents will typically describe a child's mood when discussing their temperament. It is the dimension of temperament we tend to think of first.

• *Approach/Withdrawal.* This dimension describes the child's level of engagement with new people, places, and situations. Some children have little difficulty in the presence of strangers so long as their primary caregiver is near. Others experience intense anxiety and fear, even when the primary caregiver is present. For some children, new places and situations are a cause for fear, while for others, they present opportunities to experience and explore new things.

• *Persistence.* This dimension describes a child's determination to complete a task even when obstacles stand in the way. At one end is the child who approaches the task intent upon seeing it through to completion in spite of any obstacles that present themselves. At the other end is the child who is easily frustrated by obstacles, and who, in an effort to reduce their frustration, retreats from the activity rather than confront the problem.

• *Distractibility.* This is the level of concentration a child brings to bear on a task. Is the child easily distracted by extraneous stimuli, or are they able to stay focused? This dimension is an indicator of a child's decision-making ability. Are they able to pick a preferred toy from the shelf to play with, or are they so distracted by the available selection that picking one becomes difficult? In school, are they able to focus on their assignments and classroom activities, or are they so distracted by the sights and sounds around them, or even their own thoughts for that matter, that focusing becomes impossible?

Thomas and Chess (1977) have described three general patterns of temperament in children, each based on observable patterns of behavior within the framework of these nine dimensions. The *easy* child is one who easily adapts to new experience, and has a generally positive and happy mood. These children are mild to moderate in their level of activity and intensity, and they tend to stick to a problem or activity regardless of any obstacles or setbacks. They are not easily distracted, nor do they show levels of fear and anxiety that are inconsistent with the circumstances under which these emotions are elicited. They tend to have predictable patterns of sleep and bowel and bladder activity, and they enjoy the comfort of being touched and held.

In contrast, the *difficult* child is one who is easily frustrated by change. These children do not adapt well to new situations, circumstances, or expectations, and they tend to have a negative mood that can be stressful for the parents. They are irregular in their sleeping patterns and bowel and bladder activity, and they tend to be overly active and easily distractible, making routine tasks difficult and frustrating. Difficult children prefer to withdraw from novel stimuli–things such as strangers, new family activities, even new clothes–rather than approach them with interest and a sense of discovery. For the families of difficult children, having to endure frequent fits and tantrums is a routine and stressful happening.

The final pattern of temperament proposed by Thomas and Chess is the *slow-to-warm* child. These children represent a mix of characteristics found in both the easy and difficult child. Initially, they are slow to adapt to new situations, and may show a mildly negative response to novel stimuli; however, once they begin to feel comfortable, they become more responsive. Their eating and sleeping patterns are fairly predictable, as well as their bowel and bladder activity. In terms of their mood and demeanor, they tend to be emotionally subdued and shy; however, they become more animated and sociable once they are comfortable in their surroundings.

A child's temperament helps to create a family dynamic that can be very fulfilling for all involved, or extremely stressful. In particular, the difficult child imposes new demands on the family system. These children cry more, sleep less, take longer to toilet train, and are a great deal less adaptable to the rules and expectations established by the parents in an effort to control their behavior. Any parent who has raised a difficult child will attest to the stress it causes, not just between the child and the parents, but also between the child and their siblings, and even between the parents themselves.

Each component of the family system is bidirectional in its influence. The temperament of the child impacts the quality of the parent-child relationship, and that in turn either moderates or accentuates the negative or positive aspects of the child's temperament. And it is not limited to just the parent-child relationship. The temperament of the child, especially the difficult child, can lead to sufficient stress within the family system to cause problems between the parents, which in turn can then lead to enough stress in the parents' relationship with the child to cause an increase in the child's negative behaviors. A stressful parent-child relationship can actually reinforce the negative aspects of the child's temperament.

The child's temperament is not the sole determinant of the quality of the parent-child relationship. The child brings to the equation its biologically-determined disposition; however, it doesn't yet have the cognitive capability in infancy to self-regulate and modify that disposition. The parents, on the other hand, while they each have their own temperament that can impact their relationship with the child, do enjoy a level of cognitive functioning that allows them to adapt to the child's temperament to maximize its positive expression while minimizing the negative. Thomas and Chess spent considerable time researching the interplay between the child's temperament and the parenting style of the parents.

Parenting Style

Thomas and Chess (1977) developed the idea of *goodness-of-fit* to describe the dynamic interplay between the child's temperament and the responsiveness of the parents. Goodness-of-fit occurs when the demands and expectations of the parents are attainable and not overly-stressful for the child, given the child's temperament. It occurs when the socioemotional forces influencing the parent-child dynamic are bi-directional, and when there is an adequate degree of adaptability on the part of the parents. A simple equation offered by Thomas and Chess points to the importance of this idea:

$$Temperament + Goodness\text{-}of\text{-}fit = Secure\ attachment$$

In order for the attachment bond to form, there has to be a sufficient level of responsiveness on the part of the parents, particularly the mother. If the child has a difficult temperament, then ideally the parents understand the nature of temperament and parent in a way that does not frustrate the child. For example, if the parents are easily frustrated themselves, then they may confront the child's difficult temperament with harsh punishment, or by imposing even stricter demands and expectations on the child. Or perhaps they may react in a much different manner and simply neglect the child. In either case, there is no goodness-of-fit present, and the child is on a developmental path that will likely become more problematic with each passing year. We see these situations in their extreme form with abused children. So often there is such a bad parent-child fit that the frustration experienced by the parent over the child's crying and emotional outbursts, or perhaps their inability to go quietly to bed at night, eventually takes over, and the parent either resorts to physical violence in an effort to quiet the child, or they simply choose to neglect the child. In either case, a secure attachment will not happen and the child will spend a lifetime suffering the consequences.

Diana Baumrind (1991), a clinical psychologist at the University of California, Berkeley, provided a description of four distinct parenting styles, each based on the presence or absence of two dimensions of parenting: *responsiveness* and *demandingness*. The former is the degree to which the parents are responsive to the needs of the child, and the quality of that interaction. Responsiveness implies a warm and comforting quality to the parents' interactions with the child. The latter dimension refers to the rules and expectations demanded of the child, and the degree to which the parents impose consistent discipline if those rules and expectations are not met. Demandingness implies rules and expectations that can be met by the child, with a consistent and nontraumatic system of discipline. However, in the absence of responsiveness, this dimension becomes something much different. It becomes harmful or even abusive, with expectations imposed that cannot be met, and a system of discipline that does more harm than good. According to Baumrind, the four possible combinations of these two dimensions result in four distinct parenting styles, as illustrated in Figure 2.3. Each of these four parenting styles brings a different set of variables to the family dynamic, and each interacts with the child's

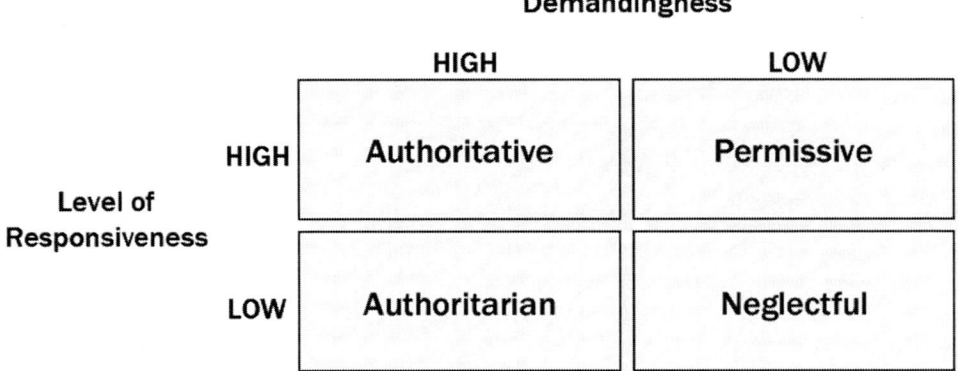

Figure 2.3. Baumrind's parenting style.

temperament in a different way to contribute to the development of a secure or insecure attachment in the child. A description of each follows:

• *Authoritative.* The authoritative parent is both demanding and responsive, however the former is moderated by the latter. Authoritative parents establish clear and attainable rules and expectations for their children, and are flexible enough to adjust those rules and expectations when necessary. Authoritative parents allow their children autonomy, and assert their authority without being overlyrestrictive. Their disciplinary style is based on the child's motivation and intent rather than only their overt behavior. These parents avoid physical punishment, and the methods they use are intended to compel the child to reflect on their inappropriate behavior, and then to seek out new behaviors that are more appropriate. Finally, authoritative parents are highly responsive to their child, and provide comfort and affection without conditions.

The authoritative parenting style is generally considered the most effective in terms of child development. By its very nature, which is flexible, responsive, and engaging, it provides a goodness-of-fit regardless of the child's temperament. Children of authoritative parents learn to respect their parents, which breeds respect for other people. They tend to be socially competent, and because of the autonomy afforded them, they learn effective problem-solving skills. And because they play an active role in establishing the behavioral parameters by which they live, they learn to self-regulate the negative behaviors and acquire a sense of self-efficacy from the positive.

• *Authoritarian.* In contrast to the authoritative parent, the authoritarian parent is highly demanding of the child with little regard for the child's ability to meet parental expectations. These parents demand obedience and allow the child little involvement in family decision-making. The child's life is structured for them, and the authoritarian parent is generally unresponsive to the child's emotional needs. Discipline in an authoritarian household is typically physical in nature. At their extreme, the authoritarian parent is physically or emotionally abusive, which ultimately strips the child of any sense of autonomy during the important developmental stages.

Obviously the authoritarian parent fails to provide goodness-of-fit regardless of the child's temperament; however, this parenting style is especially devastating for the child with the difficult temperament. It creates a situation where the child's inability to adhere to the rules only causes more rules to be established. The high intensity and activity level of the difficult child can cause the discipline being imposed by the parent to be more intense and obedience-oriented. The more frustrated the child becomes, the less responsive the parent will be, choosing instead to target their engagement in a way that reduces their own frustration level, and not the child's.

The children of authoritarian parents eventually pay a hefty price for their parents' shortcomings. They typically suffer from a lack of self-esteem because they have never been allowed the autonomy to experience success and achievement, which is so important to the development of a sense of self-efficacy. Their only measure of self-worth is the critical and oppressive nature of the parent-child relationship. The child with the easy temperament in this situation will tend to withdraw and retreat from new situations and friendships. They will lack curiosity about the world, or any spontaneity in their life. The child with the difficult temperament will react in a much different way. They will eventually begin to rebel against the authority of the parents. These children tend to perform poorly in school, and upon reaching early adolescence are quick to experiment with drugs and alcohol, usually beginning with tobacco, and to gravitate toward unhealthy peer groups. They are prone to aggressive behavior as a result of their increased intensity and frustration levels, and also because of the harsh and aggressive behavior that has been modeled by their authoritarian parents.

• *Indulgent.* The indulgent parent is high on responsiveness but low on demandingness. They place few expectations on the child, and are warm and engaging. Their primary motivation is to maintain a positive relationship with the child, and they often allow the child to control them and the situation in order to bring about that desired end. Their disciplinary methods are mild or none at all. While the indulgent parent may allow the child autonomy, they fail to teach them responsibility.

The children of indulgent parents, research shows, often grow up unhappy. They have less ability to control their emotions and impulses, and they often refuse to take responsibility for their own actions. While they tend to maintain close and loving relationships with their parents, these children typically experience problems in their own relationships due to their immaturity and lack of responsibility. The dysfunctional response patterns they learn as children, such as lying and blaming others, tend to spill over into adolescence and adulthood. These patterns of behavior are only reinforced by the indulgent parent's lack of authoritative control.

• *Neglectful.* The neglectful parent is void of responsiveness or demandingness. They simply choose to not be involved in their child's life to any significant degree. They show little affection toward the child, and ignore their need for comfort and emotional engagement. They may provide a minimal level of care needed to keep the child healthy, but at the extreme end of this parenting style, they may even ignore that. These parents establish no rules or expectations, nor do they impose any system of discipline. Like the authoritarian parent, they may engage in emotional or physical abuse, not for purposes of getting the child to adhere to the rules, but rather to get the child to leave them alone and not impede their lifestyle. This parenting style is oftentimes seen in the homes of alcoholic or drug-abusing parents, and is even more prevalent in homes where step-parents are involved.

Like the authoritarian parent, this style of parenting poses a significant threat to the psychological well-being of the developing child. The children of neglectful parents tend to grow up feeling resentment toward their parents and seldom maintain a healthy relationship with them beyond adolescence. As young children, they quickly learn the futility of communicating their needs to the parent. This in turn leads to a learned helplessness and feelings of insecurity. The child may also internalize blame for the parent's neglect, leading to feelings of self-contempt and depression. Having no healthy relationship with the parents, they also have difficulty establishing healthy friendships. They tend to experience significant problems with their self-concept and image, which translates into identity confusion during adolescence. When they reach this critical period of development, they are at risk of engaging in unhealthy peer relationships, drug and alcohol abuse, gang affiliation, and juvenile delinquency. They may actually engage in delinquent behavior as a means of seeking the attention they have been denied by the neglectful parents. A great deal of delinquent behavior is nothing more than "acting-out" on the part of the adolescent in an effort to reduce the emotional tension created by an unhealthy parent-child relationship and a dysfunctional home environment.

ATTACHMENT PATTERNS AND CRIMINALITY

The importance of the attachment process is that an adult's capacity to build and maintain healthy and stable intimate relationships is governed in large part by the quality of their attachment to a primary caregiver in infancy and early childhood. An inability to build and maintain such relationships is correlated strongly with deviant behavior, and thus, as previously pointed out, the attachment process becomes the first critical leg of the Criminal Triad.

We previously discussed the various attachment patterns in children identified by Ainsworth and Main—*secure, anxious-ambivalent, anxious-avoidant,* and *disorganized.* In adulthood, as the individual's emotional bond shifts from parent to intimate partner, the parent-child attachment that formed years earlier now has a major influence on the quality of the person's relationship with an intimate partner. The individual's partner will enjoy the fruits of good parenting and a secure attachment, and in the same respect will suffer the consequences of bad or neglectful parenting and an insecure attachment. In many respects, the manner in which an individual interacts with their opposite-sex parent during childhood is predictive of how they will interact

44   *Serial Killers*

with an intimate partner in adulthood. The parent-child relationship serves as a template for all future social relationships.

So how does each of the attachment patterns described earlier in the chapter manifest themselves in adulthood? Two researchers who built upon Bowlby and Ainsworth's work, Cindy Hazan and Phillip Shaver (1987), proposed that childhood attachment patterns translate into a series of adult patterns that reflect an individual's openness to intimate relationships, as measured along two dimensions—*avoidance* and *anxiety*. The former is an indicator of the individual's willingness to engage in intimate relationships, while the latter reflects the level of anxiety experienced by the individual at the idea of interpersonal connectedness. The two dimensions of adult attachment are illustrated in Figure 2.4.

There are four distinct patterns of adult attachment identified, each a reflection of the individual's orientation on the two dimensions. They are *secure, anxious-preoccupied, dismissive-avoidant,* and *fearfull-avoidant*. A description of each follows:

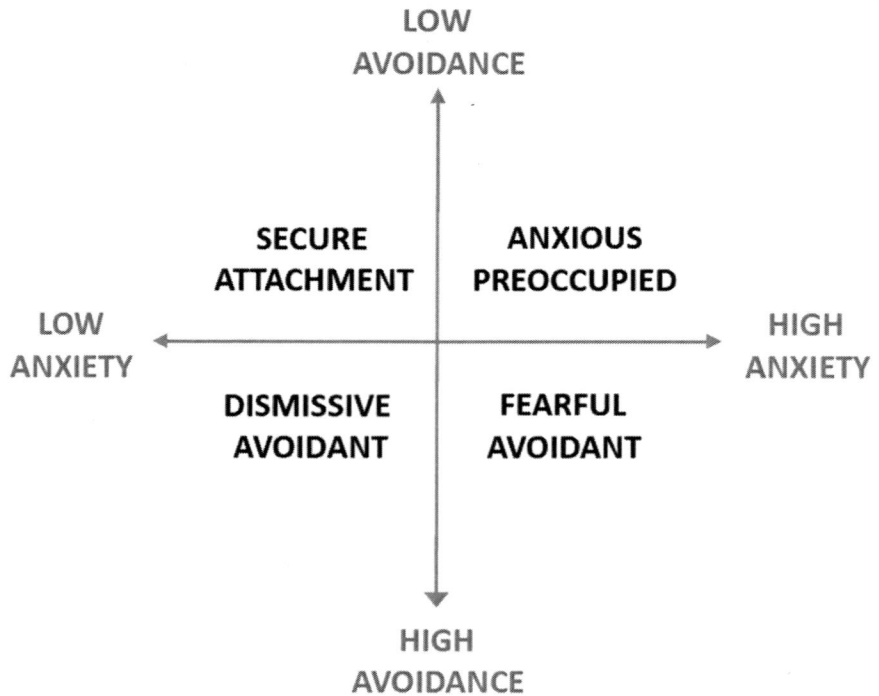

Figure 2.4. Two dimensions of adult attachment.

- *Secure attachment.* Securely attached adults have low levels of anxiety and avoidance, and experience little difficulty establishing and maintaining intimate relationships. They understand that an intimate couple is a partnership, with each party depending on the other for emotional support, one freely giving and the other willingly accepting it without condition. They tend to have a positive view not only of themselves, but also of their partners and the quality of their relationships. They are warm and respectful toward their partners, and they afford them adequate levels of independence to lead autonomous lives without fear of unsettling their relationships. Securely attached adults tend to enjoy emotional health and stability, and even increased levels of physical health due to the lower amounts of stress impacting their daily lives. Secure Attachment corresponds to the same attachment pattern in childhood.
- *Anxious-preoccupied attachment.* These individuals are high on anxiety but low on avoidance, meaning they actively seek out intimacy but fear they will not live up to the expectations of the relationship. These individuals are *clingers,* and seek not only intimacy, but also approval and validation. They become preoccupied with their relationships, and live in fear of losing their partners due to their own inadequacy. They tend to have predominantly negative views of themselves and their partners, and are less trusting and more impulsive. This form of attachment corresponds to the *anxious-ambivalent* pattern in childhood, and is most commonly associated with authoritarian parenting. As an adult, the individual is haunted by their perceived failure as a child to live up to the expectations of a critical, nonapproving parent. The result is lower self-esteem, a lack of self-confidence, insecurity, and the need for validation from whomever they select to serve in a surrogate capacity for the critical parent.
- *Dismissive-avoidant attachment.* These individuals are low on anxiety and high on avoidance. Relationships are not particularly stressful because real intimacy is avoided. They endeavor to be invulnerable and emotionally independent, and are therefore reluctant to open themselves to another person. Outward displays of emotion are perceived as weakness. These adults tend to have more positive views of themselves than their partners. When they are rejected they minimize the event, and see it as further justification for avoiding intimacy and closeness. They may view the relationship as unimportant and unnec-

essary, and participate for entirely selfish reasons. This form of attachment corresponds to the *anxious-avoidant* pattern in childhood, and is most commonly associated with the neglectful parenting style. These children adapt to the parents' absence in their lives by becoming emotionally self-sufficient, and by building walls to prevent themselves from ever being neglected or let down again. As adults, they are emotionally cold and impenetrable.

• *Fearful-avoidant attachment.* These adults are high on anxiety and avoidance. They tend to avoid close relationships out of fear of being rejected. Unlike the dismissive-avoidant attachment pattern, these people actually desire closeness and intimacy, but are so afraid of exposing themselves emotionally, they simply don't do it. They view themselves and their partners in a negative light, and perceive themselves as unworthy of a close and intimate relationship. They tend to be untrusting, and suffer from chronic loneliness and feelings of despair. This attachment pattern also corresponds to the *anxious-avoidant* childhood attachment pattern, and like the dismissive-avoidant pattern described above, is most closely associated with a neglectful parenting style. The difference however is determined by their degree of self-approval. The dismissive-avoidant individual has high self-approval. They view themselves as strong and in control. By contrast, the fearful-avoidant individual has low self-approval. These individuals view themselves as weak and unworthy, and endeavor to maintain what little control over their lives they perceive themselves as having. The dismissive-avoidant individual comes out of the parent-child relationship hardened and determined, while the fearful-avoidant individual comes out feeling abandoned and inadequate.

Each of the adult attachment patterns described above will result in a general demeanor the individual will demonstrate toward other people, from significant others in their lives to complete strangers. This demeanor, if grounded in a secure attachment, will play a crucial role in the development of the individual's internal deterrence system. However, it can also contribute to the development of a criminal personality type if influenced by an insecure attachment. It is a demeanor that is determined early on in life, externalized as an adult, and remains relatively stable across the lifespan. Each of these interpersonal response patterns can be summed up as follows:

1. Secure attachment = *Respect*
2. Anxious-preoccupied attachment = *Dependence*
3. Fearful-avoidant attachment = *Distrust*
4. Dismissive-avoidant attachment = *Contempt*

One thing must be said about the disorganized attachment pattern in childhood. Notice there is no associated adult attachment style indicated. This attachment pattern will typically carry over into adulthood without changing in form or substance. In a sense, it represents a complete lack of any internalized attachment, and therefore can best be described in adulthood as an *asocial* demeanor toward others, meaning they simply avoid social or intimate relationships altogether. Unlike the *fearful-avoidant* individual who avoids relationships for reasons of self protection and fear, the *asocial* individual simply feels no desire to even form relationships, and is thus egocentric to the extreme. They feel no emotional connection to other people, and may suffer from a mental illness. In terms of eventually developing a criminal personality type, the *disorganized-asocial* individual is typically void of the personality characteristics that can impede such a negative developmental outcome.

ATTACHMENT AND THE CRIMINAL TRIAD

The development of the Social Deterrence Mechanism is directly connected to the quality of the individual's childhood attachment. A securely attached child develops into a securely attached adult who respects other people. They desire that respect to be reciprocated, but their own is unconditional. Securely attached adults value others, and they look for the good in people rather than the bad. Their sense of self-worth is in part derived from the feedback they receive from significant others and peers. As a child, they feel shame in not living up to the expectations of the parents when they behave badly. As an adult, they experience this same emotion when they fail to live up to the expectations of significant others, friends, and society as a whole by committing crime and getting caught, by failing to meet financial obligations, perhaps by failing at business ventures, or by succumbing to the temptation to engage in any number of moral indiscretions. It is this fear of shame and public exposure that acts to deter securely-attached adults from engaging in criminality and social deviance. Thus the connection between secure attachment and the development of the Social Deterrence Mechanism is clear.

Each of the remaining adult attachment patterns is problematic for the development of the social deterrence mechanism. Each, along a continuum from mild to profound, negatively impacts the degree to which an individual is deterred from engaging in deviant behavior by the potential shame and embarrassment of not living up to the expectations of others. At one end of the continuum is the *anxious-preoccupied* individual. This individual is mildly impacted by their near-obsessive need for both intimate and close social relationships. They are motivated more by personal insecurity and a need for validation than a desire to seek interpersonal closeness for its own sake. And while these individuals do typically demonstrate a reasonably well-developed social deterrence mechanism, it is fragile at best. They can easily become obsessed with another person, and like all such individuals, are at risk of resorting to extreme measures if they become frustrated in their quest to make that person their own. Criminality becomes a real possibility if the *anxious-preoccupied* individual feels rejected. Even absent any singular obsession, this person is at risk of acting out their frustrations if they feel globally rejected.

Next on the continuum is the *fearful-avoidant* individual, whose social deterrence mechanism is moderately impacted in a negative way by their lack of social contact and intimacy. Their fear of rejection, and thus their avoidance of intimacy, may cause them to project blame for their circumstances on other people. They are distrusting of others and place little importance on how people perceive them. Their chronic loneliness can turn into despair and hopelessness, which can lead to any number of criminal acts. A sense of hopelessness tends to diminish any internal deterrence capacity the individual may have had. They become entirely egocentric, and thus they are undeterred by how others might perceive them. In fact, how others might perceive them may actually empower this type of individual to engage in criminality if they desire to make a dramatic statement to someone, or to the world in general, about the hopelessness they feel.

The *dismissive-avoidant* individual is profoundly impacted in their development of a social deterrence mechanism. They feel no emotional connection to other people, nor do they wish to. For this individual, intimacy is superficial, and engaged in only to achieve an entirely selfish end. This individual holds a positive view of themselves, but negative and demeaning views of everyone else. Thus they are in no way deterred from deviant behavior by how others might perceive them. They are not concerned about being seen in a positive light even when not engaged in deviant behavior. The opinions of others matter little. They are entirely egocentric, and thus empathic awareness is difficult, if not impossible. These individuals tend not to act out their attachment deficiencies. They seldom see themselves as deficient in that regard. Instead they become very proficient at repressing the parental neglect or abuse that led to their dismissive demeanor. When they resort to criminality, their acts tend not to be symbolic, as in the case of the *fearful-avoidant* individual. Rather, their crimes are opportunistic and hedonistic. They do what they do for personal gain or enjoyment. The potential for public shame and embarrassment if caught is not a concern, and therefore has no deterrent effect on this individual.

At the far end of the continuum of course is the *disorganized* individual. This individual is asocial and thus void of any internal deterrence mechanism where their emotional connection to other people is a factor. As adults, they typically suffer from some type of mental illness, ranging from a personality disorder to a severe thought disorder. These people can be very dangerous because they also typically lack any sense of morality, as discussed in the following chapter. Whereas in the other adult attachment patterns a social deterrence mechanism may be present to varying degrees, in this individual, it is nonexistent.

The relationship between childhood and adult attachment patterns, and the further relationship between the attachment process and the development of the social deterrence mechanism is illustrated in Figure 2.5.

In summary, the attachment process in early childhood is so critical because it is the most important determinant of social competence in adulthood, especially the ability to build and maintain intimate relationships. An adult who does not experience intimacy, whether voluntarily or due to an inability to establish such a relationship, is an individual who for the most part is isolated and lonely, or in the absence of either, egocentric to a pathological degree. Intimacy is one of the

Child Attachment	Secure	Anxious-Ambivalent	Anxious-Avoidant	Anxious-Avoidant	Disorganized
Adult Attachment	Secure	Anxious-Preoccupied	Fearful-Avoidant	Dismissive-Avoidant	Antisocial
Relationship Demeanor	Respect	Dependence	Distrust	Contempt	Erratic
Social Deterrence Mechanism	Developed	Mildly Deficient	Moderately Deficient	Severely Deficient	Void

Figure 2.5. The relationship between attachment process and the Development of the Social Deterrence Mechanism (SDM).

cornerstones of emotional health in adulthood. Not being able to enjoy it denies an individual the opportunity to experience something the long process of evolution has encoded in our DNA to desire and seek out, thus making it more than just an enjoyable pastime. As we have discussed, such an individual will not develop the capacity to self-deter from deviant behavior in order to avoid the shame and embarrassment that will result if they are caught. Such a fear is not present in sufficient levels in insecurely-attached adults. Thus the attachment process is the first critical leg of the Criminal Triad to be understood. It is the foundation upon which the other two developmental processes, *moral development* and *identity formation,* will either progress or fail.

The attachment process is critical for another reason. While an insecure attachment may cause an individual to lack a social deterrence mechanism, it may also actually motivate the individual to commit crime, even serial murder. We will discuss the three types of serial killers, including the *symbolic* killer, more in Chapter 7, and the role attachment plays in the development of that particular type of killer.

Chapter 3

LEARNING TO FEEL
The Role of Moral Development in Early to Middle Childhood

INTRODUCTION

The second critical leg of the Criminal Triad is *morality,* or the internalized system of cognitions and affective response patterns that come together in the individual to promote a sense of belongingness to the human race and an active concern for the welfare of its members. It is the part of our psychological makeup that compels us to behave in ways considered acceptable and right by the standards of our society, and to maintain a compassionate demeanor toward other people without conditions or qualifiers. Most criminals, certainly those guilty of the most heinous crimes, are void of any sense of morality. They have little ability to feel what their victims feel, they are unsympathetic to their pain and suffering, and they feel no obligation to adhere to the rules and expectations of the predominant culture. Moral development, if successful, leads to the development of the moral deterrence mechanism (MDM). It is this component of our general deterrence system that compels the individual to avoid crime because of its inconsistency with the established rules and laws of society, and because of the potential such behavior has for victimizing innocent people.

Unfortunately there has never been a universally accepted definition of exactly what morality is. Any definition is influenced heavily by one's politics, their religious faith, and their culture. Morality is also situational, making it even more difficult to define. For example, it is easy to view the taking of innocent life as an immoral act. But what if the intent of that act is to save even more lives? Such was the case when President Truman made the decision to drop two atomic bombs on Japanese cities at the end of WWII. Was it immoral to do so when the result could potentially have been the conclusion of the war, as it turned out to be? Even in the criminal domain the lines are sometimes blurred. The story of Robin Hood provides young people a confusing new moral paradigm in which bad is good and crime is virtuous. In the 1920s, the poor working classes of Chicago were fed at soup kitchens funded by the criminal enterprise of Al Capone. Did these desperate people consider it immoral when Capone brutally murdered other thugs who tried to move in on his territory? And what about those who in more recent times have bombed abortion clinics, spray painted fur coats, or created civil disorder to stop a military action? If you were to query any one of them, they would claim the moral high ground. So the question of morality can be a confusing one indeed. Our task is to understand its role in deterring crime, even those crimes considered morally good by those who commit them, and the developmental processes that lead to the internalization of a moral sensibility.

A number of basic questions must be answered in order to construct a comprehensive model of moral thought and behavior. Is morality something we think (cognition), something we feel (emotion), or is it a combination of both? Is it learned behavior, or is it part of our genetic code, the result of moral people having more successfully adapted to their environment? And what exactly are the component parts of morality? Is it a single, measurable dimension of the human personality, or is it multidimensional, consisting of multiple personality variables that combine in some particular way to make a person moral? Finally, what about the process of moral developmental? Does a moral demeanor develop through a series of qualitatively different stages, or is it a gradual blossoming that can be interrupted at various points and pushed from its developmental path?

In this chapter, we will look at the role of morality in deterring crime and deviance. We will look at the negative impact on a person when a moral deterrence mechanism (MDM) is lacking, especially when that void is accompanied by an underdeveloped or undeveloped social deterrence mechanism (SDM) and/or self-deterrence mechanism (SeDM). In short, we will look at the connection between morality, or a lack of, and the development of the criminal personality type (CPT).

DEFINING MORALITY

Before we begin a discussion of morality and its effect on a child's development and behavior, we must first define exactly what morality is. From our discussion thus far, we have seen that there is no universally-accepted definition to which researchers and theorists alike ascribe. Theories that are *cognitive* in nature tend to shortchange the role of emotion in moral reasoning and its development, and those that are predominantly *affective* tend to minimize the impact of cognition. Criminal Triad Theory presents an eclectic model of morality, one containing both cognitive and affective components. As shown in Figure 3.1, the CTT model presents morality as a combination of three internal processes: *empathic awareness, sympathetic arousal,* and *altruistic motivation;* the latter empowered by the universal principles of *justice, ethics,* and *humanity.*

These processes act together in the individual to create an emotional connection to other people—family, friends, even strangers—and a sincere and unconditional concern for their welfare, rights, and dignity. In simplest terms, when we interact with someone on a moral level, especially someone suffering in some way, first we understand

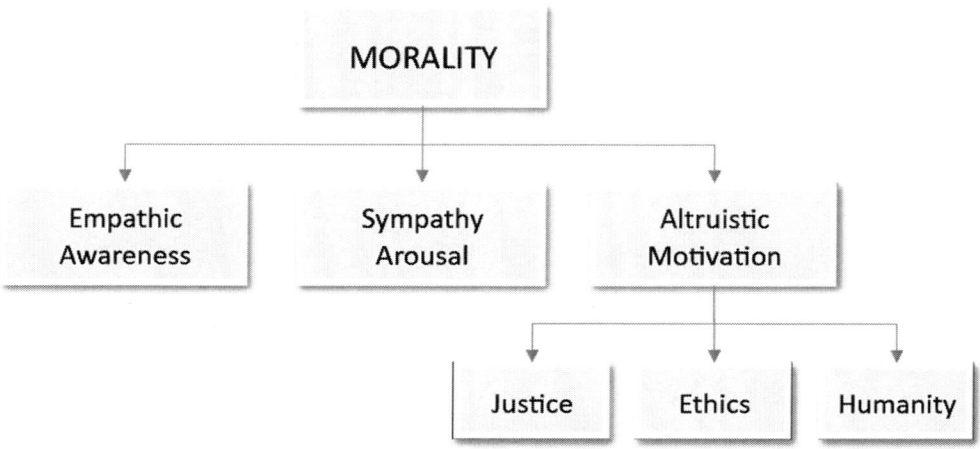

Figure 3.1. CTT Model of Morality.

their situation intellectually (empathy), then we share their situation emotionally (sympathy), and finally we confront their situation overtly (altruism). This is the CTT model of morality.

Rather than attempt to define and describe a single developmental process for morality, its multifaceted constitution requires that we understand a number of different developmental processes that eventually coalesce in middle to late childhood to bring this desired trait to the surface of an individual's personality. These processes—empathy, sympathy, and altruism—together result in the development of a moral self, and concurrently, the development of the moral deterrence mechanism (MDM) that will in part keep the individual from succumbing to the temptation to engage in crime and other forms of social deviance.

Empathic Awareness

There is a multiplicity of definitions associated with empathy. Some theorists attempt to account for its development in neurological terms. Others address it from the perspective of sociobiology. And still others define the construct using abstract philosophical terminology. Even within the discipline of psychology there has been a lack of consensus. For some, empathy is an emotional response, while for others, it is a function of cognition. The psychological theories addressing its development range from simple one-dimensional explanations to complex multidimensional stage theories.

The diversity of theoretical perspectives relating to empathy has hindered a bit its empirical study; however, two main research traditions have evolved. The first studies empathy as a function of cognition, or an intellectual understanding of another's emotions. This research tradition is interested in studying how accurately we can understand another's emotional state, and the various personality, social, and cultural factors that impact that accuracy. The other research tradition studies empathy as an emotional response. This tradition is interested primarily in the development of empathy, the situational factors that elicit it, and its relationship to altruistic behavior.

The most widely-cited theory of empathy and its development is that of Martin Hoffman (2000). He viewed empathy as a biologically-based predisposition to prosocial and altruistic behavior. This predisposition results from a combination of cognitive and affective processes that mature over time as the child's cognitive abilities and emotional sensitivities develop. He proposed a four-stage developmental scheme that begins with a newborn's instinctive crying, and ends with an adolescent's ability to empathize not only with another individual's emotional state, but with the pain and hardships of an entire class of people.

Hoffman's first stage, which he labeled *global empathy*, begins early in infancy, at a time when the child is entirely egocentric and unable to differentiate self from others. During this stage, the child will reactively cry at the sound of another doing the same. This *contagious crying* is a reflexive action according to Hoffman, and is acquired before the ability to actually understand the feelings of self and others. This reflex can be viewed as a remnant of the evolutionary process, having been selected over time due to its value as a survival mechanism. Studies of other reactive behaviors in infants, notably Andrew Meltzhoff's (1982) findings that newborn infants as young as two weeks old are able to mimic facial expressions, support the existence of this type of biologically-based reaction.

The second stage of his theory, *egocentric empathy*, begins during the second year when the child begins to experience basic empathic awareness. They remain egocentric, so while they at least begin to recognize the emotional state of another, they have not yet acquired the ability to totally differentiate the other person's state from their own. Thus, they tend to respond to the other person in a way that would alleviate their own similar emotional state. For example, a small child might try to comfort another crying child by giving them the same toy their own parent brings to them when they cry. For the egocentric child, another's emotional discomfort is indistinguishable from their own.

Hoffman's third stage is *empathy for another's feelings*, occurring typically in the third year of life. During this stage, the child begins to acquire the ability to differentiate not only their own emotional state from that of another, but also between different emotions in the same person. They begin to have a basic understanding of emotions, and can now represent them verbally in limited fashion. They are now starting to experience cognitive empathy, and with the onset of this ability, they begin to respond to another's emotional state as separate and distinct from their own. Now they may respond to the crying child by offering one of the child's own toys in an effort to console them.

Hoffman's final stage is what he refers to as *empathy for another's general condition.* He believed this stage begins in late childhood or early adolescence when the child has acquired the full ability to understand a situation from another's perspective. By this time, they have also gained the ability to understand the inner experiences of another individual. Empathy extends beyond simply an understanding of the other person's overt emotional displays. Now, according to Hoffman, the child can vicariously experience the internal state of another as if it were the child's own. They are no longer just *thinking* about another's emotional state, but now they are *feeling* it as well. Thus they are now experiencing affective empathy. They can also now understand and experience the general condition of an entire class of people, such as those living in poverty or victimized by discrimination. This final stage takes them into adulthood a fully empathic individual, able to experience the pain, discomfort, and suffering of another person on both an intellectual and emotional level. For Hoffman, morality and altruistic behavior are born of this ability.

By presenting a continuum in which the cognitive and affective processes are inseparable components of the same developmental progression, Hoffman leaves little room for a scenario in which one could develop without the other doing so. This is exactly the case with the most heinous of criminals who experience little affective engagement with their victims, yet are fully aware cognitively of their actions and the ramifications of those actions. Countless murderers, rapists, and child molesters have reported feeling absolutely nothing as they perpetrated their crimes. Hoffman suggests that by early adolescence, long before many criminals begin their deviant acts, both affective and cognitive empathy are developed (stage 4). But it is obvious that true affective empathy, as Hoffman defines it, never fully develops in many offenders. If this is so, and if those offenders never progress through Hoffman's stage 4, is cognitive development also halted? It would seem that for this reason it is important to understand the cognitive and affective components of moral behavior as two distinct processes with separate developmental progressions.

The CTT model of morality presents empathy in a slightly different light from Hoffman's conceptualization. It begins by addressing as separate constructs the cognitive and affective processes that have traditionally been included in most definitions of morality. The CTT conceptualization views empathy as the ability to understand intellectually the emotional state of another. The act of understanding is more than just a recognition of the isolated state itself. It includes an understanding of the situational context in which the state arises, and its implications for the individual's life. For example, if a perfect stranger dressed in a suit and tie were to approach you on the street and ask for money, perhaps even announcing he is hungry, it would be difficult to immediately empathize with the stranger. It would be easy enough to process the basic information of an individual asking for a handout and mentioning his hunger, but the confusion and suspicion that would result from such an individual asking for money for that purpose would likely prevent you from making any assumptions about context. Therefore, an awareness of the individual's plight would likely never rise to the level of empathic awareness without more information being introduced. Mere recognition of another's emotional state without a recognition of the context and implications is something short of empathy.

Now let's assume the individual who approaches you is dressed in layers of tattered clothing and pushing a grocery cart full of assorted junk. In this case, you immediately recognize the context in your assumption that the individual is homeless and hungry. There is little dissonance in this scenario, as in the previous example. You recognize his emotional state (hunger), the context leading to this circumstance (homelessness), and the implications of the context for the man's life (money is needed for basic sustenance). One of two things will happen in this situation. Either you will empathize with the individual, which in turn elicits an emotional response (i.e., sympathy), or you do not, in which case no emotional response occurs. In the latter case, either the person lacks the ability to empathize, or they do, but choose instead either to repress or reframe the situation in order to keep a sympathetic response from rising to the surface.

Another example may make it clearer. This time assume you are sitting on a park bench beside a man dressed in a suit and tie who has an obvious downtrodden demeanor. Immediately you recognize his emotional state. When you inquire as to what is troubling him, he tells you he was just fired from his job. With this bit of information you now understand the context, and with no further information being offered you begin to make some assumptions about the implications for the man's life. You know how devastating it is to be unemployed, espe-

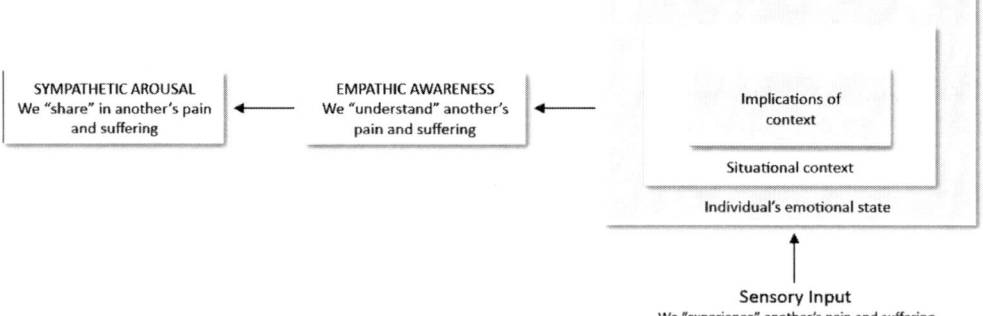

Figure 3.2. The Empathic-Sympathetic Response Dynamic.

cially at an age where having a family to support is likely. You understand about continued healthcare, paying a mortgage and other obligations, and the difficulties of finding new employment. You are now empathizing with the man as you make these assumptions, and an emotional response is elicited. This empathic-sympathetic response dynamic is illustrated in Figure 3.2.

Now let's assume for the sake of illustration that you have the misfortune of suffering from a terminal illness. In this case, you may not empathize with the man who just lost his job. You understand his emotional state and the context that led to it, but your appreciation for the implications of the man's unemployment is greatly minimized, or even precluded, as you measure his situation against the tragedy of your terminal disease. Simply put, you feel no sympathy–due to a lack of prerequisite empathy–for a man who still enjoys his good health. In this case, the negative impact of egocentrism on the ability to empathize becomes evident. The more individuals focus on themselves and their own situation, the less they are able to empathize with others. This is not to suggest however that terminally ill people always fall in this category. Quite the contrary, many become so sensitized to the hardships of others that their ability to empathize is magnified.

So the first leg of moral behavior is empathic awareness, or an understanding of another's situation that is deep enough to elicit from the individual an emotional response (i.e., sympathy). In developmental terms, empathy develops as egocentricity recedes. It is when a child learns to view the world from someone else's perspective that they begin to evaluate that perspective in its context. When their actions influence the emotions of others, especially the parents or other children, they come to understand not only the other person's emotional state, but that it was their actions that caused it. They also come to understand the implications of their own behavior for the other person's life. For example, when the child's misbehavior leads to the parent's anger, the child understands the emotional state (anger), the context in which the state occurs (their own misbehavior), and the implications of their behavior for the parent's life (continued frustration, inability to get work finished, displeasure with the child, etc.). This creates an uncomfortable emotional state for the child, one of guilt and perhaps shame. In an effort to diminish this uncomfortable state, and in the future to avoid it altogether, the child becomes more sensitive to the relationship of their actions to the emotional state of others. The child is learning to shift their evaluative focus from self to others. The child is learning to empathize.

The ability to evaluate a situation in this manner does not develop automatically, as many cognitive abilities do. It is primarily the result of effective parenting. When a parent pairs discipline with an explanation as to why the child is being disciplined, this causes the child to attend to the cause-effect relationship between their own behavior and the parents' emotional state. They are learning to evaluate context, and to empathize with the parent. Conversely, those children raised by either extremely authoritarian or permissive parents tend to remain egocentric, and thus their ability to empathize is diminished. In the latter case, where there is no discipline, the child is never forced to take responsibility for their misbehavior, nor are they confronted with the implications of their behavior, and thus their ability to empathize is already lacking at an important point in their development. The demeanor of selfishness that often results from a child being raised by permissive parents is an extreme form of egocentrism, and thus inhibits their ability to empathize with others, especially those whose interests are in conflict with their own.

In the case of the authoritarian parent, whose discipline is harsh and inconsistent, the child quickly learns that their behavior has little effect on the parent. They are disciplined regardless of the intentions of their actions, with little explanation or opportunity for self-correction. Not only do they learn that it is fruitless to evaluate the parent's emotional state and context, since nothing seems to ease their oppressive methods, but the child also begins to focus entirely on their own behavior in an effort to avoid the parent's wrath. The end result is a heightened egocentric demeanor in the child, and a lessened capacity to empathize. Whereas the permissive child's egocentrism will eventually manifest itself in the form of selfishness, in the authoritarian child, it will bubble to the surface in the form of anger and interpersonal coldness.

Sympathetic Arousal

The second leg of moral behavior, as illustrated in Figure 3.2 above, is the emotional response that results from an empathic awareness of another's distress; a response we typically refer to as *sympathy*. The distinction between this and empathy is a fine one, and the developmental context in which both unfold is similar. In fact, sympathetic arousal subsumes empathic awareness, but the reverse is not necessarily so. It is entirely possible to empathize with someone without feeling sympathy for them. The serial killer who tortures his victims certainly empathizes with them. It is his understanding of his victim's distress that motivates him to perpetrate even more violence. But the serial killer in this case is void of any sympathetic arousal for the victim.

Whereas empathy is a cognitive process that requires some amount of contemplation, sympathy is an emotional response that occurs quite automatically. It is the vicarious sharing of another's emotional state, causing some level of distress in the person experiencing the sympathetic arousal. There are many colloquialisms employed to depict this phenomenon. When a person describes being "tugged at the heartstrings," they are describing a sympathetic arousal by some particular stimulus. It is a felt emotion that many times includes a physiological response as well. The particular emotion that is felt mirrors that of the individual whose situation causes the sympathetic arousal. When you see a homeless man, you feel his despair. When you see an elderly man or woman sitting alone on a park bench, you feel their loneliness. When you see a sick child, you feel their vulnerability. In each of these cases, the sympathy is immediately preceded by an empathic awareness of the other person's situation and emotional state.

There are two explanations for a naturally occurring emotional response such as sympathy. The first is that the response is a remnant of the evolutionary process. Evolutionary psychologists will suggest that a child's emotional distress when confronted by strangers, dangerous heights, and even certain members of the animal kingdom—snakes, and other potentially poisonous critters—is the result of evolution. In Darwinian terms, those children who were naturally avoidant of such things were more successful in terms of survival, and thus their genetic configurations were passed on. Eventually, over the course of hundreds, if not thousands of generations, a genetic predisposition to experience fear in the presence of such things became *naturally selected* as an innate characteristic in newborn children. In the case of sympathy, it could be argued from an evolutionary perspective that sympathetic arousal was a survival mechanism in prehistory because it promoted communal concern and protection, and other prosocial behaviors. Thus, those who were more sympathetic survived and passed on their genetic maps more successfully.

For the second possible explanation, and the one more likely in terms of the development of a sympathetic arousal mechanism, we can turn to Pavlov's dog and the process of *classical conditioning*. When this process occurs, a previously neutral stimulus comes to automatically elicit a response because of its association with another stimulus that naturally elicits the same response. In Pavlov's case, while measuring the amount of naturally-occurring salivation in a dog (unconditioned response) following the introduction of food (unconditioned stimulus), he discovered that by pairing a bell (conditioned stimulus) with the food, eventually just ringing the bell would cause the dog to salivate. Pavlov had discovered classical conditioning. Another example is the man who feels anxiety in the presence of assertive and critical women because he associates them with his critical mother. He doesn't contemplate the association before developing the anxiety. Rather, it occurs automatically below the surface of conscious awareness.

The conditioning process for a sympathetic response pattern begins prior to the child acquiring the cognitive maturity to contemplate another's emotional state, a necessary condition for empathy. When a child becomes personally distressed, there is an emotional as well as physiological reaction that takes place in the child. The outward manifestation of this reaction is typically a distressed cry. But what happens when the child sees another in distress, especially a parent or another child? At a young age, certainly during the first three years of life, while the child is still limited by their own egocentricity, they react to

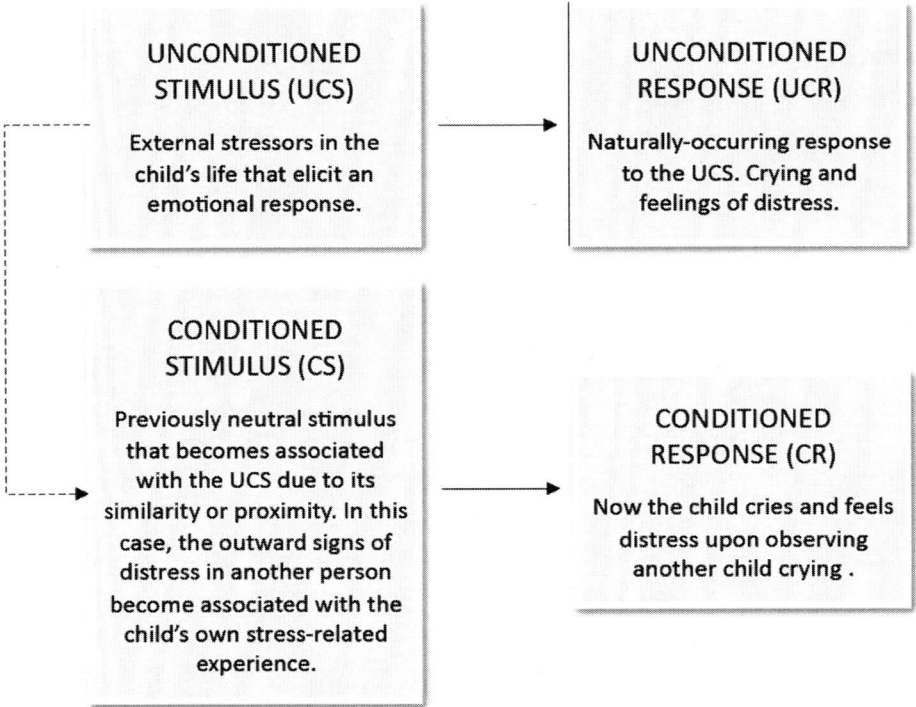

Figure 3.3. Classically conditioned distress response in a child.

the distress of others as if they themselves are distressed. While they recognize the distressed state, they are limited in their ability to understand it from other than their own perspective. This is why the crying of another child elicits their own crying. Simply put, while an external stressor in a child's life elicits a naturally-occurring reaction (distress/crying), the outward signs of distress in another child (crying) can become associated with the observing child's own stress-related experience. When this happens, simply observing the other child's behavior (crying) can elicit a similar reaction (distress/crying) in the observing child. In Pavlovian terms, it can be illustrated in Figure 3.3.

This basic distress response is typically among the first sympathetic responses to be conditioned in a child. Others, too, are created in this fashion, including fear, happiness, and excitement, all of which begin as egocentric responses, and end as classically-conditioned sympathetic responses. These conditioned responses are then strengthened and generalized to storybook characters, animals, and even inanimate objects (i.e., the man in the moon) as the child's ability to employ symbolic thought and imagination begins to develop. The more complex emotional states such as loneliness, despair, and existential pain, require the ability to empathize and think in a more abstract way in order for the conditioning process to occur. Eventually, around the age of seven, these cognitive abilities begin to gradually unfold.

So at this point, we have addressed two legs of the moral construct. To respond to another person on a moral level, first we must have the ability to empathize, or to truly understand the basis of their emotional distress or discomfort. Sometimes the other person provides us the necessary information to understand their situation, while at others, the circumstances themselves accomplish this. For example, the homeless beggar on the street need provide us no additional information in order to empathize and understand their hardship. Once we do empathize, then we experience a classically-conditioned sympathetic response, as we share in their emotional pain and discomfort by experiencing a like emotion.

The empathy-sympathy response would accomplish little as a moral mechanism without some overt response that empowers the observer's sympathy and mediates the target's emotional pain and discomfort. And that brings us to the third leg of the moral construct, *altruistic motivation,* or a desire to act-out a concern for the welfare, rights, and dignity of others by taking steps to improve their situation. It is this quality that is absent in most criminals, certainly the more violent ones.

Altruistic Motivation

What is it that compels one person to respond to someone in need but inhibits another from doing so? Most adults can empathize with someone in the throes of emotional pain and discomfort, and the vast majority will experience a sympathetic response when they do, but not all will overtly respond in an effort to mediate the situation. Those who do are motivated by a sense of altruism. We think in ways that are empathic, and we feel in ways that are sympathetic, but what exactly is the basis for the cluster of prosocial behaviors we collectively refer to as altruism? Is it a felt need, one that finds its origins in a person's biogenetic constitution, or is it one that is experienced on an intellectual level, having been acquired through some aspect of cognitive maturation?

There have been two predominant views advanced concerning altruism. The first views the phenomenon as purely egoistic in nature, meaning no one truly engages in altruistic behavior solely for the purpose of benefiting another's welfare. Rather, we do it to relieve our own distress that results from an empathic awareness, affectively experienced, of another's emotional pain and discomfort. Those who accept this particular view believe that when we engage another who is experiencing some sort of distress, we tend to experience their emotional state vicariously. Thus, our motivation to reduce that distress through some type of prosocial engagement comes not from an innate sense of morality, but rather from a desire to alleviate our own pain by first reducing the other person's.

The other predominant view of altruistic behavior is that such behavior is motivated by a sincere desire to increase the welfare of another person, even at the expense of one's own. One of the major researchers in the area of helping behavior, C. Daniel Batson (1991), wanted to know if a person could ever slip the bounds of egocentrism to help another out of a purely altruistic concern. His resulting research supported the notion that one may be motivated in that direction for other than egoistic reasons. He connected the desire to help another with the ability to empathize with that person's distress, referring to it as the *empathy-altruism* hypothesis. Batson came to believe that altruistic motivation is always and necessarily preceded by empathic concern. In fact, Batson believed the deeper the level of empathy, the greater the altruistic motivation that results.

Batson didn't deny that people at times enjoy certain benefits from their prosocial behavior. In fact, he identified three types of benefit that can potentially result. First, the helping individual can reduce their own empathic distress by reducing the distress of the person with whom they are empathizing. Second, by helping another, they are able to avoid the negative social or self-judgment that can result from failing to help. And third, the helping individual can potentially gain various social rewards from their altruistic behavior. But while Batson accepted that these benefits do occur in response to prosocial helping behavior, he believed them to be unintended consequences of achieving the ultimate goal of increasing the welfare of another.

So, if Batson is correct, and we are in fact motivated to come to the aid of another for other than egoistic reasons, even when it is not in our self-interest to do so, where does such a motivation originate? Is it genetically-based, or is it a function of cognition and learning? To answer this question, and to come to a full understanding of the nature and development of altruistic motivation, we turn to the work of Lawrence Kohlberg.

KOHLBERG'S STAGE THEORY OF MORAL DEVELOPMENT

Anyone who studies the subject of moral development will encounter the stage theory of Lawrence Kohlberg, considered among the most widely studied and cited theories in this area. Kohlberg, who did his research at both the University of Chicago and at Harvard, developed a six-stage model of moral development. Although predominantly a cognitive theorist, Kohlberg did not believe that moral development results simply from cognitive maturation. Nor did he accept the view that moral thinking, especially altruism, results from the socialization process or the influence of parents, teachers, and peers. Rather, he believed that moral thinking unfolds as we are confronted with new and more complex situations that demand us to evaluate our own viewpoints against those of others, and to do so while maintaining a fair and just system. From this process, we learn to think in moral ways. For Kohlberg, cognitive development certainly facilitates moral development; however, the latter does not progress automatically to any particular point, nor is it guaranteed that the child will ultimately progress through all six of his proposed stages.

Most of Kohlberg's research was conducted through the use of moral dilemmas. These exercises required children to read or listen to various scenarios in which a character is confronted with a choice between two opposing options, or moral imperatives. Such a choice creates for the character a moral conflict since obeying one option unavoidably causes them to violate the other. The children were then asked to evaluate the character's options, and to make a decision as to what the character should do. Of course, by doing this, Kohlberg was able to create a window through which he was able to observe the moral reasoning of the children he studied. One of his most famous scenarios was the *Heinz Dilemma* (Kohlberg, 1981). Kohlberg presented his young subjects—primarily young boys from lower- to middle-class families in Chicago—the following scenario, and then asked them to respond to a series of questions:

> A woman was near death from a special kind of cancer. There was one drug that the doctors thought might save her. It was a form of radium that a druggist in the same town had recently discovered. The drug was expensive to make, but the druggist was charging ten times what the drug cost him to produce. He paid $200 for the radium and charged $2,000 for a small dose of the drug. The sick woman's husband, Heinz, went to everyone he knew to borrow the money, but he could only get together about $1,000 which is half of what it cost. He told the druggist that his wife was dying and asked him to sell it cheaper or let him pay later. But the druggist said: "No, I discovered the drug and I'm going to make money from it." So Heinz got desperate and broke into the man's store to steal the drug for his wife. Should Heinz have broken into the laboratory to steal the drug for his wife? Why or why not?

Kohlberg was less interested in whether or not the children thought Heinz should have stolen the drug but focused more on why they did or did not consider such behavior to be the right thing to do. Their response to the initial question was followed by an interview aimed at gaining insight as to how they arrived at their answer. Kohlberg codified the children's responses in an effort to identify common themes in their reasoning, and from this data he was able to identify the six major response patterns, or moral stages, presented in Figure 3.4.

These stages represent a series of qualitatively different levels of moral thinking through which a child may develop. Taken as a whole, they represent a continuum, from a very basic type of moral reasoning typically found in young children, to an advanced level that only a small minority of people ever achieves. Each stage is described as follows:

Preconventional Morality

• *Stage 1: Obedience & Punishment.* During Kohlberg's first stage, the child has yet to internalize any system of values. They evaluate the

PRECONVENTIONAL MORALITY	CONVENTIONAL MORALITY	POSTCONVENTIONAL MORALITY
STAGE 1 The individual makes moral decisions based on the consequences of their actions. If the consequences are perceived as bad, then the behavior is viewed as bad and inappropriate.	**STAGE 3** The individual makes moral decisions based on their interpersonal relationships. Behaviors that benefit the maintenance of those relationships are viewed as good and appropriate.	**STAGE 5** The individual makes moral decisions by weighing the interests of the individual against the need for social order. Rules and laws are viewed as changeable when necessary.
STAGE 2 The individual makes moral decisions based on egocentric interests. If a behavior benefits the individual it is viewed as good and appropriate regardless of its implications for others.	**STAGE 4** The individual makes moral decisions based on the rules and expectations of society. If a behavior is against social convention it is viewed as morally bad. Law and order is given supremacy.	**STAGE 6** The individual makes moral decision based on universal human principles. The rights of the individual transcend the rules and expectations of society. Individual freedom and dignity are help supreme.

Figure 3.4. Kohlberg's stages of moral development.

rightness or wrongness of an act by its consequences. If in their mind they could potentially get punished for committing a particular act, then that act is viewed as bad by the child, regardless of intentions. Children at stage 1 view Heinz's decision to steal the drug as wrong since stealing is bad, and a behavior for which they typically get punished.

The limitations of stage 1 thinking are more the result of a child's limited cognitive development than any overly-restrictive parenting, though the latter will certainly impact later development. Until the child gains the cognitive capacity to evaluate different points of view and intentions, morality will remain external to them. Because they will invariably expand their moral reasoning capabilities with further cognitive development, it is very seldom that adults will operate from this stage, except perhaps those with the intellectual capacity of a small child.

• *Stage 2: Individualism.* Kohlberg considered stages 1 & 2 as *preconventional* since the individual at either stage views morality from their own self interest, and not as a member of a larger social group. At stage 2, the individual begins to understand that a situation can be understood from different viewpoints, but they remain egocentric in their reasoning. Rather than judging the rightness or wrongness of an act by its consequences, they now judge it by the benefits to them personally. As they evaluate options, what they consider right is what they consider best for them. A child operating at this stage could evaluate the Heinz dilemma in a couple different ways. They may consider his actions right because it is in his best interest to save his wife's life. At this stage, such a response is less about the welfare of the wife, and more about protecting Heinz's self-interests. In an actual response Kohlberg noted, a child at this stage may also say Heinz shouldn't steal the drug, because when his wife dies he may be able to marry a better looking woman (Kohlberg, 1963)! Even though the two responses are opposite, the reasoning in both cases is very egocentric, with the rightness or wrongness of Heinz's behavior determined by his own self-interests rather than those of the wife or the druggist.

Obviously, stage 2 thinking is found in much of the criminal population. Those who commit criminal acts with little thought given to the suffering of their victims, or with little ability to even empathize with their victims, can be described as operating from this stage of moral reasoning. They don't view themselves as being a member of a larger social structure, and therefore they feel no obligation to live by a system of social norms and standards. They are motivated by their own wants and desires, and thus what is considered wrong is anything that is detrimental to them personally.

Here we begin to see the impact of parenting on moral development. The child being raised by permissive parents—those who avoid any form of discipline—is at risk of missing an important developmental milestone. During stage 1, the child learns that consequences follow actions. And while their reasoning at this stage is imperfect, it is from this simple dynamic that moral development blossoms. If the child's actions are void of consequences, then the process of internalizing an evaluative system to measure right versus wrong is delayed. At stage 2 then, when the child's moral thinking is based on self-interests and by weighing anticipated benefits against potential consequences, if the child has had no history of consequences, then moral reasoning becomes based entirely on self-reward, with no mediation by the potential for consequences. The result is a demeanor of selfishness, a characteristic that negatively impacts the later development of empathy in the child.

What about the opposite of permissive parenting, the authoritarian parent? This parenting style, too, has a negative impact on moral development. At stage 1, the child of an authoritarian parent learns through a harsh system of discipline that EVERYTHING is bad, since everything seems to have negative consequences. Like the child of the permissive parent, they miss out on the opportunity to learn to evaluate a behavior. The permissive child learns that all behavior is acceptable. The authoritarian child learns that all behavior is unacceptable. Even though their evaluation at this stage is based entirely on consequences, it is *what* they are doing, and not *how* they are doing it that is important in developmental terms. They are learning to make moral judgments. Without this ability, at stage 2, the authoritarian child tends to move in a direction opposite that of the permissive child. Egocentricity is amplified in the latter, leading to selfishness, and in the former for reasons of self-protection. The end result is the same. The child of the authoritarian parent becomes so fixed on self that their development of empathy is negatively impacted, since the more egocentric a person is, the less ability they have to interpret events from someone else's viewpoint. In either case, regardless of how you define *morality,* a lack of empathy diminishes its eventual development.

Conventional Morality

• *Stage 3: Interpersonal Relationships.* Kohlberg referred to stages 3 and 4 as *conventional* because individuals at these stages view themselves as part of a larger social structure and make moral judgments based on the interrelationship between their own self-interests and the interests of society. At stage 3, which is typically demonstrated during the adolescent years, the individual bases their moral judgments primarily on interpersonal relationships, and on maintaining those relationships. The rightness or wrongness of an act is measured by its impact on the individual's relationships and friendships, or on the corporate values of a particular subgroup to which the individual belongs. It is during the adolescent years when the child makes an emotional break from the parents and shifts their emotional dependence to significant others outside the family. With this emotional reconfiguration, their sense of morality shifts from the egocentricity of preconventional thinking to the group thinking of stage 3. They are learning to become social beings.

The most obvious example of stage 3 thinking is embedded in the never-ending tension between adolescents and authority figures. In the western world, teens tend to develop their own system of values apart from those of the larger social structure. For example, society considers illicit drug use wrong, both legally and morally. This is why we have laws criminalizing the use of a wide array of drugs. But many, if not most, adolescents view it differently, especially when it comes to the possession and use of marijuana. They view the activity as acceptable, and in no way morally wrong. At stage 3, there is little interest in the values of the larger society. What's important and morally right for an adolescent is what they deem to be important and morally right for adolescents in general. Their sense of morality is further shaped by their loyalty to friends. The adolescent who helps hide his friend from the police does so even at the risk of being criminally charged because it is the right thing to do in his mind. His loyalty demands it, and thus it is morally correct. An individual operating from stage 3 would perhaps argue that it was right for Heinz to steal the drug because his relationship and loyalty to his wife demands it. This individual is not yet thinking in universal terms. If the scenario were to be changed to have Heinz stealing the drug for a complete stranger, the individual at stage 3 might suggest that it is wrong for him to do so since he is under no obligation to a stranger.

In terms of adult or juvenile criminality, stage 3 thinking can be found in criminal subgroups that place their interests and enterprises above those of the greater society in which they live and operate. Organized crime groups, regardless of their ethnicity, would fall in this category. They adhere to the laws and values of society only for reasons of self-preservation rather than any sense of moral obligation. When the interests of the group demand that the laws and values be willingly violated, they do so with little or no moral conflict since morality is measured by what is right for the group. These subgroups can also be culturally based in addition to being organized around criminal enterprises. Some examples are punk rockers, skateboarders, Goths, and drug users. All are distinct subcultures with their own set of values that define their morality.

While there is a general stage 3 morality that exists in adolescents, and to some extent tolerated by society, the children of permissive and authoritarian parents are especially at risk of allowing their developing sense of morality to be shaped by a deviant subgroup. If it is, then the individual will remain at stage 3 for as long as they remain part of the subgroup. For the permissive child, one who has never truly learned right from wrong, affiliating with a subgroup with like values only feeds their selfish egocentrism, and relieves them of the need to live by a system of rules and values which are different from their own. For the authoritarian child, one who has been precluded from internalizing their own set of values, a subgroup offers them the opportunity to do so by adopting the values of the group. These adolescents finally find acceptance and the ability to evaluate right versus wrong based on their own self-interests rather than those of the authoritarian parent(s).

• *Stage 4: Law & Order.* The individual who reasons from this stage is the exact opposite of the stage 2 individual. Whereas the latter makes moral decisions entirely from an egocentric perspective, the stage 4 individual does so entirely from the perspective of the larger society. For these people, morality is defined by those who legislate the law and make the rules to which members of society must conform. In answering the Heinz question, stage 4 individuals would invariably fault Heinz for his actions on the basis that stealing is against the law. Their overriding concern is to maintain the social order.

Few criminals operate from this stage, since it obviously precludes those who willingly violate the law. This conservative moral position however can be seen throughout the American political process, and has had a major influence on the criminal justice system. For example, on the moral question of capital punishment, those who operate from stage 4 would likely advocate strongly for its use. Their position would be that it is against the law to take the life of another human being, and those who do should suffer the ultimate justice. They would view the death penalty as a deterrent, and therefore necessary for the preservation of the social order.

Another area where stage 4 thinking has a significant impact is in the writing and enforcement of our drug laws. Many argue against the idea of criminally charging and incarcerating drug offenders, advocating instead for mandatory treatment options and programs designed to mainstream the drug user back into society. Those who operate from stage 4, however, take the more aggressive stance. They view it as morally right to arrest, convict, and incarcerate drug offenders since they are violating the law. Keeping in mind that stage 4 individuals view morality from the perspective of the larger society, in their minds, their position places them on the moral high ground because to rid society of drug users is to make the world safer for those who choose to abide by the law.

Stage 4 represents a relatively black and white view of moral issues, and is the stage where many adults end up in their moral development. In America, those who adopt a more conservative political philosophy tend to pull more in the direction of stage 4 thinking. For these people, what is right for the individual is subordinated to what is right for the nation as a whole.

Postconventional Morality

• *Stage 5: Social Contracts.* Kohlberg viewed stages 5 and 6 as *postconventional* because people who operate from these stages tend to place a higher value on the individual than society in general. The difference between this and preconventional thinking, however, is a lack of egocentricity. People who reason from these latter two stages think in universal terms. What is important, and what is considered morally good, are those things that protect the social order without diminishing the rights of all individuals.

People at stage 5 view written laws as social contracts that can changed when the situation deems it necessary. Unlike stage 4 people, who define what is morally good by the *letter* of the law, stage 5 people are more focused on the *spirit* of the law. For them, maintaining the social order is best achieved when individual rights are protected. When the rights of individuals and the goals of society come into conflict, stage 4 people will see virtue in supporting the larger societal objectives, even at the expense of individual rights. Stage 5 people, however, will pull more in the direction of maintaining the supremacy of individual rights. This argument played out in recent times in the debate over the U.S. Patriot Act following the terrorist attacks on September 11, 2001. On one side were those who felt it was worth the sacrifice to limit our constitutional freedoms for the sake of protecting the homeland. On the other were those who held to the position that to limit individual freedoms granted under the Constitution was to do more harm to the homeland than any terrorist could ever accomplish with bombs.

As for the Heinz dilemma, people at stage 5 would look for a middle ground. They might suggest that Heinz had no choice but to steal the drug—for him, the morally right thing to do—but because society must maintain safeguards against anarchy, some type of punishment is necessary, though perhaps a lighter form is in order, given Heinz's motivation for breaking the law. While the letter of the law does not make concessions for moral intentions, stage 5 thinkers look to the spirit of the law, which does allow for mitigation. To use our earlier example of capital punishment, stage 5 thinkers may accept that the death penalty is allowed under the law, and may even support its use, but they will demand that it be used equitably and judiciously, and that the validity of its deterrent effect be shown. Short of these criteria being met, especially its deterrent effect, the stage 5 thinker will likely abandon any acceptance of or support for its use.

- *Stage 6: Universal Human Principles.* Kohlberg's final stage of moral development, and the one he believed a relatively small minority of people ever attain, is one in which morality is defined entirely on the basis of universal human principles such as dignity and freedom. For the stage 6 individual, these principles transcend rules and laws, and if a conflict arises, the latter will always be subordinate to the former. These people are directed by their own inner conscience, and an action is judged morally right if it is consistent with their own system of values and ethical principles. Whereas stage 2 thinkers place themselves at the center of moral decision making, and stage 4 individuals place society there, stage 6 thinkers place humanity at the center. These individuals would never accept nor support capital punishment because in their judgment the sanctity of life transcends the need to punish. Their obvious response to the Heinz dilemma is that Heinz is morally in the right for stealing the drug since saving the life of his wife is more important than any law criminalizing such acts.

Kohlberg believed that few people ever rise to this level of moral thinking, and that those who do, don't necessarily remain there. The demands of modern society actually preclude an individual from operating from this stage at all times. In order to maintain a social structure where postconventional behavior is even possible, it becomes necessary from time to time to consider the goals of society over and above the rights of the individual. Without some degree of structure, the risk of anarchy and a breakdown in the social order increases.

Kohlberg believed a number of things about his stages of moral development. First, he believed each stage is qualitatively different from the others, and that each represents a general pattern of thinking across a wide spectrum of issues, and not just questions of morality. He also believed his stages unfold in a set sequence. Children never skip a stage in the course of development, nor do they acquire the stages out of order. And while development to any particular stage is not guaranteed, whatever their end-stage, each child will get there by following the same developmental sequence and integrating knowledge and experience from earlier stages into their current one. Finally, Kohlberg viewed his sequence as universal across cultures. He recognized that morality is defined much differently by different cultures, but he pointed out that it is not *what* they think about moral issues that make his stages universal, but *how* they think about them. He believed that regardless of the culture, or how they define right versus wrong, their underlying method of reasoning, and the cognitive-social process by which it develops, is the same regardless of the culture.

Kohlberg's theory is certainly the most widely cited theory in the area of moral development, but he is not without his critics. First of all, Kohlberg says much about moral thinking, but not a lot about moral behavior. As we know, how people think and how they actually behave are sometimes two different things. Furthermore, as a cognitive theorist, he says little about the emotional aspects of morality. Internal states and mechanisms such as empathy and sympathy are never mentioned. One wonders if a person would simply choose on an intellectual level to employ postconventional thinking if they didn't feel something inside that compels them to move in that direction.

Finally, although Kohlberg believed his theory to be universal, there are those who believe it to be both culturally and gender biased. His highest level of moral thinking, postconventional, places the rights of the individual on an equal or higher plane than the goals of the larger society. American democracy was established on this principle. Critics point out, however, that in some cultures, especially the more primitive ones, behaviors that insure the continued viability of the community are at the moral pinnacle. Individualism is neither aspired to nor considered morally good. Conventional morality in these types of cultures is therefore the desired goal.

In terms of gender, some have argued that Kohlberg's stages reflect a male orientation. Most notably, Carol Gilligan (1982), an associate of Kohlberg's, has argued that the justice and ethics orientation of Kohlberg's concept of morality fails to adequately address the female moral dimension, which is centered more on interpersonal relationships and compassion. Consequently, women tend to score artificially low on Kohlberg's scale, typically at stage 3, where moral judgments are based primarily on interpersonal relationships and group affiliations. In reality, however, most would agree that in terms of actual behavior, women tend to be the more moral sex, at least in Western society. This is certainly supported by nearly all quantitative measures of moral and deviant behavior that are broken down by sex, not the least of which is the annual crime statistics.

Gilligan argues that men and women develop along different moral lines. She believed that Kohlberg's theory, which views morality as a confluence of justice, ethics, and equality—a *morality of justice*—fails to adequately address and measure the *morality of care* that she believes is dominant in women. According to Gilligan, moral reasoning in women is based on principles of nonviolence and interpersonal connectedness. Thus, while men endeavor to *treat* people in moral ways—equitably and fairly—women endeavor to help people in moral ways—compassionately and sympathetically. Gilligan views the two moralities as separate and distinct from one another, and attributes their differences to the eventual separation by adolescent boys from their mothers, and the continued identification with their mothers by adolescent girls.

The CTT model of morality supports Gilligan's views, however, rather than two separate and qualitatively distinct moralities, Kohlberg's justice-oriented model and Gilligan's care-oriented model are both viewed as being part of a single moral continuum, with Kohlberg's configuration being a lesser and included component of Gilligan's. In other words, the CTT model views a *morality of justice* as being a step along the developmental pathway toward a *morality of care*. Why is a morality of care elevated to a higher moral position than a morality of justice? Because the former compels the individual to move in the direction of altruistic engagement for its own sake, while the latter compels the individual to do so within a system of rules, laws, and social expectations. To illustrate the differences, let's return to the Heinz Dilemma. You will recall that someone operating from Kohlberg's highest level of moral reasoning, stage 6, might respond to the dilemma as follows: *The sanctity of life transcends the law, therefore I would steal the drug to save her life regardless of the possible ramifications.*

As you can see, by focusing on the drug, the dilemma forces an answer based on the principles of justice and ethics. Is it fair to the pharmacist to steal his drug? Is it worth violating the law to save a life? Gilligan argued that for the most part women do not reason in this manner on issues of morality, and therefore on the scales used by Kohlberg, women naturally score lower. For example, a woman might respond to the dilemma as follows: *I couldn't steal anything, but I would comfort her in any way I could, and I would care for her through her illness, and be there for her.*

A response such as this under Kohlberg's formulation would be seen as a stage 4 response, and would be interpreted as a morality that measures right versus wrong by the written law. But this is not the case with most women, at least according to Gilligan. Can it be said that caring for a sick person through an illness is as moral as stealing a drug to save her life? Certainly it can. Arguably, under Gilligan's formulation of a morality of care, stealing the drug is not even an option, so therefore it creates no moral dilemma. The moral dilemma is whether or not to care for a terminally ill individual. It can even be argued that this person has chosen a higher moral position. Not only did they not violate the rights of the pharmacist, but they have chosen to sacrifice themselves to provide care and comfort to a dying person. So by measuring this response against the principles of justice and ethics upon which men tend to base their sense of morality, it appears to fall way short, morally speaking, of the decision to steal the drug. But by measuring it against the principles of compassion and care upon which women tend to base their sense of morality, it is a response that demonstrates the highest level of moral engagement.

Now we can begin to understand the nature and development of *altruistic motivation* by first understanding the differences between men and women in terms of moral reasoning. What Carol Gilligan has described with her morality of care is the innate biologically-based instinct women enter the world with in preparation for their maternal calling. It is an instinct that is absent in men. For them, the evolutionary process has selected other instincts—physical strength, aggression, territoriality—that are important for the survival of the group as opposed to the individual. It can be argued that in prehistory males who survived and passed on their genetic configurations were those who were most successful at protecting the group from the dangers of the day. A morality thus developed in men based on what was best for the group. What was considered morally right was considered so after being measured against a system of rules and social expectations. In our modern day, this translates into the principles of justice and ethics by which we live as members of a larger society.

Arguably, altruism was not selected at all in males, since by its very nature, altruistic motivation would at times, if not most of the time, be at odds with the goals of the group. To slow down the nomadic movement of the group for a sick member only placed the entire group at risk. To carry away a severely wounded male after a tribal conflict only reduced the available manpower and resources for the next fight. To place the welfare of the individual above that of the group would not have been a successful strategy in prehistory anymore than it would be in our modern world of geopolitical conflict.

For women, however, the evolutionary pressures followed a different course. While the men were concerned with the welfare of the group in prehistory, women were charged with the welfare of the individual, namely their own offspring. Those women who actively cared for their children were more successful at raising them to the age of sexual maturity, and thus they more successfully transmitted their genetic code to future generations through their children. The children of women who were less inclined to care for them, or not inclined at all, were less apt to survive, and thus the genetic configurations of those mothers were slowly lost to the evolutionary darkness. The end result was the natural selection of a maternal instinct in women that compels them to care for, console, and comfort their offspring. And from this instinct, a morality developed that was based on the welfare of the individual, as opposed to the group. What was considered morally right was considered so after being measured against the rules and expectations of personal care. While the men insured the survival of the group by protecting it from outside dangers, the women insured its survival by protecting and caring for its individual members from inside the group. In our modern day, this translates into the principles of compassion and humanity that are woven into the female psyche.

As for altruistic motivation, defined as the felt need to increase the welfare of others, it is an instinct that has been naturally selected in women, an instinct that eventually becomes the maternal instinct at sexual maturity. It can be said that until the female child reaches the point when this instinct becomes naturally focused on her own offspring, it remains free-floating, directed at no one specifically and at everyone generally. The maternal instinct manifests itself in childhood as an interpersonal connectedness, and a demeanor of caring.

This then is the basis for altruistic motivation in women. It is a biological remnant of the evolutionary process, and because of this innate characteristic women are in fact morally hard-wired to respond in a manner men can only achieve through learning and cognitive maturation. Men, on the other hand, are hard-wired to respond territorially and protectively, and thus they are genetically mapped with a group-orientation that elicits a response pattern based on the principles of justice and ethics. The differences can be illustrated in Figure 3.5.

Kohlberg and the Criminal Triad

So are women more moral than men? Well that, of course, depends on how you define morality. If you equate it with altruistic motivation, then the answer is most certainly yes! This should be obvious to any

	WOMEN	MEN
Evolutionary Outcome	Person-orientation	Group-orientation
Purpose	Survival of the individual	Survival of the group
Instinct	Maternal Innate characteristics include compassion and altruism	Territorial Innate characteristics include protectiveness and aggression
Inherent Morality	Morality of Care A sense of justice becomes a learned response	Morality of Justice A sense of humanity becomes a learned response

Figure 3.5. Gender differences in moral reasoning.

casual observer of history and human relations. But if we equate morality with a sense of justice and ethics, then it becomes less clear. Under Kohlberg's conceptualization, approaching morality from a justice orientation, men might perhaps be seen as defending the moral high ground. For Carol Gilligan, however, viewing morality from a care orientation, women are viewed as the more principled sex.

The CTT model of morality, as previously stated, views both orientations as being part of the same developmental continuum. The model presents two of the three components of morality—*empathic awareness* and *sympathetic arousal*—as being identical in men and women in terms of their nature and development. It is only the third component, *altruistic motivation,* which sets the sexes apart. It is here where Kohlberg's morality of justice and Gilligan's morality of care come face to face. It is here where evolutionary pressures brought the sexes to a fork in the road, with men having followed an evolutionary path that had no need for a sense of maternal-like caring, and thus it was selected out of the male genetic code. Such a demeanor, which we refer to as *humanity,* is an acquired characteristic in men. Women, on the other hand, followed an evolutionary path that required a maternal posture for survival, and thus this same sense of humanity was eventually selected as a biologically-based instinct in women.

Criminal Triad Theory presents a model of altruistic motivation that consists of three structural components—*justice, ethics,* and *humanity.* Each is part of a general pattern of behavior that compels the individual to endeavor to increase the welfare of some or all of society's members. Before we discuss their relationship to each other, and to morality in general, we first must define each of these component parts. The definitions that follow are specific to Criminal Triad Theory, and may deviate from other accepted definitions.

• *Justice:* This is a desire on the part of the individual to do what is right, as right is defined by the rules and statutory expectations of a particular society. It elicits in the individual a desire to increase the welfare of some, but not all, since it necessarily puts the individual at odds with those who violate the rules and expectations. A sense of justice is altruistic in that it empowers a belief that those who are harmed should be restituted, and that the rights and quality of life of the law-abiders should be protected from the deviant acts of the law-breakers. Using capital punishment as an example, a sense of justice would likely compel the individual to support the idea of executing those who kill in premeditated ways, since by taking the life of such an individual, no further harm can be perpetrated against innocent people by that person. Furthermore, justice demands a policy of deterrence, so for that reason, a person who is influenced by a sense of justice would likely be accepting of a system of punishment that doles out consequences commensurate with the acts committed.

• *Ethics:* This is a desire on the part of the individual to do what is right, as right is defined by the higher principles of human relations–namely fairness, honesty, fidelity, and equality, among others. A sense of ethics compels the individual to increase the welfare of others by establishing and maintaining a transparent and equitable protocol for social exchange. It is altruistic in that it leads the individual to adopt a pattern of behavior that actively avoids the exploitation of another person or entire class of people. While a just demeanor is adversarial in nature, an ethical demeanor is prosocial. Its effect is to help create a level playing field where people can pursue opportunity, advancement, and an acceptable quality of life without having to traverse the chasm created by a lack of ethical purpose in our interpersonal relationships and social institutions.

Using our previous example of capital punishment, a sense of ethics may lead the individual either to agree or disagree with its use, and for principled reasons, however, regardless of the position taken, the individual with a sense of ethics will recognize that true justice demands a fair and equitable distribution of consequences, and further, that there are at times mitigating circumstances that must be weighed when doling out those consequences. Thus ethics demands an adherence to the *spirit* of the law, rather than the *letter* of the law as demanded by justice. It can be said that justice is a lesser and included characteristic of ethics. A sense of justice compels us to adhere to the established rules. A sense of ethics compels us to interpret those rules, and when necessary, to adjust them for the sake of fairness and equity. A sense of ethics also guides our behavior when no particular rule or statutory law is prescribed.

• *Humanity:* This is a desire on the part of the individual to increase the welfare of all people based on the universal human principles of life, freedom, and dignity. In the context of Criminal Triad Theory, humanity is exactly that which we previously discussed as *altruism.* A sense of humanity is essentially synonymous with Carol Gilligan's morality of care. In women, it is the biological instinct that compels them to care for their offspring in an unselfish and sacrificial manner, an instinct that is generalized to varying degrees to all people. It represents a sincere desire to alleviate the pain and suffering of others, including entire classes of people. A sense of humanity is void of egocentrism. Women who are compelled to act in such a manner do so instinctively, led by the personal anguish that is sympathetically experienced in response to the pain and suffering of another.

Unlike women, men acquire a sense of humanity through cognitive mechanisms and learning. It is likely that men come to experience another's pain affectively through the process of classical conditioning. Are men capable of experiencing a sense of humanity in the same way as women? Certainly many do, but generally speaking, there is a difference in how the sexes respond. Because men acquire their sense of humanity through cognitive means, they are much more successful at using cognitive measures to disallow its expression. For example, opinion polls, especially in America, have repeatedly shown that men are much more inclined than women to accept the idea of war, even preemptive war, as a means of solving international conflict. When evaluating its necessity, women generally do so from a humanitarian perspective, whereas men do so from a justice perspective. Even faced with the prospect of killing thousands of women and children with our modern-day weapons, men will generally hold to a justice perspective and justify such "collateral damage" as an unavoidable means to a moral end, relying on their sense of ethics to minimize the damage to the extent possible.

If we return once again to our example of capital punishment, a sense of humanity would likely compel the individual—male or female—to disavow the practice, regardless of the crime committed. For someone operating from this perspective, to take another life violates the universal human principles upon which humanity is based. The individual may separate the act of the execution from the individual being executed, and thereby advocate on behalf of all humanity rather than the killer specifically, but the result is the same. A sense of humanity demands that the sanctity of human life be viewed as transcending all principles of justice and ethics, and for that reason, both are viewed as lesser and included characteristics of humanity.

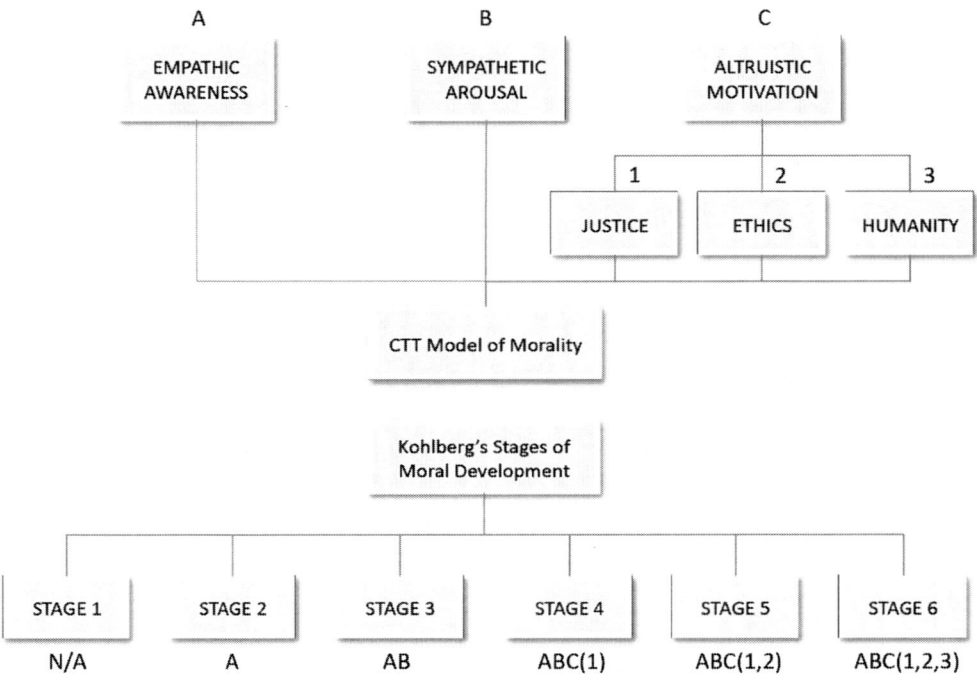

Figure 3.6. A comparison of the CTT model of morality and Kohlberg's model.

Now that we have a clear picture of altruism, we can piece together the component parts of our morality model and reconcile it to Kohlberg's. Again, while Gilligan viewed her morality of care, including its development, as qualitatively different from Kohlberg's morality of justice, the CTT model incorporates both, and views them as two points on the same continuum. Figure 3.6 illustrates the similarities between the CTT model and Kohlberg's, and clearly accounts for Gilligan's morality of care.

Like Kohlberg's model, the CTT model provides for six different stages of moral reasoning which are essentially the same, though with some definitional differences. Under the CTT model, a morality of justice can be abbreviated as "ABC(1)." In this case, both empathic awareness and sympathetic arousal are present, but altruistic motivation is limited to the subcomponent of justice. This would essentially be consistent with Kohlberg's stage 4. In contrast, a morality of care can be abbreviated as "ABC(1,2,3)." In this case, both empathic awareness and sympathetic arousal are present, with altruistic motivation being defined by the presence of the subcomponent of humanity, with justice and ethics being necessarily present as lesser and included characteristics. This highest stage of moral reasoning is essentially consistent with Kohlberg's stage 6; however, it is not to be viewed from a justice orientation, as Kohlberg does. Rather, it is to be viewed in a manner more consistent with Gilligan's care orientation.

In the middle of these two stages is the ethics-orientation, abbreviated as "ABC(1,2)." Consistent with Kohlberg's fifth stage, this mode of moral reasoning is characteristic of an individual who transcends the law and order orientation of ABC(1), but falls short of the universalism of ABC(1,2,3). This individual is one who understands the balance that must be maintained between the universal rights of the individual and the goals of the larger social group. For this person, the spirit of the law outweighs the letter of the law in importance, but the law itself is seen as important for maintaining the social order. This individual experiences empathic awareness and sympathetic arousal, and their altruistic motivation is person-oriented. They may, however, lack a sense of universal connectedness that compels a desire to increase the welfare of all people. In fact, they may not feel the need to increase anyone's welfare except those with whom they come in contact. Their moral engagement may thus be reactive. In contrast, a person operating from the higher ABC(1,2,3) position will proactively seek out opportunities for increasing the welfare of others.

Now that we have a clear understanding of what altruistic motivation actually is, we can complete our model of the moral response (see Figure 3.7).

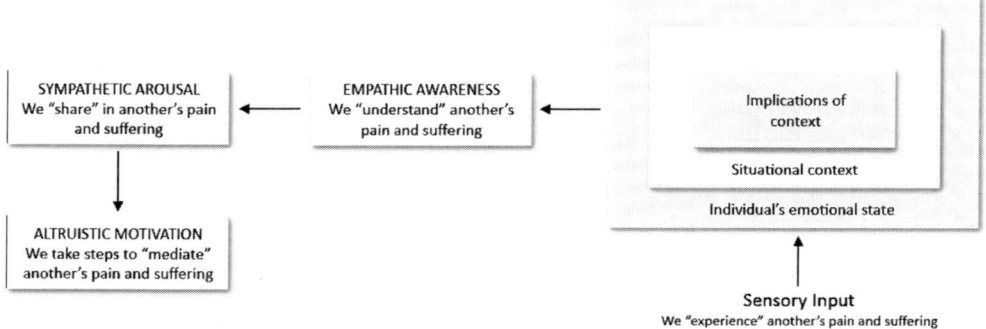

Figure 3.7. CTT Model of the moral response.

THE MORAL DETERRENCE MECHANISM (MDM)

Under the CTT model, an individual is morally deterred from engaging in criminal activity if they function from at least the ABC(1) level, or Kohlberg's stage 4. With at least minimal altruistic motivation, the individual respects the rights of others, and seeks to increase the welfare of at least some members of society. On the low rung of the altruism ladder, they may be motivated to do so by a desire to adhere to the letter of the law for the good of the social order, and on the high rung, by a desire to respect the universal human principles of life, freedom, and dignity. Either way they are compelled to avoid criminality for moral reasons.

Those who operate from below this level, or at Kohlberg's first three stages, do so from either an egocentric or subgroup orientation. Their moral reasoning is based on what is best for themselves or the group to which they are affiliated. Empathic awareness and sympathetic arousal may be present, but there is a lack of altruistic motivation. Therefore, behaviors that violate the rights of individuals or the laws and expectations of society are not seen as necessarily bad if those behaviors benefit their own goals, or those of the particular subgroup to which they belong. Members of street gangs, drug cartels, and organized crime families are all examples of the latter orientation ("AB"). And while not all members of such groups lack a moral deterrence mechanism, those who place their loyalty to the group above that of the larger social order, or the universal human principles upon which the social order is built, certainly are indicative of a personality type that lacks moral deterrence.

The person who operates from an entirely egocentric perspective ("A") is one who has the capacity to empathize, but feels neither sympathy nor altruistic motivation. It can be argued that most career criminals fall into this category, which parallels Kohlberg's second stage. They are motivated only by their own need for excitement, gratification, or windfall. If the individual lacks even the ability to empathize, consistent with Kohlberg's first stage, then they are void of any sense of morality, and obviously undeterred from engaging in criminality for moral reasons. Typically what distinguishes this individual from the type "A" individual is some form of mental illness or an extreme deficit in cognitive functioning. This complete lack of moral purpose can also be brought on by chronic drug and alcohol use. When the individual abuses either to the point of becoming physically or psychologically dependent, and when reality is turned on its head so that a sense of normalcy can be maintained only in a drug-induced state, then the individual becomes so singularly focused on the substance itself—egocentrism to the extreme—that empathic awareness is a near impossibility.

SUMMARY

The second leg of the Criminal Triad, moral development, occurs in middle to late childhood, and is a combination of both cognitive and affective psychological mechanisms that come together to compel the individual to act in prosocial ways, and to elicit a sincere desire to increase the welfare of others to varying degrees. When we engage another person on a moral level, we first understand their emotional pain cognitively; then we share their emotional pain affectively; and finally we confront their emotional pain overtly in an effort to reduce or eliminate it. We empathize, then we sympathize, and finally we act in an altruistic manner. Our sense of altruism can be either *justice-oriented* or *care-oriented,* but either way, it acts to deter us from engaging in criminality. The person who is not motivated to act altruistically, even though they may experience both empathic awareness and sympathetic arousal, is undeterred, at least by a moral sense and purpose. At best, they are deterred by the social relationships that have formed as a result of a successful attachment during early childhood, as well as by a well-defined sense of self formed during adolescence. At worst, they are a cold and calculating criminal offender who shows neither respect nor concern for the laws and expectations of society, nor the universal human rights of their victims.

Chapter 4

WHO AM I?
The Role of Identity Formation During Adolescence (Part I)

INTRODUCTION

By the time a child reaches adolescence, it is hoped that a healthy parent-child attachment during early childhood has by now led them to become socially adept and comfortable. If this is the case, then during middle to late childhood, they were likely successful in establishing friendships, building self-confidence, and preparing themselves to become their own person independent of their parents. The important consequence of developing a secure attachment is that the child enters adolescence free of the egocentricity of early childhood, and with an internalized array of values that reflect an understanding of their place and purpose in the larger social order.

Another important consequence of a secure attachment is that the child has likely gained the ability to empathize, and to become sympathetically aroused when confronted with the pain and suffering of another person. And while a fully developed sense of altruism likely will not manifest itself until the child has gained the cognitive ability to think in more abstract and universal terms, it is hoped that by this stage, at least a glimmer of humanity is becoming evident in the child's behavior. They are becoming not only a social animal, but also a moral one. And the combination of these two characteristics, assuming a normal course of development, will act to deter the adolescent from engaging in delinquent behavior while they busy themselves carving out their own unique identity.

Just as a secure attachment in early childhood contributes to moral development in middle to late childhood, both will contribute to the child's identity-formation in adolescence. If the child fails to securely attach to a caregiver early in childhood, then they won't have the socioemotional assets later on to build healthy relationships apart from the family. And if they haven't the ability to establish healthy relationships, which in middle to late childhood are primarily same-sex friendships, then they are lacking one of the tools necessary to build two of the three structural components of their identity: the *social self* and the *sexual self*. Further, if in early childhood they fail to emotionally bond to the parents to the extent that they become sympathetically aroused when the parents are distressed, then they likely will demonstrate a deficit in sympathetic arousal later on when circumstances demand a moral response. Such a deficit will negatively impact the third structural component of the adolescent's identity, the *ideological self*. Before we discuss the development and implications of identity formation, we first must further define these component parts. To do this, we turn to Erik Erikson's *psychosocial* theory of development (Erikson, 1964).

Erikson (1902–1994) is one of the most important psychologists in the history of modern psychology. He was trained in psychoanalysis—his only academic training—at the Vienna Psychoanalytic Institute under the tutelage of Anna Freud, daughter of Sigmund Freud. Unlike Freud's *psychosexual* theory of development, which argues that biological drives and instincts, to include the sex drive, are the primary factors influencing the development of personality, Erikson's *psychosocial* theory, in contrast, argues that the primary influences are social relationships—parents, siblings, and peers.

According to Erikson, when a child reaches adolescence, the primary developmental task becomes the establishment of a personal identity. It is a time when the adolescent, perhaps for the first time, asks the challenging question, *who am I?* Few if any enter adolescence with that question already answered. It is a question typically accompanied by an indescribable angst that compels the young person to begin a journey of sorts; a journey begun out of an existential fear of forever fading into the crowd and never being noticed. It is a time when the adolescent's focus shifts from living for the present to planning for the future. In Western culture, adolescence is a period of transition. It is a time when the adolescent attempts to slip free of the restraints of childhood to fly from the family nest and into adulthood.

For Erikson there are essentially three component parts that make up an adolescent's personal identity. These component parts answer the questions, (1) *what do I want to believe?* (2) *what kind of intimate relationships do I want to have?* (3) and, *what role do I want to play in society?* When these questions are successfully answered, then it can be said that the adolescent has established a well-defined self-concept to carry them into adulthood. If they are not successful in this endeavor, then identity *confusion* can result. This will translate into a host of potential problems during early adulthood, including problems with relationships, moral reasoning, and in becoming a productive member of society. At the extreme end, identity confusion can lead to a type of anxiety that will lead the person to act-out in various ways, including deviant sexual and criminal acts, to relieve the anxiety. The lack of an identity creates an existential void in the person that ultimately can lead to despair, self-contempt, and even self-destruction. For this reason, identity-formation serves as the third and final leg of the Criminal Triad.

Before we discuss the actual process of identity-formation, the role of others in that process, and the consequences of not meeting with success, we first must define each of the three structural components of identity. Each is a separate and distinct piece of *self* that defines one aspect of the whole. The components are the social self, sexual self, and the ideological self. Each has a separate developmental track that is influenced heavily by the adolescent's attachment in early childhood and their moral development in middle to late childhood. Further, these aspects of self do not develop independent of one another, but have a bi-directional and circular influence. They are interconnected and inseparable components of the unified whole of personality. Problems with one will negatively impact the others. Given that all three develop along a concurrent timetable, it is easy to understand the emotional difficulties adolescents experience during their identity-formation years. It is a constant juggling act between who they are, who they wish to be, and how they believe others perceive them. Hopefully, at the end of this process, having entered it an innocent child with no identity apart from the parents, they come out the other end with a healthy and robust self-image to begin adulthood with.

SOCIAL IDENTITY

This component of the adolescent's identity represents how they wish to present themselves to society, and how they wish to contribute to the larger social order as one of its adult members. It is the outward and pragmatic component of self. It involves the education and vocation to which the adolescent aspires, the type of family structure they wish to build for themselves, the type of outward appearance and style they intend to portray, and even the type of material possessions they hope to obtain and be identified with. The social self is that part of our identity we want others to see and judge us by. It is the part that compels one person to withdraw from society to live a hermit's existence, and another to aspire to start a business and become wealthy.

One of the most important components of the social self is the vocation the adolescent chooses to pursue. Just what we choose is one of the most important decisions we will make in our lifetimes. The decision we make is reflective of our personalities, and becomes one of the components that anchors our identity. During adolescence our identity is shaped in part by what we hope to become vocationally, and in adulthood by what we actually do become. Our vocational interests will dictate the type of college education we pursue, and perhaps even the college we select to attend, if we attend at all. It may impact our decision about when to marry and start a family. As we begin planning our vocational pursuits during adolescence, the job or profession we select will impact how we dress, the types of friends we choose, and how we carry ourselves in a social setting.

An example here will illustrate the impact of vocational interests on the adolescent identity. Let's assume adolescent A, a male, aspires to be a police officer. Such an aspiration will begin to influence many aspects of the boy's outward presentation. He dresses conservatively, cuts his hair short, and perhaps even begins an intense exercise regimen to build up his chest and biceps. In his interactions with other adolescents his age, he attempts to maintain an assertive and forthright demeanor, one that is politically conservative and somewhat intolerant of those around him who might be labeled juvenile delinquents. For this boy, the idea of being a police officer has a significant impact on his self-esteem. He has dated a number of different girls, and is not interested in maintaining a relationship with only one. After all, he has heard many stories about the sexual conquests of police officers, and how such extracurricular activities are part of the police culture. Some of the young people around him have even labeled him as arrogant at times.

In contrast, adolescent B, a girl, wants to be a medical doctor. She is dedicated to her studies, and in terms of her education is fully aware of the long and difficult road ahead. Her friends are few in number, and because she is so serious about her studies, she finds little time for social events, especially with boys. She has no boyfriend, nor is she interested in having one at this point. She finds purpose and meaning in her vocational interests. She feels a burden for the underprivileged, and hopes one day to provide healthcare to the disadvantaged. Her friends describe her as quiet, intelligent, and humble. Her vocational interests have greatly impacted her self-esteem and her self-confidence.

From the foregoing, you begin to see how vocational interests can potentially impact the adolescent identity. The social self is typically the first component of identity to spring to life, and the vocational aspect is typically where it starts. When a young adolescent begins this process, his or her vocational goals are typically *fantasy-motivated.* At this young age, the child may endeavor to become a super-hero, a cowboy, or perhaps even the President of the United States. They haven't yet developed a realistic view of most vocations, nor do they understand their own limitations or the limiting nature of many professions. It is likely they will demonstrate an interest at this point in the profession that appears to them to be the most fun.

As the adolescent reaches the middle teens, with further cognitive development giving them the ability to think in more abstract and realistic terms, their pursuit of vocational interests becomes *internally-motivated.* Now they are attracted to particular jobs and professions for reasons that are reflective of their personality and developing identity. In fact, it can be said that vocation follows personality, and identity, at least in part, follows vocation. But while this is so, the actual vocation selected by the adolescent may depend on their motivation for pursuing one in the first place. There are four different orientations from which an adolescent carries out this endeavor. They are:

• *Interest-oriented:* This adolescent chooses a particular vocation strictly out of interest. They find it fascinating for any number of reasons. Using the example of a police officer, this adolescent may wish to pursue that option because they are interested in guns, or the technology involved in criminal investigations. They read books on the subject, and attempt to learn all they can about law enforcement. They may join a law enforcement explorer post, or have a police scanner in their bedroom. They know exactly what it takes to get hired as a police officer, and have already started making plans for their education and training. In terms of personality, this orientation is reflective of self-confidence, a healthy and secure attachment that has led to a strong sense of self-efficacy. This adolescent fully believes they are capable of achieving the vocation they have selected.

• *Purpose-oriented:* This adolescent chooses a particular vocation because they feel a calling, such as our future medical doctor from the previous example. They believe they can have a positive impact on some segment of society, and they are motivated to select a particular vocation more so by the opportunity it provides to have such an impact than by their personal interest in the job or profession. This young person would choose to be a police officer because in their minds, it will allow them to make a difference in the lives of those they are sworn to protect. They hold an idealized view of the vocation, and are not swayed by its negative aspects. In terms of personality, such an orientation can have a complex set of variables. On the positive side, it may be reflective of a highly developed sense of morality, and the secure attachment necessary to translate the positive aspects of their attachment experience into an altruistic motivation to serve others in a humanitarian way. On the negative side, this orientation may reflect an insecure attachment, and the adolescent's attempt to sublimate their negative attachment experiences with something positive. The downside to the latter motivation is the real opportunity that professional burnout will occur when they realize this sublimation is short-lived, as the negative emotions associated with their attachment experience once again bubble to the surface.

• *Prestige-oriented:* This adolescent is attracted to a vocation by the benefits it provides. His or her selection is less about interest or purpose, and more about appearance, and the social benefits of being associated with a particular vocation. This individual may aspire to become a police officer because of their perception of how the police are viewed by other members of society. They may be attracted to the power that accompanies the badge and gun. Their desire may be heavily influenced by media portrayals of the police. In terms of personality, this orientation may represent a lack of self-confidence and an underdeveloped self-image. The adolescent may view their choice of vocations as a means of compensating for their deficits. It may also represent an artificially-inflated sense of self-confidence, itself indicative of a high degree of egocentricity and perhaps a lack of moral development.

- *Obligation-oriented:* This adolescent is motivated to select a particular vocation out of obligation to others, primarily the parents. In some cases, they are simply precluded from any internal motivation, and instead willingly defer to the wants of their parents for their vocational future. This is typically seen in either a family-owned business where the children are expected to operate the entity once the parents retire, or in families with a generational tradition of working either for or in a particular company or industry. The latter scenario is seen in many blue-collar towns dominated by one particular factory or type of manufacturer (i.e., auto-makers, steel, etc.). This adolescent may choose

Orientation	Motivation	Personality	Potential Negative Outcomes
Interest	Motivated by their personal interest in the job or profession.	Self-confident, secure attachment, strong sense of industry, high self-efficacy	Not correlated with negative outcomes beyond typical job dissatisfaction
Purpose	Motivated by the relationship of the job or profession to other people. A sense of mission.	Highly developed sense of morality, secure or insecure attachment is possible, high self-efficacy. Higher than normal cognitive functioning. Typically the desired job or profession is a major component of identity.	Job burnout when their sense of mission is continually compromised by reality. If their sense of purpose is motivated by a need to compensate for deficiencies in their life, then burnout happens even quicker. In this case job failure is likely.
Prestige	Motivated by the relationship of the job or profession to how they wish others to perceive them.	Typically a lack of self-confidence, underdeveloped self-image, egocentric, underdeveloped sense of morality.	Lack of commitment and dedication to job or profession. Uses it only as a conduit for egocentric goals. Job burnout and disciplinary action is likely.
Obligation	By the expectations of family and society. A sense of tradition.	May reflect a secure or insecure attachment, a lack of self-confidence and autonomy, underdeveloped sense of identity.	Lack of contentment and feelings of stagnation if job or profession is inconsistent with personal interests.

Figure 4.1. Vocational orientations.

to be a police officer because his father, brothers, and grandfather all entered the profession, and thus he feels obligated to do the same. This orientation could reflect a loyal and secure attachment, or it could reflect an insecure attachment and a lack of self-confidence and autonomy. The latter would be the case when the adolescent's sense of obligation is inconsistent with their personal interests and goals.

It has been said that in our modern society, the *socialization* of children has been replaced by their independent search for identity. Until the post-war 1950s, children in America were in fact socialized. This meant they were essentially indoctrinated with the values and beliefs of their parents, which were then expected to be internalized as their own. In terms of vocation, adolescents pursued a choice primarily from an obligation-orientation. Identity was found in family tradition, and for the most part, vocation was viewed as being an important component of the family's identity and tradition. If the father worked at the local factory, it was expected that the son would follow in his footsteps. Women were not yet a significant component of the workforce, but if the mother did work, say as a nurse, a bank teller, or as an operator, then the daughter was expected to proudly pursue this same vocation.

In the 1950s, however, this all began to change, and the turbulent 1960s all but guaranteed that the change would be lasting and complete. Suddenly young people were rebelling against the indoctrination of their parents. It was no longer considered important to safeguard the family identity by following in the parents' vocational footsteps. Adolescents suddenly sought independence and autonomy at an early age. They began to make their own vocational decisions, and even to exercise their right to delay or avoid making such a decision altogether. Of course, the downside to this newfound autonomy was that many simply didn't bother pursuing a vocation until the fun and freedom of being young had run its course, a circumstance that has lingered to the present day in many young people. The two negative consequences of this chosen course are that a person may be forced to *accept* rather than *choose* a vocation—likely one they have no interest in—and they may lose out on the opportunity to have one of the important components of identity impact their life in a positive way.

If we look at the correlation between vocational interests, or a lack of, in adolescence and the development of criminality, the importance of this component of social identity becomes abundantly clear. One of the powerful inhibitors of criminality in adolescence is a well-defined vocational goal. The reason is twofold. First, it is commonly understood that a criminal record, especially a serious one, is an insurmountable obstacle to pursuing a career. For the vast majority of vocations, such a record simply makes it impossible. And second, a clear vocational goal will be internalized as a component of identity, and the stronger an adolescent's identity, the stronger its deterrent effect on criminality. It can be shown that the vast majority of adults convicted of criminal offenses had no stable vocation prior to their convictions, and if they did, it was likely one they were forced to accept for pragmatic reasons, and not as the fulfillment of vocational goals established and internalized during adolescence.

SEXUAL IDENTITY

The second component of an adolescent's identity, and in many ways the most volatile, is their sexuality, or the way they wish to express themselves as sexual beings. It involves not only the type of intimate relationships they choose to pursue—heterosexual, homosexual, asexual—but also their physical appearance, their attracting and dating behaviors, and any other aspect of their lives that relates to intimacy and sexual activity. It is volatile because our culture places so much emphasis on it as an element of personal identity. In many ways, especially in America, we are what we are sexually. We are bombarded daily with movies, music, advertisements, and many other types of media that reinforce this social reality. Our culture is also extremely critical of any form of sexuality that is not considered normative by the majority. This criticism tends to burrow its way into the deepest parts of an adolescent's psyche where it can have the most toxic effect. If others ridicule our vocational interests, it is easily overcome. But to have our sexuality called into question can be psychologically devastating for an adolescent.

There are many models of sexuality that attempt to break it down into its component parts. The CTT model looks at sexuality as consisting of four component parts, each progressing along separate developmental pathways, and then coming together to form this most critical part of our identity. The four components are *sexual expression, sexual efficacy, sexual image,* and *sexual portrayal.* Each develops along a continuum of self-perception, ranging from self-loathing at the low end, to a narcissistic view of oneself at the high end. A further discussion of each follows.

Sexual Expression

Every child at some point discovers the pleasurable aspects of self-stimulation. As puberty awakens the child's body to the new experience of autoeroticism, they very quickly find themselves confronted by a very complex and confusing set of emotions. They are torn between the sheer physical pleasure of the activity and the guilt and shame that Western society tends to condition children to associate with it. Just how successfully an adolescent confronts this conflict will in part determine to what extent they are comfortable with their sexuality later on when they begin to initiate intimate relationships.

While society tends to address the issue of masturbation as a secretive activity that is not to be openly discussed or admitted to, the real danger comes from the moral agents that are present in an adolescent's life, namely their parents and their church. The danger is that an adolescent has not yet internalized their sexuality to any significant degree. So when they are taught that masturbation is dirty and sinful, the message they internalize, since the act itself is rather unavoidable, is *I am dirty and sinful.* And when that happens, then the adolescent begins to juggle a complex set of emotions that cognitively they are not yet prepared to handle.

Essentially all adolescents must work through this conflict at some point, and the vast majority are successful at resolving it. The danger comes when this conflict is coupled with either an authoritarian parent or a spiritually-abusive church. When that happens, then the likelihood of the adolescent entering adulthood with a dysfunctional view of their sexual nature increases dramatically. With such a poor self-perception, they may repress sexual urges and desires, or act them out anonymously with nameless strangers who make no judgments or evaluations. They may avoid intimacy out of shame or a lack of self-worth. And even when engaged in intimate relationships they may experience sexual dysfunction or pursue alternative forms of sexual activity that are kept hidden from their partner in the same way their autoeroticism was kept hidden from their parents.

Conversely, an adolescent who is successful at resolving this conflict will likely move into adulthood completely comfortable with their sexual nature. Sex is something to be enjoyed and talked about openly between intimates. There is no shame or guilt associated with it. They are free to try new things without fear of embarrassment or judgment. The message they have internalized as part of their sexual identity is *I am free to express myself sexually*. Sex is not seen as an activity that demands a cold secrecy for reasons of ego protection, but rather one that demands a shared openness between intimates and secrecy only to protect the unspoken beauty and mutual trust intimacy inspires.

Sexual Efficacy

While sexual expression relates to the extent an individual feels they are free to engage in sexual activity without fear of judgment, shame, or guilt, *sexual efficacy* relates to the individual's level of confidence in their ability to engage in sexual activity and build intimate relationships. A low sense of sexual efficacy will inhibit the adolescent from pursuing intimate relationships. They are plagued by feelings of insecurity and inadequacy as a sexual being. For them, sexual expression may not be problematic. They may have no reservations about engaging in sexual activity, they just simply don't believe anyone will desire them as an intimate partner if they are at the low end of the efficacy scale.

It is true that most adolescents experience some deficit in sexual efficacy at one time or another. Most will have doubts about their desirability. For boys, sexual efficacy is heavily influenced by the *introversion-extraversion* dimension of personality. More specifically, sexual efficacy is correlated with the amount of shyness, or social anxiety, the boy feels in situations involving interaction with members of the opposite sex. This lack of confidence leads to feelings of awkwardness, intimidation, and apprehension about proactively seeking out this type of social interaction. Many boys in this situation simply delay dating and intimacy, and instead shift their focus and energy to same-sex friendships, academic endeavors, or extracurricular activities they find fun and fulfilling. This type of strategy is completely normal. The problems arise for those boys who are not able to effectively cope with their low self-confidence. Their desire for social engagement with an intimate, and their inability to do so, can combine to create feelings of contempt toward all members of the opposite sex, and even toward themselves.

In girls, sexual efficacy is related more to appearance than any internal dimensions of personality. In Western culture, girls are taught from an early age that appearance is the key to all things. They are bombarded by a cultural message that says males dominate, and that beautiful females are what motivate them. Practically before boys can even dress themselves, little girls are already obsessing over their clothes and the look of their hair. It doesn't take much for the cracks to begin forming in their fragile self-concept. Kids can be extremely cruel to one another, and the sexes tend to attack each other where it hurts the most. Boys will attack each other's strength, athletic and physical prowess, material belongings, and their popularity among primarily the other boys. Girls, on the other hand, will attack each other on the basis of personal appearance, clothes, hair, facial features, and rather than their popularity with the other girls, it is more likely they will focus on each other's popularity, or lack of, with the boys of their social group. For girls this can be especially devastating. They are much less successful than boys at disengaging and shifting their energy and focus to activities other than engaging members of the opposite sex in dating and intimacy. As adults, this difference is clearly reflected in where men and women typically look to for their source of self-esteem. For adult men, it is primarily their jobs and accomplishments, while for adult women, it is their relationships.

For both boys and girls, the message that is internalized when plagued by a deficit in sexual-efficacy is dependent on exactly how deep the deficit runs. For most, especially boys, the message is, *someday I will find a partner who will want me.* This, of course, is a completely normal and healthy demeanor. This young person has an understanding of the transient nature of adolescent dating problems. More damaging is the young person with an extreme deficit. The message they internalize is, *no one will ever want me.* These adolescents tend to direct blame for their situation inward. Such self-blame can ultimately lead to self-contempt, which can then lead to self-destruction in the form of eating disorders, self-mutilation, drug and alcohol abuse, and even suicide. At the very least, this message will lead to significant problems with self-esteem that will impact every aspect of the young person's life.

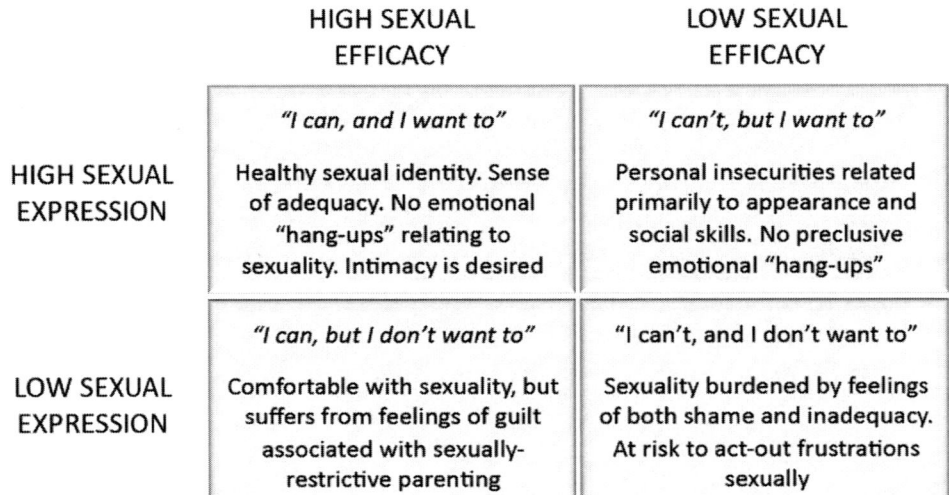

Figure 4.2. The interaction between sexual expression and sexual efficacy during adolescence.

In looking at the dynamic between sexual expression and sexual efficacy, you begin to see just how complex sexual identity becomes during adolescence. When we look at the various combinations possible, we see four distinct behavioral patterns begin to emerge. Figure 4.2 illustrates the potential implications of these variations.

In terms of criminal potential, the *low efficacy-low expression* adolescent is of particular concern. This is a young person, primarily a boy if discussing criminal potential, who feels he is unworthy of being wanted by a member of the opposite sex, and who acts as his own worst enemy by repressing sexual urges and avoiding intimacy out of fear of being judged too harshly by self and others. He is an adolescent who likely developed significant attachment problems long before reaching the point of identity development. At its extreme, such a personality type may become dangerous as an adult. They may attempt to symbolically kill their parent(s) by killing surrogate victims. They may blame all women for their inability to form intimate relationships and retaliate by sexually assaulting many. They may seek sexual gratification in the dark world of child exploitation where they can avoid the dual risks of rejection and judgment. They may even identify with their young victims, and seek out children from broken or impoverished homes in an effort to convince themselves they are actually helping them in some perverse way by exploiting them.

Sexual Image

This component of sexuality is the adolescent's perception of his or her own physical and sexual attractiveness. Unlike sexual efficacy and expression, which are primary factors in the development of sexuality due to their relationship to other important psychosocial processes, sexual image is a secondary factor. Regardless of the type and quality of our attachment experience or the attitudes of our parents on issues relating to sexual expression, the type and shape of our body is genetically determined. Simply put, we are stuck with the cards we are dealt. Therefore our self-perceptions of attractiveness and body image are not dependent on earlier psychological processes. We can be perfectly well adjusted and still think we are unattractive when we look in the mirror. In fact, the better adjusted we are psychologically, the more realistic our perception of self will be when we do look in the mirror, be it good or bad.

Now it is true that a low sexual image is common during adolescence, especially among girls, and that this low self-perception can negatively impact sexual efficacy, but the negatives are typically not severe or lasting unless compounded by insecure attachment or other psychosocial deficits. By itself, body image will not disrupt the other developmental processes associated with identity-formation. But when other problems exist, especially with the person's perceived sexual efficacy, a negative sexual image will only add to and compound the problem.

Sexual Portrayal

This component of sexuality relates to the gap that exists between the adolescent's outward portrayal of his or her gender role, and the stereotypical gender role demanded by cultural norms. The effeminate boy and the tomboy girl are two examples where the adolescent may have a low sense of sexual portrayal, especially if problems with sexual efficacy or expression exist. Like sexual image, sexual portrayal is a secondary factor in the development of sexual identity. In many cases, adolescents who do not fit the cultural norm are perfectly comfortable with their sexual portrayal, even though they may experience some negative social consequences. Many athletic girls, for example, do not follow the stereotypical gender role of a young woman and are quite comfortable with that. In fact, as our modern society continues to evolve, gender roles are beginning to blend into each other in some respects, making sexual portrayal less an issue in the formation of identity. Arguably though, for adolescent boys, the blending of gender roles has not occurred as easily as it has for girls. The social costs are still greater for a boy than for a girl when their gender portrayal comes closer to the opposite sex than their own.

In terms of criminality, a serious problem can percolate beneath the surface when an adolescent, especially a boy, has a low opinion of his own sexual portrayal, and the social costs have been significant. An example might be the boy who is labeled a homosexual because of his effeminate demeanor, when in fact he is just a shy and reserved heterosexual who has not yet developed a sufficient level of social competence to establish intimate relationships. Some in this situation remain comfortable with their sexual portrayal regardless of the consequences, but those with a low self-assessment to begin with will only have their self-contempt reinforced and strengthened, especially if attempts to change their portrayal meet with failure. While the psychological trauma of being labeled in this manner can be devastating, assuming a positive view of sexual efficacy and expression, the negative effects will begin to subside once they are able to form a stable and fulfilling relationship with an intimate partner. The more dangerous situation is the individual who has a very low view of their sexual efficacy, as well as their sexual expression. The humiliation of being labeled by peers, in addition of having a poor view of their sexual portrayal, may push the adolescent to the breaking point. They may choose to retaliate against those they blame for their humiliation, or even worse, they may feel the need to make a statement to the world, and to prove themselves through some particularly dramatic act in which they demonstrate their power over others. In this case, we could potentially have a school shooting with many innocent victims, such as the one that occurred at Columbine High School in April, 1999.

Perhaps just as devastating for the adolescent than not being able to live up to society's gender expectations is being forced to adopt a *sex* role that is not natural for them. This has been a perennial problem for gay and lesbian adolescents. Even in our modern and somewhat tolerant culture, this difficulty still persists for many young people who are afraid and confused about their emerging sexuality. They are forced to play the role of a heterosexual to avoid the social costs that come with being labeled a homosexual by their peers. These young people have a very low self-assessment of their sexual portrayal. The continuous tension and stress from having to continue their false portrayal, and in the process not allow themselves to experience the intimacy they desire, can be especially devastating. A number of gay and lesbian adolescents have committed suicide as a result of the emotional devastation that can result from keeping one's sexuality hidden out of fear or confusion.

In total then, our sexual identity is a confluence of self-perceptions relating to our sexual *expression, efficacy, image,* and *portrayal.* Each can easily be measured through the adolescent's self-report and placed on a continuum ranging from self-loathing to narcissistic. In merging these four dimensions, we can see the possibility for a large number of different combinations, each representing a particular type of sexual identity. The closer the individual moves toward self-loathing, the greater the possibility for the development of criminality as a means of retaliation and self-authentication. For these individuals, criminality, especially violent crimes against other people, becomes a way of acting-out their anger on the world for their inability to feel normal. In the end, however, their deviance only justifies their self-loathing. In seeking to feel normal, they only perpetuate their feelings of abnormality.

At the other end of the sexual identity continuum is the adolescent who has a narcissistic view of their sexuality. These young people, boys and girls alike, have an inflated view of their sexual attractiveness, their freedom to engage in sexual behavior, and the degree to which they portray their particular gender role. They tend to be very egocentric and quite unable to experience true intimacy and interpersonal connectedness. They view sexual efficacy in purely sexual terms rather than measures of intimacy. At their extreme, these individuals may engage in criminality as a way of validating their inflated self-perceptions. They may engage in sexual assault out of a belief that their victims actually desire that type of aggressive interaction. Date-rape is a real risk with this type of adolescent boy, especially if their advances are initially rejected by their victim. Like all narcissistic personalities, they have a very fragile self-concept. They cannot handle rejection, because it quickly begins to erode their false perceptions of self. While the self-loathing individual may engage in criminality for reasons of *ego authentication,* the narcissistic person may do so for reasons of *ego protection.* In the mind of the former, there is nothing to protect. In the mind of the latter, there is nothing to authenticate.

Sexual identity is considered by many to be the most critical component of identity, because it is the component most connected to the early attachment experience. It is made even more critical by our western culture's obsession with it; an obsession that is quickly internalized into the psyche of an adolescent trying to figure out their place and purpose in the world. Essentially, every modern serial killer who has been widely studied by criminologists and forensic psychologists has been found to have severe deficits in the area of sexual identity. Jeffrey Dahmer engaged in homosexual sex, and later hated himself for it. He confessed to killing as many as 17 men and boys after having sex with them. Edmund Kemper felt entirely incapable of intimacy, and killed six young girls before finally murdering and dismembering his emotionally-abusive mother. And Aileen Wuornos, one of the few female serial killers to gain notoriety, was purportedly sexually abused repeatedly as a young child by her own family members before getting pregnant at age 13, the result of a stranger rape. She eventually gave herself over to prostitution and murdered seven of her male customers before getting caught.

Sexuality is a powerful motivator in our lives. It can lead to happiness, or it can lead into the darkness of deviance. But it isn't the only component of identity that if derailed in some manner can result in a direct pathway to violence. There are times when what we choose to *think* is as powerful as what we *feel* as a determinative factor in our decision to engage in socially unacceptable and harmful behaviors. To understand this, we next turn to the third and final component of identity, the various ideologies we choose to adopt as our own.

IDEOLOGICAL IDENTITY

What is it that compels a young Muslim man from a seemingly normal family to fly a hijacked plane into a building for the sole purpose of killing innocent people? What makes a Christian man so crazy about the issue of abortion that it leads him to bomb abortion clinics with little regard for innocent people who may be harmed in the process? And what causes a young woman to risk jail by approaching people on the street wearing expensive coats of animal fur and ruining them with an indelible spray paint?

All of these crimes, among countless others, are the result of a person's *ideology,* or a set of beliefs the individual adopts in support of a particular religious, political, or philosophical orientation. During adolescence, a young person endeavors to break free of the parental oversight that has guided them since birth in order to become their own person. Part of that endeavor involves figuring out exactly what it is they want to believe as a free-thinking human being. Ideology becomes a powerful motivator in the young person's life. Once an ideology is adopted, a young person will conform their behavior and beliefs to that ideology. It becomes a type of guiding light on their journey to adulthood, and several ideologies may be adopted and abandoned by the time they get there.

While there are many different ideologies from which an adolescent can choose, they can essentially be broken into three major categories: *religious, political,* and *philosophical.* We can think of an individual's religious ideology as a system of beliefs that defines their relationship to a higher being or absolute truth. Philosophical ideology is a system of beliefs that defines the individual's relationship to the world, and guides their interactions with its various physical and metaphysical components. And finally, political ideology is a system of beliefs that defines a person's view of government and its obligations to those it governs. Each of these general categories of thought come together to form the whole of an adolescent's ideological identity. Before we discuss the dynamic interplay between these three components and their critical role in the development of the self-deterrence mechanism (SeDM), we first must define each and discuss the course of their development from childhood to adolescence.

Religious Ideology

A young person develops a religious ideology out of a quest for understanding. Adolescence is a time for discovery, when a young person endeavors to understand their place and purpose in a world that becomes increasingly more difficult to understand as their cognitive development reaches a point where abstract thought begins to bubble to the surface. As they become more introspective, they discover an existential component of self that creates an indescribable emotional discomfort, or *angst*. In an effort to understand and relieve this discomfort, the adolescent begins a period of searching in an effort to answer the question, *why am I here?* A young person will settle for nothing short of an absolute answer to this question, and those who set out on this journey will continue until either their answer is found, or they abandon their search in favor of accepting a more pragmatic view of life, complete with all of its unanswered questions.

The easiest place for an adolescent to discover an absolute answer, and perhaps the only place, is through a faith-based belief in a higher power. Faith replaces proof, and acceptance replaces searching. Suddenly in religion, the adolescent can answer the important questions, and the angst that initially gave rise to their journey now becomes latent. Religion is a powerful motivator for an adolescent. At the very time they are becoming frightfully aware of their own mortality, and its ultimate finality, they are learning through religious awareness that it may in fact be possible to transcend that mortality. Their belief in this transcendence can become the absolute by which the adolescent defines their life and empowers it with meaning and purpose.

Criminal Triad Theory views religious ideology as progressing through three developmental stages (*obedience, doctrinal,* and *existential*). Moving from one stage to the next is dependent on the child's level of cognitive functioning and their expanding ability to think about God in more abstract terms. As a child moves closer to this ability to think abstractly, they experience a number of qualitative changes in their cognitive abilities that facilitate this movement. They move from being egocentric, and with no ability to work through a basic operation in their mind, to having the ability to perform complex and abstract mental operations from multiple perspectives. Given the abstract nature of any religion based on a transcendent god, it goes without saying that even a basic ability to understand and internalize its many precepts requires a higher level of cognitive ability. Until that ability is achieved, however, the child is still socialized and conditioned in ways that will directly influence how they internalize issues relating to God and religion when they reach adolescence.

During the early childhood years, or the *obedience stage,* the child understands God in very simple terms. During this period, parents tend to use God as a tool for socialization. He is portrayed as a sort of watchful eye in the sky, always there, even when the parents are not. At this stage, the child has no ability to think about religion per se, and about God only as the white-bearded, grandfatherly figure who is easily confused with Santa Claus. In the Christian faith, they may have an easier time with Jesus, since his picture is prominently displayed throughout our culture. But the young child has no ability to understand the relationship between the two, except that one is the son of the other. To the young child, God is human, and he demands obedience to his rules, which are identical for the most part to the rules established by the parents. A child is taught to pray at a young age before meals and bed, but they do so out of obedience and a fear of retribution if they fail to comply.

When a child reaches middle childhood, assuming church attendance is a family function, they enter the *doctrinal* stage of religious development. During this stage, the child begins to understand that God is part of a religious system. They can now understand basic religious practices, and that there are differences in how different denominations practice their religion. They can now relate the practices to the idea of God, however God is still something external to them, influencing their behavior from some physical place in the sky. Obedience is still a factor, but unlike the very young child, who is obedient for the sake of avoiding retribution, the child in this stage is obedient to fulfill the expectations of the religious system. They now understand that there is a final outcome to obedient religious adherence, that being their ascension to heaven following death, but they remain unable to separate their understanding of God and heaven from the physical world. God still exists in the flesh, and heaven remains a place somewhere beyond the clouds. A child in the doctrinal stage has not yet gained the ability to grasp the more abstract concepts: things such as transcendence, omnipresence, omniscience, and eternity. Nor have they yet internalized their religion.

When a child reaches adolescence, they enter the final stage of cognitive development. They are now able to think abstractly. In terms of religious development, the adolescent now enters the *existential* stage. They are now able to internalize the idea of God, and to understand the transcendent nature of his existence. God no longer is a man with a white beard who guides their behavior from a place in the clouds. The adolescent understands that spiritual nature is qualitatively different from physical nature. They understand that God guides them from within, and that spiritual obedience is subject to the exercise of their own free will. Whereas the *obedient* child is motivated by the desire to avoid retribution, and the *doctrinal* child by the perceived expectations of their religious paradigm, the *existential* child, now an adolescent, is empowered by an internal need to understand their relationship to God, and thus answer the question, *why am I here?* By internalizing the idea of God, they are able to internalize the attributes of God: things such as compassion, tolerance, peace, and love. They thus make those attributes their own rather than continuing to understand them as merely the expectations of their particular religious system. Obedience to God thus becomes inseparable from obedience to self.

This is not to suggest that all children progress through this sequence of stages. In fact, many do not. Many children are never exposed to religious practices by their parents. Will this preclude them from any type of spiritual discovery during adolescence? Absolutely not! Many adolescents with no religious involvement at all become deeply spiritual during adolescence. Some do it within the walls of a denominational church, while others do it totally apart from organized religion. In many cases, a lifelong involvement in a religious system can actually be a hindrance to internalizing a healthy spiritual ideology during adolescence. Legalistic churches that focus primarily on strict obedience to rules and doctrines can so indoctrinate the child during the obedience and doctrinal stages that during adolescence they are incapable of separating themselves from their religious system. What they end up internalizing is the legalism that has been forced upon them during their important childhood years. They either accept this and attempt to answer the question of why they are here with the religious system itself, or they rebel against it and leave the question unanswered. In the former case, the adolescent quickly discovers how difficult it is to live up to the expectations of a religious system best suited for a fully-developed adult. When they internalize the religious system itself as the reason for their existence, then they are at risk of reaching a point where they sadly conclude that they are unworthy of their own existence. Many have fallen victim to this type of spiritual legalism, and in many cases, it has contributed to later criminal conduct.

A strong and well-defined religious ideology can contribute significantly to a person's ability to self-deter from criminality, but it can also have negative implications, especially when combined with an extreme political ideology. Many are led by their political beliefs to advocate on behalf of a particular cause or issue, but when they believe God is fully supportive of their efforts, and that they owe a higher obligation to God than to the secular law, then sometimes they are emboldened to cross the line into criminality. Such is the case with those who bomb abortion clinics, burn churches supportive of gay marriage, or attack and torment interracial couples who move into a particular neighborhood. Each of these forms of deviance can result from a toxic mix of religious and sociopolitical ideologies. Let's turn now to the development of a political ideology.

Political Ideology

During late adolescence, many young people suddenly feel compelled to adopt a particular political ideology. The one they choose will be reflective of their personal views about government, and about its relationship to those it governs. Unlike religious ideology, which acts to calm the existential angst of adolescence, political ideology can agitate the innocence of youth, and lead a young person to be confrontational and socially active. Political ideology leads a young person to shift their concern away from self, perhaps for the first time, and onto the welfare of others. Just who the *others* are depends on the ideology. At its extreme, it can lead a young person to resort to violence in the form of sociopolitical radicalism, either from a left- or right-wing perspective.

Some extreme political ideologies can be viewed as good-intentioned, with the ultimate goal of promoting such admirable social values as peace, racial equality, and equal opportunity. Such was the case with many of the more radicalized factions of the youth movement of the 1960s-1970s. Groups such as the *Weather Underground* and *Black Panthers*, both espousing a left-wing political ideology, sought respectively to end the war in Vietnam and bring racial equality to African-Americans. To further such goals, these groups took the position that the ends would justify the means in their struggle to bring about the greater good for society. Thus, it became acceptable in the minds of these radical young people to bomb banks and government buildings, or to promote armed conflict with the police, who were viewed as agents for the oppressive ruling class.

Other types of extreme political activism are anything but good-intentioned. Whereas the left-wing radical groups of the day sought to be *inclusive,* and to empower their respective ideologies for the betterment of all members of society, right-wing radical groups have tended to be *exclusive.* Chief among them are the KKK and the various white-supremacist groups that have endeavored to further only the goals of their limited segments of society. These groups, too, adhere to the belief that the ends justify the means, and in some cases, the ends and the means are one and the same. Such was the case with much of the violence perpetrated against African-Americans in the South during the days of the Civil Rights movement. The right-wing groups responsible for much of this violence had no goal beyond terrorizing African-Americans. Even in recent times, we have seen the destructive results of right-wing radicalism in America. In 1995, Timothy McVeigh, an antigovernment, right-wing extremist, bombed the Alfred P. Murrah Federal Building in Oklahoma City, killing 168 innocent people, including 19 children.

Before we discuss how a young person crosses the line into political radicalism and criminality, we first need to understand the various levels of political involvement pursued by young people, and the role ideology plays in their decision to participate at the levels they do. We start with the politically *passive* adolescent. Many adolescents simply have no interest in political ideology. They may individually, or as part of a particular subgroup, have little or no interest in the plight and welfare of the masses, nor in issues relating to social policy. They may see no benefit in registering to vote upon reaching the required age or feel any connection to a larger community or political class. For many adolescents, there is a natural cynicism that takes root toward the political system that governs them, mainly because most social policy is designed to benefit adults and young children, while maintaining maximum control over adolescents. There has always been a tension between adolescents and adults, primarily parents. That tension is easily generalized to all adult institutions, namely governments, churches, and corporations. Some adolescents will adapt to the rule and authority of these institutions, some will rebel in various ways, and still others, the politically-passive, will simply renounce or avoid any allegiance or connection to them. They thus identify with no political party or ideology, and for the most part, hold a very jaundiced view of the political process in general.

The politically-passive adolescent may also be part of a disenfranchised minority population that has been conditioned to be apolitical. A learned helplessness will result when a person is subjected long enough to an unresponsive political system that limits opportunity and involvement. Many adolescents in the lower socioeconomic classes of American society see little usefulness in the political process for them personally. They quickly learn that the system is designed to benefit the majority class. Once they come to the conclusion that the political system has turned its back on them, some will simply give up and abandon any political ideology they may have adopted and view it as a failed ideal. Others in this situation may never adopt a political ideology in the first place, but rather, may be conditioned from a young age to stay at arm's length from the political process, both intellectually and practically.

This is not to suggest that the absence of a political ideology in adolescence will unavoidably lead to criminality. Many adolescents do just fine without seeking out and adopting a political ideology. In fact, to what extent adolescents in general engage the political system changes over time. Since the 1960s, we have moved from a period of high involvement by adolescents in the political process, to the 1990s, when that involvement tapered off dramatically. During periods when youth involvement in politics and social activism is low, there is less of a perceived need on the part of adolescents to incorporate some political ideology into their self-identity. Thus political passivity becomes more common, and more accepted by the youth culture.

The political culture in America is essentially the ongoing tug-and-pull between two opposing ideologies. At one end of the political spectrum we find liberal Democrats, and at its opposite end, conservative Republicans. Adolescents who are politically *mainstream* are those who have adopted one political ideology or the other, or remain somewhere in the middle with aspects of both ideologies incorporated into their own. These adolescents understand the political process, willingly cast their vote when they reach the proper age, remain attentive to the political debate, and take positions on social issues that are in line with their chosen ideology. They tend to have a clear, though not always well-informed, opinion about how government should govern, and about how the relationship between government and the people it governs should be structured.

The greatest influence on the development of an adolescent's mainstream political ideology is the ideology of the parents. The choice of a political party, like the choice of a denominational church, is among those traditions that will be passed from parent to child, absent a compelling reason on the part of the child to disavow it. This passing of tradition is more likely in the child who finds identification with the parents, especially the same-sex parent, to be a source of self-esteem. It is also more likely in the child who has been precluded by authoritarian parents from developing their own ideology, instead having the ideology of the parents forced upon them. In this latter case, although the adolescent may adopt the ideology of the parents, and at some point even become politically active, eventually an imposed ideology will burn itself out unless the young person internalizes it and makes it their own. In the former case, where the adolescent finds positive reinforcement in the form of heightened self-esteem by identifying with the parent, then there is a good chance the parental ideology will be internalized by the young person and become lasting.

Not all adolescents who choose to become politically active, either in thought or action, do so from the perspective of either of the mainstream political ideologies. Some choose an *alternative* political ideology. These tend to be ideologies that are viewed as lying beyond the outer fringe of either of the mainstream ideologies. On the left, a young person may choose to adopt either a socialist or Marxist ideology. And on the extreme right, a libertarian or strong nationalist ideology. Adolescents who adopt an alternative ideology tend to be even more politically active than their mainstream counterparts. Those who espouse alternative political beliefs are seldom in agreement with the beliefs of their parents. Such beliefs are typically adopted and internalized after much searching and consideration. Whereas young people who adopt a mainstream political ideology may do so out of a sense of familial obligation, or perhaps simply a need to conform to society's norms and expectations, the young person who adopts an alternative ideology does so in response to some intellectual need. If that need is indeed met, then the ideology they adopt and internalize will likely become a more powerful component of their identity than had they just dispassionately decided to become either a Democrat or Republican

Alternative political ideologies were a mainstay of the youth movement of the 1960s. Young people simply became disillusioned with mainstream politics. Most adopted leftist ideologies that espoused Marxist ideas. It was not uncommon to see politically-active young people wearing Ché Guevara t-shirts and handing out literature that advocated revolution at the ballot box. By the 1980s, many predominantly white adolescents were searching for answers in extreme right-wing ideologies. One important characteristic of those who follow an alternative political calling is that they endeavor to become relevant in the mainstream political debate. They do not advocate violence, but rather seek acceptance and assimilation. They truly believe their positions on the issues are correct, and they tend to be empowered more by the issues themselves than by simply their membership in a particular political subgroup.

Sometimes adolescents veer even further off the beaten path of political ideology by adopting a *radical* view of things. These young people tend not to be concerned about assimilating themselves into the mainstream debate. They are more concerned about eliminating the mainstream debate altogether. Many radicalized young people have given up on changing things through the power of the ballot box. Here is where the opportunity for criminality arises. In the 1970s, left-wing groups took up arms in their goal of inciting revolution. In the 1980s, we saw the advent of radical right-wing groups such as *skinheads* and *neo-Nazi* groups. Whether their ultimate goal is the betterment of society or its further segregation, radical groups are not interested in political debate or negotiation.

Those young people who become radicalized in their political beliefs typically do so in response to some level of frustration. They are lashing out at the government, or some segment of society, and they view themselves as holding the ideological high ground, thus justifying their radical tactics. They may be frustrated by society's lack of concern for animal rights, leading them to join a radical group that firebombs animal research facilities. They may be frustrated by the government's decision to allow logging on federal lands, leading them to join a radical environmental group. Perhaps they lost out on a job to a minority candidate, and in response decide to join a radical right-wing group with exclusionary objectives. Many adolescents adopt an alternative political ideology. The nature of the adolescent psyche makes adolescence a time when the young person is highly susceptible to alternatives. But to cross the line into radicalism requires some impetus beyond intellectual curiosity. Most radicals do not start out that way. They are young people with varied belief systems who reach a point where they feel trapped in a corner—morally, intellectually, politically—with no alternative but to fight back. Once they convince themselves then that they do in fact hold the moral high ground, then radical thought can very easily turn into criminal action.

To look for one particular personality type that is more prone to radicalism is fruitless. It is simply not a homogenous group. In the 1960s and 1970s, many people from small town America were shocked to discover that the boy or girl next door who had gone off to college so full of promise and excitement about the future had landed themselves on the FBI's most wanted list for bombing government or university buildings. Many of those young people had come from completely normal and loving families. Others took a different path, shedding the innocence of their church upbringing to join a radical right-wing group espousing violence against African-Americans and Jews. There simply is no psychometric tool or behavioral indicator available that can effectively predict a young person's descent into the abyss of radicalism. It is not a personality characteristic that develops over time, but is more often a sudden change that results from a life-changing event. It is culture that creates the social milieu that fosters the rise of radical ideas. It is personal experience that causes a young person to adopt those ideas.

Like its religious counterpart, political ideology can both deter a young person from criminality, and lead them into it. Certainly those who adopt a mainstream view of things will internalize with it an appreciation for the rule of law, since social order is the primary goal of any mainstream political system. Even those with an alternative ideology will likely be deterred from criminality since they are to some degree socially conscious, although not always advocating on behalf of all segments of society. They tend to be goal-oriented, and recognize that to cross the line into criminality will preclude them from achieving those goals. At the other end of the spectrum are those who adopt radical ideologies. And while not all radicalized youth choose to cross the line into criminal conduct, it certainly creates a situation where they are accepting of it from others advocating on behalf of their goals. They may even provide aid and comfort. They have given up on the political process as a mechanism for change, and view themselves as holding the moral high ground in their efforts to force change through other than political means.

Philosophical Ideology

Just as an adolescent's identity can in part be defined by their views on the relationship of government to the individual, it can also be defined further by their views on their own relationship to the world. Philosophical ideology is a bit more difficult to define than its political counterpart. Whereas the latter may influence how an individual chooses to vote or voice their political dissent, the former will influence how they choose to live their life. A philosophical ideology defines the individual's view of their place and purpose in the social apparatus, and how they are to relate to it. Do they isolate themselves from society, or do they engage it? If the latter, do they do so through assimilation or confrontation? Do they live their lives at the expense of others, or do they sacrifice for the good of others? The answers to these and other questions can be found in an individual's personal philosophy of living.

There are a number of predominant philosophical types that an adolescent will choose from. Unlike political and religious ideologies, which require a conscious recognition of the defining aspects of those paradigms, a philosophical ideology can happen quite naturally and with no consideration given to a particular lifestyle as an ideology. In fact, whereas political and religious ideologies are voluntarily adopted, and can be avoided altogether, a philosophical ideology is involuntary, and cannot be avoided. It is only a matter of whether an individual has the insight to understand the underlying philosophical ideology that empowers them, and its implications for their life.

Some of the predominant philosophical typologies are as follows:

• *The Aesthetic:* These adolescents endeavor to experience the beauty and wonder of their existence. They give primacy to experience over knowledge. At the core of their being is a love of the arts. They may be musicians, artists, or thespians, or they may be naturalists who love the outdoors, and see themselves as just one component of a complex whole composed of man, animal, and nature. The Aesthetic is a lover of life who seeks peak experience and self-actualization through sensory stimulation and shared experience with like-minded individuals. True friendship is considered as important as intimacy. They are almost always nonviolent individuals, and the Aesthetic ideology is seldom correlated with criminality. The stimulation potentially provided by criminal conduct is counterproductive to the Aesthetic's need for positive sensory experience.

• *The Stoic:* These adolescents are easily recognized by their lack of emotionality and pursuit of knowledge. Unlike the Aesthetic, who seeks experience over understanding, the Stoic gives primacy to understanding over experience. These young people typically do very well in school, participate in nonathletic extracurricular activities, and may have difficulty establishing intimate relationships due to their lack of social skills or their prioritization of personal goals over relationships. They set high self-expectations, and are easily devastated when those expectations are not met. These young people tend to be very future-oriented and have clear academic/vocational objectives in mind before most other adolescents of their age group. They are dependable, forthright in their opinions, and are better than most at reading the overt and ulterior motives of other adolescents.

The danger for this type of adolescent is that they may set self-expectations that are unrealistically high. Their self-esteem is almost always tied to their success in meeting those expectations. Failure can lead to a diminished perception of self, which in turn can lead to feelings of self-contempt. This, of course, can lead the adolescent right into destructive behaviors that are correlated with criminality: drug and alcohol abuse chief among them. The presence of a critical authoritarian parent will only exacerbate the adolescent's sense of failure and contribute to their slide into deviance when they become overwhelmed. Their level of achievement may be internally motivated, or it may be an attempt to please a critical parent. If the latter, any amount of failure will be internalized as shame and guilt, which in turn will only magnify their feelings of self-contempt.

- *The Hedonist:* These adolescents endeavor to enjoy life to the fullest extent possible. They, too, give primacy to experience over understanding, but they seek experience for its own sake, and not out of any existential motivation. The Hedonist lives for the moment, and is little concerned about the future. They typically consider school a necessary evil since it provides so little stimulation for them. They tend to be focused entirely on what pleasures them, and are very egocentric in that attitude. They enter relationships primarily for the opportunity to engage in sexual activity, and not out of any need for intimacy. In fact, they are oftentimes cold and manipulative in their interpersonal relationships. The hedonistic adolescent is not focused on the consequences of their actions, but rather the benefits. They tend to be competitive, at times aggressive, and because of their egocentrism they typically have some amount of difficulty with empathic awareness and sympathetic arousal.

A hedonistic pattern of behavior in an adolescent is typically found in response to either an indulgent or neglectful parenting style. The indulgent parent imposes few rules or behavioral expectations on the child, and thus the child never learns about behavioral boundaries. And because their actions seem to seldom impact the parent negatively, since discipline and negative consequences are absent, they never fully learn the emotional cause and effect necessary for the development of a moral self. The result is an egocentric demeanor that demands gratification. These adolescents are ripe for delinquency. They lack the judgment to properly weigh the potential consequences of their actions because they were never subjected to consequences during the important years of their development.

In the case of a neglectful parenting style, the adolescent's hedonistic behaviors may be related more to the emotional trauma of being neglected than to the poor judgment associated with permissive parenting. The adolescent's pleasure-seeking behaviors in this case may be acting-out behaviors, or a way for the adolescent to release the frustration and emotional tension that result from the neglectful parent-child dynamic. The adolescent may act-out as a way of expressing the painful and confusing emotions they are unable to verbalize. We see this type of behavior often in dysfunctional households where violence or drug and alcohol abuse is present. It is strongly correlated with juvenile delinquency and criminality.

It is important to point out that not all hedonistic adolescents turn into juvenile delinquents. Many, especially those who come from stable and healthy family situations, are able to keep sight of the boundaries. They may push the limits of what is considered acceptable behavior by their family or school, but they are able to avoid the temptation to cross the line into criminality. When they do, it is typically minor infractions such as curfew violations, possession of marijuana, underage drinking, and the like. They tend to avoid behaviors that victimize innocent people. The healthier the parent-child dynamic, the stronger the sense of morality that develops in the child.

• *The Nihilist:* When we speak of nihilism, we are referring to the philosophical view that there exists no real justification for things like values or morality. The nihilistic adolescent is one who is essentially amoral and void of any values or guiding principles. Whereas the hedonist may unavoidably cross the line into criminality as a consequence of their pleasure-seeking activities, the nihilist may willfully and quite wantonly commit crime because they are simply undeterred from doing so. They tend to function at a very basic level intellectually, and may even be diagnosed mildly retarded or suffering from a personality disorder. These adolescents simply have no respect for the rights of others, and are almost entirely egocentric. They invariably fail in school, have very few close friends, and come from families where violence and alcoholism are commonplace. Their philosophy is very simple. They want what they want, when they want it, and are willing to go to any lengths to get it. They see no moral issue in stealing the property of another individual. Some, the "natural born killers" among them, may even enjoy committing violent crimes. Seldom do these adolescents avoid the criminal justice system before reaching adulthood.

• *The Anarchist:* This has become a popular ideology among youth during the last 25 years, especially among those who are into the punk rock scene. The Anarchist is an adolescent who disavows all forms of authority, and who views the rights and desires of the individual as holding supremacy over the need for maintaining social order through the imposed restriction of those rights and desires. The anarchist is not inherently evil, nor even deviant. Many of these adolescents are very respectful of the rights and desires of other individuals as well. They are typically part of a subculture, and they establish friendships and intimate relationships within that subculture. And while there is almost always tension between adolescents and the agents of social order, namely the police, the Anarchist creates an increased tension by denying the authority of police, teachers, and parents on a philosophical level. They tend to withdraw from mainstream society, and they avoid any connection to the popular culture. The music they listen to and the literature they read are typically "underground." They may or may not perform well in school, and they tend to use their physical appearance to symbolize their personal philosophy. Tattoos and body piercing are common, as well as alternative hairstyles and clothes.

The vast majority of these adolescents eventually grow out of this philosophy when they are confronted by the reality of adulthood. The need to assimilate into mainstream society becomes apparent when the need for a career or secondary education becomes obvious. Many will maintain some semblance of the anarchist identity, but abandon the ideology for a more utilitarian approach, as defined below. The danger in this ideology lies in its potential connection to various political ideologies. The anarchist lifestyle combined with a radical left-wing political ideology may produce a domestic terrorist at its extreme. When combined with radical right-wing politics, it may present itself in the form of a neo-Nazi or "skinhead" ideology. Either of these extremes can result in the adolescent's involvement in criminality, and perhaps even violent criminality.

• *The Utopian:* This adolescent is on a peaceful, intelligent, and philosophically-based search for their own "nirvana," or a higher form of existence beyond the routine of everyday life as a member of the popular culture. The utopian adolescent is considered a "dreamer" by friends and teachers. They are highly stimulated by the arts, but unlike the Aesthetic, who enjoys the beauty of art for its own sake, the Utopian sees it as a conduit to this higher plane of existence. They feel an existential restlessness that compels their search for self-actualizing experience. The Utopian is often said by adults to have their "head in the clouds." They may find comfort in the *New Age Movement,* or perhaps the Eastern religions, or even the works of Shakespeare. They tend to have a well-developed sense of morality, and typically function at a high level intellectually. Since the 1960s, these adolescents have been known to use mind-altering drugs in their search for a nirvana state, and while they are intellectually stimulated like the stoic, they tend to be less focused on academic or vocational goals. The Utopian seeks relationships with like-minded partners who can share their journey. Intimacy is not an end state in itself, but rather a socioemotional conduit to the desired end state.

While this particular philosophy is not correlated with criminality, the greatest danger these adolescents may face at some point is the cold bite of reality. They quickly learn when no longer under the protective care of their parents that the utopian mindset does not get a person a job or pay the bills. Some will grieve the perceived end of their journey by turning to substance abuse. Others, the majority, will simply accept as a more realistic end state things like intimacy, parenthood, and a career. Very few will resort to criminality because it neither satisfies nor quiets their existential restlessness.

• *The Utilitarian:* This philosophical perspective is the one most promoted by our sociocultural institutions. The utilitarian adolescent is one who is realistic and pragmatic. They tend to find happiness and self-esteem by taking the necessary steps to become a productive member of society. They disavow alternative ideologies as being counterproductive to the goals of carving out a career, getting married and starting a family, and perhaps buying a house and establishing a savings plan. The utilitarian sees the benefits in education, but may see equal benefit in learning a trade or joining the military. They typically belong to some organization (i.e., Scouts, FFA, 4H, etc.), and they come for the most part from stable homes with effective parenting. They seek out opportunities for intimacy, and are prone to early marriage and parenthood to fulfill societal expectations. In terms of political ideology, they almost always adopt the ideology of their parents, which tends to lean toward nationalist-conservative. The utilitarian seldom resorts to criminality. They almost always support the police and the need to maintain social order.

Figure 4.3 summarizes the philosophical orientations described above. It is important to point out that an adolescent can adopt and live by a combination of these philosophies. For example, it is not uncommon for an adolescent to seek a utopian existence in the anarchist ideology. The utilitarian adolescent may derive much enjoyment from the aesthetic qualities of art, music, or poetry. It is quite normal for an adolescent to live by a hybrid philosophy, but almost always one particular philosophy dominates. The transient nature of adoles-

Philosophical Orientation	Motivation	Relationships	Predominant Parenting Style	Criminal Correlate
Aesthetic	Internal sensory stimulation	Intimacy for its beauty	Authoritative	NO
Stoic	Intellectual stimulation	Intimacy is secondary	Authoritative Indulgent	NO
Hedonist	External sensory stimulation	Avoids intimacy	Indulgent Neglectful	YES
Nihilist	Egocentric desires	Unable to experience	Indulgent Neglectful	YES
Anarchist	Social separation	Intimacy with like-minded	Neglectful Indulgent Authoritarian	YES
Utopian	Existential stimulation/ Self-actualization	Intimacy as a conduit to self-actualization	Authoritative Indulgent	NO
Utilitarian	Pragmatism/ Social convention	Intimacy per social expectations	Authoritative Authoritarian	NO

Figure 4.3. Adolescent philosophical orientation.

cence, however, is such that with little provocation the young person can change their thinking and behavior to fit a new philosophy. This usually comes about through some type of peer interaction or a significant event that takes place in the family. Some of these changes are themselves transitory, while others become internalized as lifelong patterns of behavior.

CHAPTER SUMMARY

We have looked at the three major components of an adolescent's identity: *social, sexual,* and *ideological.* We have discussed how the parent-child dynamic contributes to each. We will now turn to the actual process of identity-formation, and the process by which an adolescent chooses which identity types and styles to mix and match to suit their particular needs and desires. Unlike many other aspects of development, particularly those occurring in the preadolescent years, identity formation doesn't happen in large part below the surface of conscious awareness. Adolescents craft an identity through trial and error. Immediately after their awakening into adolescence it's as if they decide to walk into the identity store to go shopping; choosing some products, rejecting others, and even returning a few for a refund when they don't work.

As we turn now to the developmental process of identity formation, we will look also at the role of identity in the development of the criminal personality type. As the third leg of the Criminal Triad, it is here where the conscious decision to engage in juvenile delinquency occurs. The child has little ability to change the course of their own moral development in middle childhood, and even less control over the quality of their parent-child attachment, but they have much ability to determine the outcome of their identity-formation process. They are at a point in their cognitive development where abstract thought is possible, and a point in their socioemotional development where emotional independence from the parents is critical. The ball is now in their court to take in hand the identity palette and paint a picture of who they will be from this point forward. For some, the process is easy and uneventful. For others, it is wrought with frustration and tension. And for still others, it can be so emotionally devastating that they spend their remaining days dealing with its lingering effects.

Chapter 5

CLOSING THE GAP
The Role of Identity Formation During Adolescence (Part II)

INTRODUCTION

As we discussed in the preceding chapter, there was a time in America, prior to the latter half of the 1950s, when adolescents were *socialized* rather than being self-motivated to carve out a personal identity. What an adolescent ultimately became was dictated by cultural and parental expectations. The developmental task of adolescence was to finish the process of sculpting oneself in the image of the parents. For a boy, the expectations were to carry on the trade or profession of their father, perhaps after a stint in the military, and then in short order marry, purchase a home, and have children. The expectations of an adolescent girl were even more limited. They were simply to get married, have children, and to support their husband. If a girl decided to work, it was typically because her mother worked, and the job she chose was typically the same type of job. The end result was young people who exited the other end of adolescence into adulthood without their own sense of identity. They had been socialized to adopt the predominant persona created by their culture for people of their age group.

In the latter half of the 1950s, however, something interesting happened in America. In 1956, Poet Allen Ginsberg's "Howl" was published, and the following year, writer Jack Kerouac's "On the Road" was put into print. These works, among others, represented the beginnings of the American *Beat Movement.* This cultural phenomenon had a lasting impact on America's youth. For the first time, young people refused to be socialized and molded in the image of their parents. After two recent wars, and nuclear annihilation fast becoming a real possibility, young people had had enough. Their parents had failed them, and now it was time to try figuring things out on their own. Their collective angst compelled them en masse to abandon the status quo in favor of throwing caution to the wind and following their youthful and at times hedonistic yearnings. Adolescents were hungry for spontaneity, and an end to the psychological repression perpetrated against them for decades by a utilitarian American culture that demanded conformity. With the construction of a new national interstate system underway, true freedom was just an automobile and a full tank of gasoline away.

American youth never returned to the days of their die-cast socialization. The Beat Movement of the 1950s became the counterculture of the 1960s, and the sociocultural fate of America's youth was sealed for decades to come. As those who passed through adolescence during this colorful period in contemporary history became the parents of the generation to follow, the standard shifted. Young people no longer were expected to follow a predetermined pathway into adulthood. The sociocultural expectation shifted from socialization to identity formation. Henceforth young people would be expected to determine for themselves how they wished to enter adulthood. They would now craft their own belief system (ideological self), workout their own sexuality (sexual self), and determine for themselves their vocational or academic goals and objectives (social self).

A child begins the process of identity formation long before they set out on their adolescent journey to discover themselves. It all starts when they begin to identify with other people or fictional characters. This typically begins when they start to fantasize about being someone else, or at least being like someone else. It may be based in reality, but more than likely, at least early on in their development, it will be a character from a movie, a book, or in our modern age, even a video game. This fantasy play serves an important function for the child. It causes them to become aware of self as a unique being with unique and malleable characteristics. It further teaches them to self-evaluate, and for the first time to formulate some semblance of an *idea-self.* This idealized self-portrait becomes the object of their aspirations; however, early on in their development, prior to gaining the full ability to self-evaluate, there is no gap between this idealized self and their *perceived-self.* Through fantasy play and make-believe, they are able to be whomever they wish to be. Their cognitive immaturity makes this fantasy play quite adequate in terms of calming the socioemotional tension associated with the development of a self-concept. Eventually though, when their cognitive development makes self-evaluation easier and more realistic, this ideal-self will become the yardstick by which they begin to measure their perceived-self. Closing the gap between the two will eventually become the major developmental task of adolescence, and their success in doing so will be positively correlated with self-esteem. Coming to the realization that this gap, which is illustrated in Figure 5.1, even exists represents the starting point of the identity-formation process.

Eventually the child's fantasy play is replaced by their identification with real people. It may be a sports figure, a musician, or perhaps a movie or television star. It may also be a pastor or a teacher, or a police officer or fireman. And certainly, it may also be the parents. Typically the person or persons with whom an adolescent identifies is one who possesses certain characteristics they wish for themselves. Boys identify with other males based primarily on their occupation or physical abilities. Girls, on the other hand, tend to identify with other

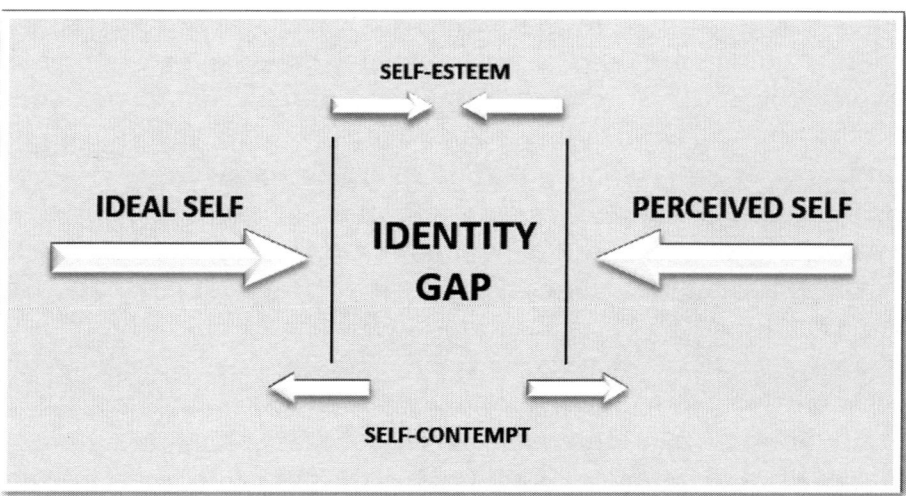

Figure 5.1. The adolescent identity gap.

females based primarily on physical and stylistic attributes. When an adolescent identifies with another individual, they are essentially incorporating that person's desirable characteristics into their own version of an ideal-self. This ideal-self then is what compels the young person to seek out a personal identity in an effort to close the identity gap. In short, a successful childhood is one in which a secure attachment leads to the personal autonomy and efficacy necessary to enter adolescence and begin to establish a well-defined personal identity. A successful adolescence in turn is one in which the young person closes the identity gap enough to quiet the emotional storm and enter adulthood with the necessary ego strength to successfully transfer their attachment from the primary caregiver(s) to a significant other. Thus, a personal identity has a dual function in that it allows the young person to effectively disengage emotionally from the parents and then re-engage emotionally with an intimate partner.

In American culture, when an adolescent enters the period of identity formation, society tends to give them the room and the flexibility to experiment with many different roles and components of identity in order to determine what works best for them. Psychologist James Marcia (1973) referred to this as a *psychological moratorium.* It is a time when the young person is allowed the freedom to dye their hair, wear strange looking clothes, embrace alternative lifestyles, or even adopt as their preferred mode of transportation a skateboard without serious or lasting consequences. In contrast, imagine someone thirty-something showing up for work one day with a nose-ring or purple hair! Obviously our culture does not afford adults the same level of freedom to express themselves. They are held accountable for their identity, and if the outward expression of that identity is not in accord with prevailing cultural expectations, then there are consequences.

Erik Erikson described another important variable in the identity-formation process—the *identity crisis* (Erikson, 1968). It is a term used widely in our popular culture, typically to describe an individual who is confused about who they are or what they want out of life. For the adolescent, a crisis occurs when they are internally motivated to experiment with new identity roles, expressions, or ideologies. This typically occurs when the young person feels as if they are being lost in the crowd, a sentiment experienced by most adolescents at one time or another. This crisis can be brought on by a particular life event, or practically anything that is meaningful to the adolescent. It can be a movie, a song, a book, or even a sudden flash of clarity about life's deeper meaning. To use our earlier illustration, a crisis is experienced either when the adolescent is focused on narrowing the identity gap, or when they are in fear of the gap widening. There are two things that are true of adolescents. First, they have this sense that their lives are being played out on a stage. And second, they tend to believe that everyone around them is watching their every move. Consequently, self-portrayal, or the outward expression of their efforts to narrow the identity gap, is greatly increased during adolescence. Because of this heightened egocentricity, and the adolescent's almost singular focus on how they are perceived in the eyes of their peers and potential intimates, identity crises tend to occur rather frequently, even in those adolescents described as securely-attached and emotionally healthy.

When a crisis is experienced, that is when the adolescent is compelled to try something new. For some, it may be a new vocational or academic goal, or perhaps a new religious experience. Others may become vegan or involve themselves in the punk rock scene. Still others may turn to reading poetry, or participate in some sport or activity. Some adolescents may even make the difficult decision to announce that they are gay. The possible options are limitless. What they all have in common, however, is that they allow the adolescent to portray themselves in a new and expanding way in order to close the identity gap and facilitate their search for self.

As most of us know from our own adolescent experience, not everything a young person does to define themselves meets with success. At times, adolescents have been known to veer quite widely from the beaten path in their attempt at self-discovery. Marcia (1973) expanded on Erikson's earlier ideas by suggesting that a young person carves out their identity gradually and over time by committing to those things that seem to work, and discarding those that do not. For Marcia, this *crisis-commitment* dynamic is critical to the adolescent achieving a well-defined sense of who they are before entering adulthood. Those who do not commit to various roles and expressions of identity during adolescence enter adulthood in a state of *identity confusion.*

Marcia identified four different identity statuses based on the presence or absence of crisis and commitment in the adolescent's life. They are:

• *Identity diffusion:* For this young person, neither crisis nor commitment is present. The adolescent is simply not motivated to figure out who they are. They are lost in the crowd, and they wish to stay there. This identity status is typically reflective of an insecure-attachment on the part of the adolescent, and may be the result of a *neglectful* parenting style. The adolescent may not wish to figure out who they are out of fear of what they will find. They may experience feelings of self-contempt and engage in self-destructive behaviors like self-mutilation, purging, or drug and alcohol abuse. The identity gap for these adolescents seems insurmountable. At its extreme, it can lead to suicidal ideations. Young people who have suffered any type of abuse at the hands of their parents will almost always suffer from identity diffusion.

In terms of criminality, the identity-diffused adolescent may act out their existential despair by seeking identity through participation in an unhealthy peer group. These adolescents are followers, and easily enticed to join a group, especially when they feel some amount of acceptance and positive regard. They easily adopt the predominant persona of the group since they have none of their own to stand in the way. Apart from some type of group affiliation, the identity-diffused adolescent may also act out their emotional tension by engaging in solitary criminal activity. If they project their self-contempt on others, then they may transition from self-destructive acts to perpetrating violence against others in an effort to reduce that tension.

• *Identity moratorium:* This adolescent is one who experiences crisis, but fails to commit to any particular role or expression of identity. This is typical during the early stages of identity-formation, as the young person experiments with many different facets of identity. One can sit for a time at a mall, a skate park, and any other place where adolescents congregate and watch the process as it is occurring. You will see young people expressing themselves in many colorful and bizarre ways, at least by adult standards. In most cases, this self-expression is completely normal and healthy. As they do, they are getting feedback from other adolescents. This feedback facilitates their self-evaluation and leads the adolescent to commit to various identity components.

For some adolescents, however, commitment doesn't happen when it typically should. Our culture affords the adolescent a psychological moratorium, but at some point, the adolescent is expected to begin figuring things out and taking steps toward adulthood. These steps are taken with each commitment the adolescent makes. The young person who never commits is one who never makes a serious effort to plan their future. At 19 they are still doing the things they were doing at 15. They have no interest in being an adult with adult responsibilities. They tend to bounce between minimum wage jobs, and they struggle in college because of their inability or refusal to commit to academic goals. In terms of parenting, it is common for this type of adolescent to have *permissive* parents who failed to establish well-defined goals and expectations during the adolescent's childhood years. In this case, the child never internalizes the success of meeting those goals and expectations, and thus they miss an important opportunity to learn how to live their lives in a goal-oriented manner. The parents may be responsive and loving, and so the adolescent may enjoy a secure attachment, but the adolescent's inability to commit to any expression of a permanent identity tends to be enabled, more so than discouraged, by the parents' indulgent demeanor toward them and their lifestyle.

There is not a strong correlation between this type of identity status and criminality unless other factors are present, and the young person's inability to commit to identity is a response to some internal conflict they may be experiencing. Unlike the identity-diffused adolescent, who feels no crisis, and thus no desire to even experiment with different identity roles and expressions, this adolescent does feel crisis. They are interested in self-portrayal and are therefore concerned somewhat with how others evaluate them. The more concerned an adolescent is about self-portrayal and peer feedback, the less likely they are to engage in socially deviant behavior.

• *Identity foreclosure:* Typically the result of an *authoritarian* parenting style, this adolescent commits to identity, but not in response to any precursory crisis. These young people are under the complete control of their parents, and they are simply not willing to challenge their authority. They are socialized rather than being given the freedom to shape their own identity. The parents decide for them what their career and academic goals will be, what school and social activities they will be involved in, and in some cases, even whom they will date. For some ethnic groups in America, Middle Easterners and South Asians predominantly, this type of socialization is culturally accepted, and even demanded. At its most extreme, even marriages are arranged by the parents. In these families, the child's identity is not to be distinguishable from that of the family's. Individual happiness takes a backseat to family honor.

In the predominant American culture, this type of socialization is neither accepted nor demanded, and thus many young people who are subjected to this type of commitment without crisis pay an emotional price. Even in the less extreme cases, where the parents perhaps demand only a particular profession, course of study, or university choice, it still runs the risk of creating emotional tension by disallowing the adolescent the full opportunity to close the identity gap. When a young person is denied this opportunity, they lose out on the chance for self-discovery, a process so critical to the development of a healthy self-concept and a happy adulthood. They never fully develop a sense of self apart from the parents, and as a consequence they may experience problems exercising personal autonomy, and may maintain an emotional dependence on the parents even into adulthood.

The greatest risk for these adolescents resorting to some form of deviant behavior is when the emotional strain of their identity-confusion overwhelms them, and they act out in order to reduce the tension. While most will choose simply to break away from the parents and deal with the lingering emotional effects as best they can, others may resort to self-destructive behaviors, including criminality, as a way of rebelling against, and symbolically denying the authority of the parents. Drug and alcohol abuse is not uncommon. In the most extreme cases, these individuals may either experience such an existential void that it leads them to attempt suicide, or to murder innocent victims as a way of symbolically killing the authoritarian parent. These most extreme cases typically include some form of abuse on the part of the parent.

• *Identity achievement:* Certainly the ideal situation is the adolescent who experiences crisis and readily commits to those components of identity that seem to work. The young person who commits to identity is one who gradually develops a self-concept, which in turn will carry them into adulthood with a sense of confidence and self-efficacy. Along the way, they will commit to various ideologies, the outward expression of their sexuality, and certain vocational and academic goals. They may choose a religious or political affiliation. They may decide to live in a rural setting, or perhaps instead in a large urban environment. They may aspire to aggressively build wealth, or to forsake wealth for a life of humble means. Typically they have been exposed to *authoritative* parenting, which has been found to be the most effective parenting style.

Criminality is rare for the adolescent who is actively committing to various aspects of their identity. They are moving forward in a goal-oriented manner and making commitments in response to positive feedback, narrowing the identity gap each step of the way. As the gap narrows, self-esteem is increased, and this alone will deter the adolescent to a significant degree from engaging in deviant behavior.

IDENTITY AND THE CRIMINAL TRIAD

The formation of a well-defined personal identity is key to the adolescent developing a self-deterrence mechanism (SeDM). It is this internal mechanism that deters the individual from engaging in crime not for reasons of morality, nor a fear of being judged by others, but rather for purely internal reasons. For the individual with a well-defined personal identity, to engage in criminal conduct unavoidably creates a dissonance between their ideal-self and their perceived-self. Simply put, it has the effect of widening their identity gap, thus lowering their self-esteem and causing their self-concept to begin to crumble. It is the anticipation of this happening, and the expected emotional discomfort that will unavoidably follow that empowers the individual's SeDM. They choose not to engage in deviance because such behavior is simply inconsistent with who they are. They are not individuals who will commit criminal acts only when no one is looking. Rather, like the majority of individuals in our society, their sense of identity is like a perennial mirror that keeps a reflection of self focused in front of them. By having a keen sense of who they are, and by being content with that identity, they are more likely to continue moving forward toward their ideal-self.

The question must be asked if it is possible for someone to have a well-defined identity, one perhaps they are quite comfortable with, and still be a career criminal. Are all criminals simply acting-out in an effort to reduce the emotional tension associated with identity diffusion or foreclosure? The answer to the latter question is no. In fact, some criminals are very comfortable with their lifestyle, and willingly choose an identity role that incorporates a criminal demeanor. To understand, we must look at the possible end-states of the identity-formation process. There are four potential outcomes: the *congruous* identity; the *discordant* identity; the *antisocial* identity; and the *deficient* identity. Each is reflective of the level of success or failure the adolescent encounters in the course of responding to the crisis-commitment dynamic.

It is important to understand that culture is largely responsible for dictating what is considered a normal and well-defined identity. After all, our identity is the software that allows us to interface with other members of our society. If that interface is to be effective, then our identity must be compatible with society's corporate identity. The sociocultural norms that define an acceptable identity are what allow us to be compatible. So the success of an adolescent's identity-formation is determined by more than just the degree to which the adolescent is happy with their perceived-self. There is a social component that must be included in the evaluation, or the degree to which the adolescent's identity is compatible with society's demands and expectations.

The *congruous* identity is one in which the adolescent is comfortable with their perceived-self, and the various aspects of ideology, sexuality, and sociality to which they have committed are within sociocultural norms. This does not necessarily mean that the adolescent's identity gap has been greatly narrowed. In fact, the adolescent may still feel quite incomplete in their identity, but they are at least moving in the right direction. They have experienced crisis throughout their identity-formation years, and they have actively committed to certain roles and expressions of identity along the way. Their congruous identity translates into ego strength. Regardless of the distance present in their identity gap, their perceived-self is congruous with their ideal-self. They are at least on the same path so to speak, and heading in the same direction. The individual with a congruous identity feels capable of managing their identity gap. Their ideal-self tends to be realistic, and their perceived-self tends to be an accurate assessment of who they are. Their expression of identity is also congruous with societal expectations. The congruous identity is strongly correlated with the presence of a self-deterrence mechanism (SeDM).

The *discordant* identity, on the other hand, is found in the individual who feels incapable of managing their identity gap. Their ideal-self may be unrealistic and unachievable, and their self assessment may be unduly critical. These are people who have not successfully committed to components of identity during their adolescent years, or they committed at the behest of an authoritarian parent (foreclosure). The discordant identity is marked by an emotional discomfort and a lack of a defined self-concept. At its extreme, they may suffer severe psychological problems from the self-contempt that can result when an adolescent enters early adulthood without a sense of who they are. This may result in a type of spiritual or existential crisis, confusion relating to their sexuality, and a lack of academic or vocational goals.

The individual with a discordant identity, though they may perceive their identity gap as overwhelming, is still in many cases self-motivated to narrow it. The congruous identity is so because both their ideal and perceived-self is consistent with their self-expectations and those of the particular sociocultural system in which they live. Thus the ideal-self and perceived-self are said to be congruous, though possibly separated to some degree. For the discordant identity, the ideal-self, though seemingly unattainable, is still consistent with societal expectations. Consequently, the individual's self-identity may still have a deterrent effect on any temptation to engage in criminal activity. It is their perceived-self that is the problem. It is incongruous with their ideal-self because of their lack of a well-defined self-concept. Because of this circumstance, they essentially have no roadmap for achieving a sense of congruity with the ideal-self. If their identity gap is so overwhelming that they have essentially given up any efforts to commit to new identity roles and expressions, then their ability to self-deter from criminality may be greatly diminished or gone altogether. When this happens, then the individual may begin to act-out in an effort to reduce their frustrations and tensions, and this may involve deviant behavior.

But can an individual actually enjoy committing crime, and can criminality be an expression of identity to which they have committed? The answer is yes. The individual with an *antisocial* identity is one who may be completely comfortable with who they are, but their identity expression is inconsistent with societal demands and expectations. These individuals tend to have a very narrow identity gap or none at all. They are typically narcissistic and unable to empathize, or to be sympathetically aroused. These individuals have no SeDM, and are deterred only by potential consequences. They are typically guided by a hedonistic or anarchistic ideology, and they seldom demonstrate any sense of spirituality. Their social identity is typically lacking to a large degree. They feel no need to conform to society's expectations, so vocational and academic goals are of little consequence.

This type of identity is a result of a failure to commit to acceptable identity roles during adolescence. Typically the product of either *permissive* or *neglectful* parenting, these adolescents acquire their self-esteem through identification with unhealthy peer groups. The values of the group become internalized as their own. Further, their ideal-self is defined by the group rather than society, thus making it easier to narrow the identity gap by simply meeting the expectations of the group. We see this today in gang affiliation, where members have a strong sense of identity, but are in no way deterred from engaging in crime.

The final identity outcome is the *deficient* identity. This individual has no ideal-self, and their perceived-self only instills self-contempt. They have no identity gap, and they make no effort to commit to any particular expression of identity. In James Marcia's terminology, they are identity-diffused. These individuals have no SeDM, and are guided by no particular ideology. They tend to engage in drug and alcohol abuse, and seldom maintain a career. Rather than conform to sociocultural norms, they choose instead to retreat from society and its demands. They have difficulty establishing and maintaining healthy relationships.

People with deficient identities are typically those who had their opportunity for identity-formation taken from them through neglect or abuse during childhood. Children who are victims of sexual or physical abuse commonly suffer from identity-diffusion. The emotional abuse wrought upon the child by an extreme authoritarian parent can also lead to this circumstance. In terms of criminality, these individuals tend to engage in deviant behavior as a way of reducing psychic tension, and to symbolically lash out at the parents who contributed to their feelings of self-contempt. Many serial killers fall in this category. Unlike the antisocial individual, who commits crime because they have reasons for doing so, perhaps only because they enjoy it, the individual with the deficient identity does so to protect a fragile and

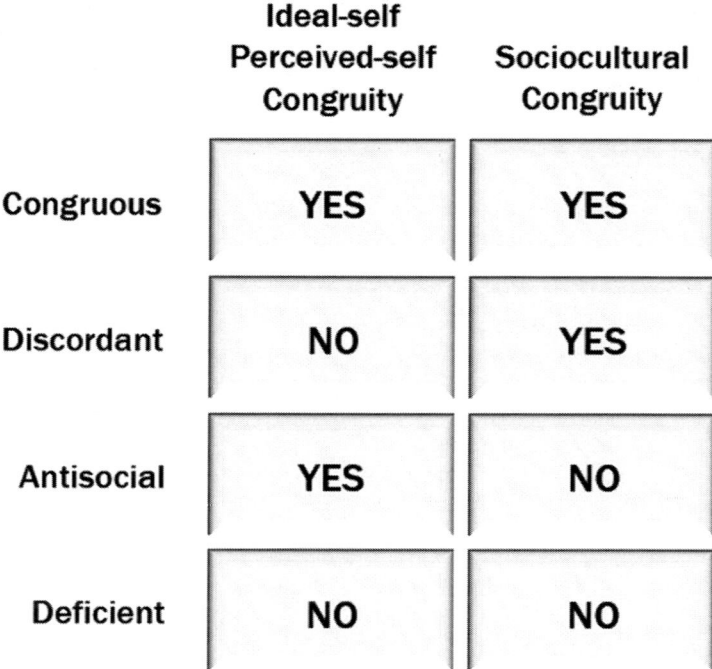

Figure 5.2. The four identity outcomes.

unguarded self-image. And when the temptation or need to engage in crime for this purpose presents itself, there simply is no SeDM to prevent it.

The four identity outcomes can be described in terms of their congruence with both the ideal-self and the sociocultural expectations that define an acceptable identity. Figure 5.2 illustrates the four potential outcomes.

CHAPTER SUMMARY

The journey to the development of a criminal personality type begins with the parent-child relationship during infancy and ends with the development of a personal identity during adolescence. The former will directly impact the latter. Those who enter adulthood with a well-defined self-concept, and who have committed to a socially-acceptable set of ideologies, an expression of their sexuality they are comfortable with, and the necessary vocational or academic goals that will lead them to a productive life as an engaged member of society, are entirely less inclined to engage in criminal behavior and other forms of deviance. With the development of a personal identity, one that is congruous with both the individual's ideal-self and the expectations of society, comes an inner strength, and with it the ability to effectively mediate the demands of society and the impulsive desires of self. This inner strength results in the development of the SeDM.

We turn now to the onset of criminality during the offender's juvenile years. We will look at the role each of the developmental processes discussed thus far—*attachment, moral development, identity formation*—plays in the adolescent's decision to engage in criminal conduct when the opportunity presents itself, a decision that can lead to a deviant pattern of behavior that may last well into adulthood.

Chapter 6

CRIMINAL BEGINNINGS
A Killer Is Born

INTRODUCTION

Crime is found wherever the criminal personality type comes into contact with the necessary environmental stimuli to cause it to bubble to the surface in the form of deviant behavior. Thus far we have said much about the development of this type of personality, but little about the stimuli that compels it into action. Criminality is not inherently potential in an individual. It requires the individual's interaction with other people and situations in order for it to develop as a pattern of behavior. Inevitably a young person who has developed a criminal personality type, as we define it herein, will come face to face with the situational variables that will stress their ability to self-deter. When they succumb to this temptation, and when they are subsequently caught by the police, as most juvenile offenders are, then they find themselves labeled and subjected to a juvenile justice system that in many ways is less about rehabilitation, and more about warehousing the violent offenders among them, and placing the rest on a conveyor belt through a system that has neither the time nor the money to care much about them. Many young people who enter the system with some hope of turning away from a life of crime and deviance unfortunately exit the other end labeled, abandoned, and identity-diffused.

From this point forward, we will focus on those young people who meet our criteria for having a criminal personality type, meaning at least two of the deterrence mechanisms are absent in the individual. We will look primarily at the motivating variables that compel this population to engage in criminality. While they may appear as a homogenous group to a juvenile court system that tends to focus on their crimes rather than their socioemotional development, juvenile delinquents are anything but a homogenous group. Their reasons for engaging in delinquent behavior are quite varied; however, we can easily categorize them into one of three groups—the *opportunistic, ego-directed,* or *symbolic* offender. Each represents a different type of motivation for the young person, and each can be discussed in terms of its relationship to the three developmental legs of the Criminal Triad: *attachment, moral development,* and *identity-formation.* We will begin our discussion with the juvenile offender who engages in criminality for opportunistic reasons.

THE OPPORTUNISTIC OFFENDER

Those juvenile offenders who engage in criminal conduct for reasons related to the actual or potential benefits of their criminal acts are referred to as *opportunistic* offenders. They are extremely egocentric offenders who are motivated by their own selfish wants and desires, including the desire to sexually assault and murder innocent victims. Their conduct is not motivated by any internal ego needs or deficits. They simply enjoy their particular style of criminality, in some cases to the point of obsession, and they lack the requisite moral deterrence (MDM) to resist the temptation to engage in such behavior. Their crimes are thus *act-focused,* meaning the act itself is what is important to the offender.

This type of offender is typically the child of a permissive or neglectful parent—neglectful in the sense that the parents are entirely uninvolved—and a single parent household is not uncommon. In this type of parenting environment, the child never learns the proper boundaries, and their behavior is left unchecked by any significant rules or expectations. Because they seldom receive negative or critical feedback from a permissive or absent parent, this child fails to learn critical self-evaluation, and thus they remain egocentric beyond the point when a child should begin to develop an understanding of how their behaviors can be viewed by others in a negative light. With egocentricity comes a demeanor of selfishness and an inability to effectively empathize with others. Of course, without empathic awareness, the child has little ability to sympathize, which in turn inhibits their altruistic concern for others. So the downside to permissive parenting can potentially be the child's inability to fully develop a sense of morality, and when we pair this with a heightened level of egocentricity, then opportunistic offending as a juvenile becomes a real possibility.

If we look at the attachment process in infancy and early childhood, we find that the children of permissive parents are typically securely attached. These are not bad parents, at least not in terms of their responsiveness to the child. They tend to be highly responsive and may be very loving parents who are loved by their children. But they shortchange their children by not establishing rules and expectations, and even more so by not providing critical feedback when the child fails to follow the rules or meet the expectations. The classic permissive parent is one who comes to their child's defense even they have done wrong. They essentially teach the child that there is no wrong, at least not in terms of the child's behavior, and that any criticism by other adults, teachers, or authority figures can be discounted.

With a neglectful parent, or one who is reactive rather than responsive, and otherwise not involved in their child's life, these children are typically insecurely attached, though not always, and the lack of moral development that results from not learning the acceptable boundaries of behavior is no different than it is for the children of permissive parents. We will look at the more serious outcome of neglectful parenting, where some type of physical, sexual, or emotional abuse is involved, when we discuss the *symbolic* offender.

In terms of identity-formation, these individuals tend to be comfortable with who they are. As discussed in the preceding chapter, they tend to have a very narrow identity gap, or none at all. They are almost always guided by a hedonistic or anarchistic ideology, and while some may have had a church upbringing, their sense of spirituality tends to diminish when they reach adolescence. If we look at such opportunistic offenders as serial killers John Wayne Gacy and Theodore "Ted" Bundy, we find that both were entirely comfortable with who they were, even to the point of having a high opinion of themselves. They may be sociable, albeit manipulative so, and they may even be able to develop and maintain intimate relationships; however, those relationships will tend to lack any degree of transparency or emotional commitment.

Juvenile to Adult Progression

One thing that is true of most minor juvenile offenders is that they eventually grow out of their criminal behavior patterns. The Washington State Institute for Public Policy (1996) found that of those 18-year-olds who during 1988 committed a nonviolent misdemeanor, only 1% were subsequently convicted of a violent felony by the age of 25. Another 8% were convicted of nonviolent felonies. In contrast, of those juvenile offenders who had committed a violent felony (3%), 20% were later convicted of a violent felony as an adult. Another 27% were convicted of nonviolent felonies. The authors concluded the obvious, that the more serious the juvenile offender's crimes, the greater the likelihood that they will become an adult offender.

The opportunistic juvenile offender who becomes a chronic adult offender is typically one whose egocentricity and lack of moral development leads to a pattern of behavior that meets the DSM-IV criteria for *Antisocial Personality Disorder* (ASPD). This diagnosis requires that three or more of the following criteria be present in adulthood (18 years of age or older):

- A failure to conform to social norms with respect to lawful behaviors as indicated by repeatedly performing acts that are grounds for arrest;
- Deceitfulness, as indicated by repeated lying, use of aliases, or conning others for personal profit or pleasure;
- Impulsivity or failure to plan ahead;
- Irritability and aggressiveness, as indicated by repeated physical fights or assaults;
- A reckless disregard for the safety of self or others;
- Consistent irresponsibility, as indicated by repeated failure to sustain consistent work behavior or honor financial obligations;
- A lack of remorse, as indicated by being indifferent to or rationalizing having hurt, mistreated, or stolen from another.

When we speak of "personality disorders," we are referring to a group of disorders that manifest themselves in the form of pervasive and inflexible behavior patterns that result in the individual's inability to function in ways that are consistent with cultural expectations. People diagnosed with a personality disorder often have significant difficulties with relationships, academic achievement, and employment. They are different from the more serious psychiatric disorders that are marked by significant emotional or cognitive impairment (i.e., schizophrenia, bipolar disorder, major depression). People with personality disorders are not significantly impaired either emotionally or cognitively; however, their behavior patterns preclude them from interacting normally with other people. Also, whereas people suffering from the more serious disorders know full well they are sick and psychologically abnormal, people with personality disorders tend to view their behavior as quite normal.

Of the personality disorders, Antisocial Personality Disorder is the most highly correlated with criminality. Young people whose behavior is consistent with this diagnostic category have been conditioned by developmental processes to impulsively seek gratification. Because they remain very egocentric, most have failed to develop an adequate sense of morality. A loss of egocentricity is necessary in order to experience the world from another's point of view. Without this ability to empathize, the young person never fully develops the ability to experience on an emotional level the pain and suffering of others, especially the victims of their deviant acts.

THE EGO-DIRECTED OFFENDER

This offender type is motivated much differently than the opportunistic offender. The ego-directed offender is one who engages in deviance because of a deficient self-concept. For this young person, criminality becomes a way of filling the void, albeit temporarily, in their sense of self. Whereas the opportunistic offender is *act-focused,* the ego-directed offender is *self-focused,* meaning it is not necessarily the crime itself that is of utmost importance, but rather the effect the crime has on their deficient self-image. They lack a well-defined sense of self and are likely identity-diffused. These young people are insecure and lack any degree of self-efficacy. They crave positive strokes to feed an otherwise fragile self-concept.

The primary objective of the ego-directed offender is to lessen the impact of a deficient self-image by manifesting its opposite. They typically do this by seeking power and control. They commit crime to prove their social prowess, both to themselves and to the other members of the group. They are coldly aggressive in relationships to prove their sexual prowess, all the while feeling terribly uncomfortable with intimacy. They compensate for their lack of social identity and poor academic achievement by being tough-minded and rebellious. While many young people affiliate with gangs purely for opportunistic reasons, the ego-directed offender does so for reasons related to self-image. They enjoy being feared by others, and perceived as someone who is unafraid of authority figures.

The crimes committed by the ego-directed offender are diverse, and run the entire gamut of crime types. Unlike the opportunistic offender, however, who commits crime for the material and psychological benefits, and thus has a vested interest in maintaining a low profile, the ego-directed offender derives maximum benefit from maintaining a high profile. For them, their criminal conduct is of less value unless it can be worn like a badge of honor for others to see and admire. They may achieve some degree of ego-gratification in the crimes themselves, but it is fleeting given their fragile sense of self. What is more important for the ego-directed offender is to be seen and heard, and to be connected to the crimes they commit. They may arrogantly play a game of cat and mouse with the police, daring the police to try to catch them. Whereas the opportunistic offender attempts to protect their criminal enterprise with silence and stealth, the ego-directed offender attempts to protect their ego with a sense of arrogant disregard.

What makes this type of offender dangerous is the perceived *ego-death* they face if they allow the crack in their self-concept to widen. It is not uncommon for these offenders to resort to violence either to strengthen their self-image through acts of power and control, or to prove to others by the same means their social prowess. They may be followers who will carry out any order, including those requiring violence, to preserve their status in the group; sexual offenders who engage in date rape to compensate for their deficient sexual identity; or bullies and fighters who instill fear in others in order to hide the chinks in their own social armor. In short, the ego-directed offender resorts to a delinquent lifestyle in order to hide the reality of their own identity gap from self and others.

In terms of development, and specifically the parent-child dynamic, the ego-directed offender is typically the product of neglectful parenting. A parent who is unresponsive or absent precludes the child from enjoying the positive feedback that is so critical to the development of self-efficacy and a healthy self-image. A child who has no rules or expectations never has the opportunity to benefit from successfully meeting those rules and expectations, a consequence of which is the development of a sense of self-efficacy. The outcome is the same for the child who has rules and expectations imposed upon them, but receives no positive reinforcement or feedback from the parents for successful outcomes. Without gaining the ability to measure success and failure, the child is left unable to properly mediate their wants and desires against sociocultural demands and restrictions. A neglectful or unresponsive parent results in an insecure attachment and an underdeveloped self-concept.

As previously stated, an unresponsive or neglectful parenting style can also lead to the development of an opportunistic offending pattern. What is the difference? Recall that we described the neglectful parent, excluding those who are abusive, as reactive rather than responsive. They are relatively uninvolved in the child's life, and when they are, it is typically because they are reacting to some particular circumstance that requires their involvement. It is the quality of that reaction that affects the development of the child. The more negative and critical the interaction, the more deleterious the impact it has on the child's development. At one end of the spectrum, unresponsive parenting with a neutral to positive reaction style can lead to the child simply not learning the boundaries of acceptable behavior, and thus resulting in a lack of moral development and an opportunistic offending pattern. At the other end, a predominantly negative to critical reaction style can directly impact the child's development of a self-concept and result in an ego-directed offending pattern.

Juvenile to Adult Progression

The adolescent offender who engages in crime in an effort to seek identity and strengthen their deficient sense of self will enjoy only transient benefits. Eventually, the weight of societal expectations and restrictions will come to bear as the adolescent passes into adulthood. Most will eventually abandon the criminal lifestyle as it loses its effectiveness in bringing about the desired outcome it was able to produce in adolescence. Suddenly, behaviors intended as a display of power and social prowess are no longer reinforced as they once were. The individual quickly learns that the criminal justice system is terribly unbending once they are no longer considered a juvenile. The behaviors that once propped up their self-image now contribute to its decay. Whereas adolescents enjoy somewhat of a moratorium in terms of social criticism for deviant behavior, a view grounded in the optimistic belief that all but the most violent adolescents can eventually grow out of their deviance, adults are not afforded the same level of tolerance. And thus, most will turn away from the criminal lifestyle, although in all probability their lack of identity will manifest itself in other ways.

Obviously, there are those who never turn away from their deviant lifestyle. There are those whose lack of self-confidence, self-efficacy, and a well-developed identity becomes a chronic and lifelong problem. Whereas the opportunistic offender lacks a moral deterrence mechanism (MDM), the ego-directed offender lacks a self-deterrence mechanism (SeDM), and possibly, too, any significant degree of moral deterrence; the latter making the former even more dangerous and chronic. The ego-directed offender who maintains their lifestyle into adulthood typically meets the diagnostic criteria for either the *Histrionic* or *Narcissistic* personality disorder. Like the Antisocial personality disorder discussed previously, both disorders manifest themselves in the form of a pervasive and inflexible behavior pattern that causes the individual significant problems in social interactions.

The DSM-IV describes the *Histrionic personality disorder* as a pattern of excess emotionality and attention seeking. In order to meet the diagnostic criteria, at least five of the following must be present in adulthood:

- Uncomfortable in situations in which he or she is not the center of attention.
- Interaction with others is often characterized by inappropriate sexually seductive or provocative behavior.
- Displays rapidly shifting and shallow expression of emotions.
- Consistently uses physical appearance to draw attention to self.
- Has a style of speech that is excessively impressionistic and lacking in detail.
- Shows self-dramatization, theatricality, and exaggerated expression of emotion.
- Is suggestible, i.e., easily influenced by others or circumstances.
- Considers relationships to be more intimate than they actually are.

The presence of the above criteria does not guarantee that the individual will engage in criminal conduct; however, those adult offenders who do engage in criminality for reasons related to self-image will no doubt display a number of these criteria. The justification and reinforcement they seek as adolescents turns into excessive attention-seeking in adulthood. Their adult crimes tend to be related to this attention-seeking, and the frustration that results when they do not get the attention they demand. Sex crimes are common with the histrionic offender. Crimes that can facilitate the offender's desired social image are also prevalent, such as the individual who embezzles money from his company or commits other types of fraud in order to buy the material things that will prop up his or her image and stature. The Histrionic offender is also prone to follow others in order to gain approval, especially when they are incapable of doing so on their own. They are thus drawn to adult organized crime groups; however, they seldom end up in leadership positions within those groups due to their excessive emotionality and theatrics, behaviors typically not conducive to the group's need to maintain a low profile in order for their criminal enterprise to remain viable.

In contrast to the Histrionic offender, who is given to excessive attention-seeking, the Narcissistic offender is less concerned about receiving approval and positive strokes from others, but instead endeavors to seek self-approval. Whereas Histrionic offenders make good followers, Narcissistic offenders make good leaders. They have little sense of morality, and may even be entirely incapable of empathic awareness or sympathetic arousal. They are grandiose in their thoughts and actions, and rather than seeking attention, they instead seek admiration, which in turn feeds their need for self-approval. The DSM-IV lists the following criteria, any five or more of which will result in a diagnosis of *Narcissistic personality disorder:*

- Has a grandiose sense of self-importance (e.g., exaggerates achievements and talents, expects to be recognized as superior without commensurate achievements).
- Is preoccupied with fantasies of unlimited success, power, brilliance, beauty, or ideal love.
- Believes that he or she is "special" and unique and can only be understood by, or should associate with, other special or high-status people (or institutions).

- Requires excessive admiration.
- Has a sense of entitlement, i.e., unreasonable expectations of especially favorable treatment or automatic compliance with his or her expectations.
- Is interpersonally exploitative, i.e., takes advantage of others to achieve his or her own ends.
- Lacks empathy: is unwilling to recognize or identify with the feelings and needs of others.
- Is often envious of others or believes that others are envious of him or her.
- Shows arrogant, haughty behaviors or attitudes.

The Narcissistic offender can be extremely dangerous, not only because of their deficient sense of morality, but because they will avoid at all costs even the slightest appearance of failure or of backing down. For them to fail is to become vulnerable, and to do that is to expose their fragile ego to the world, or even worse, to themselves. The Narcissistic offender is also unconcerned with potential consequences since they seldom believe they will be caught. For them, the power to control the situation and circumstances are what is important. Their crimes, too, may include sexual offenses, including even serial rape. They mistake power and control for intimacy, and cannot handle being rejected sexually. They may engage in various types of fraud and financial exploitation. Unlike the Histrionic offender, however, who commits financial crimes in order to facilitate their attention-seeking activities, the Narcissistic offender does so for the challenge of it, and to facilitate a lifestyle high in stature; one that will attract the envy and admiration of others. Of most importance to the Histrionic is social approval. For the Narcissist, it is self-approval.

The ego-directed offender is egocentric, lacks a fully developed sense of morality, and is typically insecurely-attached due to neglectful parenting. Whereas the opportunistic offending pattern is typically the result of a child being improperly rewarded, and thus conditioned to engage in behaviors that provide self-gratification without regard for societal rules and restrictions, the ego-directed offender is more the result of abnormal personality development. It can be said that the ego-directed offender is one who likely never enjoyed the necessary autonomy and initiative as a child to venture out and become their own person, confident in their ability to achieve and master their environment. They end up identity-diffused, suffering from a lack of purpose and direction in their lives, an inability to develop intimate relationships, and without having adopted any particular ideology strong enough to buffer them against the temptation to engage in crime and other forms of deviance.

THE SYMBOLIC OFFENDER

This offender type is typically the product of *authoritarian* or *abusive* parenting. Like the ego-directed offender, they commit their crimes as a way of relieving psychic tension, what we usually refer to as "acting out." However, while the ego-directed offender is *self-focused*, the symbolic offender is *other-focused*. The crimes they commit are either intended to symbolically hurt their abusive parent by hurting someone else, or to gain mastery over an authoritarian parent by engaging in behaviors that symbolically deny the parent power and control over them. Another way of saying it is that their sense of self becomes lost in the emotional turmoil of their helplessness.

The abuse that leads to this offender type can come in various forms. It can be emotional, physical, or sexual in nature. The end result is the same; the young person goes through adolescence identity-diffused, and then enters adulthood with a *deficient* identity. They have no ideal self they hope to achieve, and they dislike their perceived self. Some may even engage in criminality as a way of unconsciously destroying themselves. The sad reality of child abuse is that it strips the child of the tools needed to form a healthy identity. Rather than internalizing the positive strokes and feedback of a loving parent when they reach adolescence and the point of identity-formation, they instead internalize the emotional pain and suffering inflicted on them by the authoritarian or abusive parent. They are precluded from committing to healthy expressions of identity by the fear and lack of self-worth instilled in them by their abuser's actions. Their sexual identity is impacted by their fear of intimacy, and if they were the victim of sexual abuse, then their sexual identity becomes jumbled and confused. And as their self-image continues to be eroded by their lack of identity commitment, it can eventually turn to self-contempt. It is at this point when the adolescent is most at risk of offending.

The symbolic offender is certainly the product of insecure-attachment. There is little chance of a healthy attachment in an abusive parent-child relationship. However, the child may in fact develop a sense of morality. Through their own pain and suffering, they may become sensitive to the pain and suffering of others. By identifying with others, they increase the likelihood of experiencing empathic awareness and sympathetic arousal for potential victims in advance of their own criminal acts. This becomes the moral deterrence mechanism (MDM) that can potentially cause them to redirect their psychic tensions into healthier expressions. For many, however, the tension is simply too intense, or they have not yet learned through education, therapy, or experience, ways in which they can effectively redirect the outward expression of that tension. In this case, the individual begins a cycle of behavior that will only intensify as they enter adulthood. The tension builds, they resort to some deviant act to relieve their anxiety, the tension subsides for a period of time, and then some event takes place that causes it to build once again. On top of that, the guilt they feel for having victimized an innocent person, and knowing they are about to do so again, only intensifies the tension as it builds once again toward its crescendo.

Oftentimes the symbolic offender abuses drugs and alcohol as a way of deadening their emotional pain. This, of course, has the opposite effect, as their substance abuse further alienates them from anyone who could potentially have a positive impact on their life. Substance abuse also makes effective therapy impossible, and further contributes to the individual's lack of self-worth by causing significant problems in areas that typically serve as important sources of self-esteem and identity; namely relationships, employment, and education. And while the individual may become so focused on the drug that they do in fact refrain from criminal behavior, the chances are extremely high that the individual in this situation will become addicted or alcoholic in a relatively short amount of time.

The progression of the symbolic offender's pattern of deviance differs from that of the other two offender types. If they have been the victims of abuse, then they tend to be loners. Their lack of self-confidence and self-worth causes them to isolate from all but a few friends. If they are the product of an authoritarian parent, and their deviance is aimed at gaining power and control over the parent, albeit symbolically, then they may affiliate with a deviant peer group to have greater access to criminal opportunity. Either way, the symbolic offender suffers the same consequence as the drug addict who needs more of the drug over time to get the same effect. For the symbolic offender, the petty crimes that begin their criminal career eventually are insufficient as a means of reducing the tension and anxiety they feel. Consequently, their crimes become more serious as time goes by. And while the majority of adolescents turn away from criminality before graduating to violent crimes, those who enter adulthood without having broken free of the symbolic offending cycle are at real risk of becoming violent offenders.

Juvenile to Adult Progression

Many serial killers, serial rapists, and other violent offender types can trace the onset of their deviant behavior patterns back to an abusive or authoritarian parent. Many report having experienced the very cycle of violence previously described, and having had to elevate their level of violence in order to reduce the tension and anxiety. Most, through whatever therapy made available in the prisons where they are incarcerated, come to understand the symbolic nature of their crimes. It is almost always during early adulthood when their jump from petty to violent crimes takes place, mostly because it is then when the full impact of their identity-diffusion is felt.

Like the other offender types, the symbolic offender typically meets the diagnostic criteria for certain personality disorders, namely *Borderline Personality Disorder* and *Avoidant Personality Disorder*. The DSM-IV further addresses the issue of extreme anger with a diagnosis of *Intermittent Explosive Disorder*. If the adolescent's offending pattern continues into adulthood, then it will surely significantly impair their ability to be a normal functioning member of society, and thus they can be described as having a personality disorder. Again, as previously stated, these disorders are not to be confused with the significant impairments of thought or emotion found in the major psychiatric disorders that require medical intervention. Rather, they are patterns of behavior demonstrated by people, criminals, and noncriminals alike, who for the most part fail to recognize the pervasiveness and consequences of their thoughts and actions.

The DSM-IV describes the Borderline individual as one who experiences instability in their relationships, self-image, and emotions, and is very impulsive. To meet the diagnostic criteria, five or more of the following must be present:

- Frantic efforts to avoid real or imagined abandonment.
- A pattern of unstable and intense interpersonal relationships characterized by alternating between extremes of idealization and devaluation.
- Identity disturbance: markedly and persistently unstable self-image or sense of self.
- Impulsivity in at least two areas that are potentially self-damaging (e.g., spending, sex, substance abuse, reckless driving, binge eating).
- Recurrent suicidal behavior, gestures, or threats, or self-mutilating behavior.
- Affective instability due to a marked reactivity of mood (e.g., intense episodic dysphoria, irritability, or anxiety usually lasting a few hours and only rarely more than a few days).
- Chronic feelings of emptiness.
- Inappropriate, intense anger or difficulty controlling anger (e.g., frequent displays of temper, constant anger, recurrent physical fights).
- Transient, stress-related paranoid ideation or severe dissociative symptoms.

Individuals with a Borderline personality tend to suffer an intense fear of abandonment and rejection. The result of abusive or authoritarian parenting, these individuals fail to develop a sense of self, nor the sense of security that accompanies that development. They fail to develop a sense of trust, and consequently they become overly dependent on others. Because of the inconsistent parenting to which they were exposed, however, their view of others, even those upon whom they depend, can change dramatically without provocation. They may imagine an impending separation, or in a marriage may obsess over the imagined infidelity of their spouse. Their extreme fear of abandonment causes them to become obsessed with preventing it. These individuals can be dangerous in a relationship, and are prone to over-controlling, manipulating, and even abusing their intimate partners. In its extreme form, these individuals may be loners who deal with abandonment issues by kidnapping and sexually molesting children who are incapable of leaving or being critical of them.

The Borderline individual also suffers from an extremely unstable self-image. Having missed the critical periods for the development of a healthy self-image, and having been denied the emotional tools for doing so, these individuals tend to have a very poor image of self, and may even consider themselves bad or evil. This reality is only compounded when their abusive childhood is paired with a fundamentalist religious upbringing. These children tend to accept and internalize the blame for their own abuse. Nothing is more devastating to their emotional development. As adults then, they tend to drive away nurturing caregivers with their own abusive behaviors, oftentimes becoming self-critical and judging themselves unworthy of nurturing relationships. Their self-criticism leads to self-pity, which leads to self-contempt, which begins the tension-building phase of their offending cycle all over again.

While the Borderline individual actively seeks relationships, albeit toxic ones, for reasons related to emotional dependency and their own insecurity, the symbolic offender can also manifest a pattern of behavior consistent with the DSM-IV diagnosis of Avoidant Personality Disorder. These individuals tend to avoid relationships rather than crave them. They are socially inhibited and demonstrate an intense fear of criticism and social rejection. The Avoidant individual is plagued by feelings of inadequacy, and thus avoids intimate relationships out of fear of rejection. They are extremely shy and oftentimes struggle with sexual dysfunction. To meet the DSM-IV diagnostic criteria, at least four of the following must be present:

- Avoids occupational activities that involve significant interpersonal contact because of fears of criticism, disapproval, or rejection (For children, the DSM-IV reference to occupational activities can apply to school. Children with APD often have marked difficulty, especially with new classes, presentations in front of the class, and less-structured times such as recess or lunch.)
- Is unwilling to get involved with people unless certain of being liked.

- Shows restraint within intimate relationships because of the fear of being shamed or ridiculed.
- Is preoccupied with being criticized or rejected in social situations.
- Is inhibited in new interpersonal situations because of feelings of inadequacy.
- Views self as socially inept, personally unappealing, or inferior to others.
- Is unusually reluctant to take personal risks or to engage in any new activities because they may prove embarrassing.

Like the Borderline personality, the Avoidant personality, too, is a product of abusive or authoritarian parenting. A child who has never been given positive feedback, or is given positive feedback but in an inconsistent context, is never able to develop a sense of self-efficacy. In *Eriksonian* terms, they never developed a sense of trust or personal autonomy in childhood, and thus they suffer from identity confusion in adolescence. Both are descriptive of an individual who simply has no confidence or self-esteem. When they look in the mirror, they do not like what they see, and they have no sense of their own worth or capabilities. They are typically loners, and in early adulthood when the primary developmental task becomes the establishment of intimate relationships, it is then when their risk of acting-out symbolically in the form of criminality is heightened.

Like the Borderline individual, the Avoidant adult will engage in criminal conduct in order to reduce the psychic tension that consumes them. The danger is that the level of deviance required to reduce the tension is commensurate with the amount of tension they are experiencing. If it is extreme, then chances are their level of deviance will match it. Here, too, in its extreme form, we find serial killers, rapists, and pedophiles. The symbolic offender seeks emotional equilibrium, and they can only achieve this transiently by projecting their contempt for the abusive or critical parent onto innocent others, and then seeking retribution symbolically by lashing out at them. Unfortunately, such deviance only justifies and magnifies their sense of worthlessness and void, which in turn feeds the dangerous cycle of their offending pattern.

In its less extreme form, at least in terms of violent victimization, the Avoidant individual may turn to drugs and alcohol as a way of reducing or suppressing the emotional tension they experience. Substance abuse is highly correlated with this personality type. In this case, their crimes may be limited to shoplifting and burglary in order to fund their drug habit. They will, however, resort to violence to protect their ability to secure the drugs they need. Both the Avoidant and Borderline personalities have highly addictive qualities. Once addicted, the drug becomes their intimate partner, and acts as a surrogate for the parent they never had. Its emotional benefits are quite fleeting, however, and once the drug's effects wear off, the individual only falls deeper into the emotional abyss from which they are trying to escape.

One final personality disorder must be mentioned in relation to the symbolic offender. That is the individual diagnosed with *Intermittent Explosive Disorder*. These individuals are characterized by impulsive acts of aggression and destruction of property. Their episodic aggression typically follows the precipitating stressors by just a short period of time, sometimes only minutes or hours. They seldom plan out their actions to any significant degree. These individuals differ from the Avoidant personality type in temperament. They are typically individuals who had a difficult temperament as infants, and an extremely low frustration threshold. There is a strong probability that violence and aggression were common occurrences in their home environment, and that they have been conditioned to react to stressful situations in such ways. They most likely were the victims of physical abuse as children, and now manifest the same aggression modeled by their abusive parent.

The symbolic offender who is consumed by anger can be very unpredictable and dangerous. They are angry at the world for having allowed them to be victimized, and they play the role of the persecuted victim. With the introduction of the least amount of stress they can explode like a pressure valve. It is then when they are overcome by the need to destroy in an effort to symbolically destroy that part of self that was victimized by the abusive parent. In adolescence, these individuals tend to become involved in delinquent behavior at an early age, and typically begin their criminal careers with fighting, truancy, and destruction of property. The more their aggression reduces their psychic tension, the more they are conditioned to engage in aggression as a coping mechanism. As adults then, what began as fighting and destruction of property can easily erode into murder, rape, and serial arson.

In many ways, the personalities of both the symbolic and ego-directed offender may look similar. But the distinction is found in the motivations underlying their crimes. While the ego-directed offender is compelled by a need to feel better about themselves, however perverse it may be that their crimes can at least temporarily bring about that desired end, the symbolic offender is spurred on by a need either to destroy or gain power over what compels their internal emotional turmoil, typically an abusive or authoritarian parent.

CONCLUSION

The onset of criminality is precipitated by both internal and environmental factors and events. The crime itself cannot be looked at as simply a deviant act apart from the offender's developmental history, at least not if we are to understand and prevent its reoccurrence. Crime may end with the commission of a deviant act, but it begins long before that with the quality of the offender's parent-child relationship. We have discussed three potential offender types, each based on a particular parent-child dynamic. They are summarized in Figure 6.1.

There have been many theories that attempt to account for criminality. Many are sociological theories that approach the offender from the outside looking in. They tend to concern themselves mostly with social and environmental factors such as poverty, social strain, and a lack of educational and vocational opportunity. But these theories fail to tell us why some in these stress-inducing situations choose to engage in deviance, while others, the vast majority, do not. To answer this question we must turn to psychology and approach the offender from the inside looking out.

In this chapter, we have looked at the various offender types as they progress from adolescence to adulthood. But exactly why when the individual reaches that fork in the road leading to a criminal lifestyle they make the fateful decision to follow it, is and always will be a bit of a mystery. We can certainly look at a young person's developmental history, and we can even psychometrically measure their level of morality, their self-evaluation, and the quality of their attachment. From this, we can get a fairly accurate picture of the strength of their internal deterrence system. We can even say whether the indi-

	Psychosocial Components of the Criminal Triad				
	Primary Source of Motivation	Attachment	Moral Development	Identity Formation	Related DSM-IV Diagnoses
Opportunistic Offender	Motivated by the potential rewards of their criminal activity. Includes material rewards as well as internal rewards related to excitement and pleasure-seeking.	Indulgent parenting style. Lack of rules, lack of sharing behaviors and respect for others. Egocentric.	Low empathic awareness due to egocentricity. Greatly reduced ability to experience sympathetic arousal.	May have a well-developed sense of identity but incongruous with social conventions. Antisocial.	Antisocial personality Disorder
Ego-Directed Offender	Motivated by the positive psychological effects of their criminal conduct, especially on self-esteem and their perceived-self.	Typically the result of neglectful or authoritarian parenting. A lack of autonomy precludes self-development.	May or not have a developed sense of morality depending on severity of identity deficits.	Deficient self-identity. They may seek validation of self in unhealthy peer groups or power-oriented criminality.	Histrionic personality disorder Narcissistic personality Disorder
Symbolic Offender	Motivated by a need to relieve psychic tension by victimizing surrogates for the sources of their negative emotions.	Insecure attachment resulting from abusive or authoritarian parenting.	May or may not have a developed sense of morality. If so, remorse will lead to self-guilt, which causes psychic tension to increase once again.	Deficient self-identity. They may experience self-contempt related to their development. No sense of self in extreme cases.	Borderline Personality Disorder Avoidant Personality Disorder Intermittent-Explosive Disorder

Figure 6.1. The three offender types.

vidual has a criminal personality type, at least as we define that construct. And finally, we can understand the stimulus-response mechanisms and conditioning processes that can energize such a personality type to engage in socially-deviant behavior. But what we may never know for certain is why a young person, at that critical moment when faced with the option of either engaging in or avoiding a behavior that could potentially impact the remainder of their life, chooses one course over the other. Our best efforts, in terms of ongoing research and study, should be directed not at the decision-making processes of young people who choose crime as a means to some desired end, but rather at gaining a fuller understanding of those young people for whom crime is never considered as a viable option. Once we understand why, which is perhaps best explained by the presence of an internal deterrence system, then we can work backwards from there in an effort to understand the phenomenon of crime.

We will now look at each of these offender types in the context of serial murder, and by looking at specific serial killers who have been identified and apprehended over the years. We will look at their crimes and what is known about their psychosocial development in an effort to classify each. We will then end with a look at the "Zodiac Killer," a serial murderer who has never been identified. Perhaps by applying Criminal Triad Theory we can narrow the population of suspects in this brutal series of murders that occurred over four decades prior to the writing of this book.

Chapter 7

DAVID BERKOWITZ: THE SON OF SAM
An Ego-Directed Killer, Subtype: Deficient Sexual Self

INTRODUCTION

Few will debate or deny the evil nature of essentially all serial killers, at least during the period when they are carrying out their heinous crimes. But much debate has taken place about certain of these killers relating to their postconviction years; specifically, the extent to which their rehabilitation is probable or even possible at all. One individual who has been the subject of such debate is David Berkowitz, New York City's infamous *Son of Sam* killer. Today, over 35 years since he was convicted and incarcerated for life for killing six individuals and wounding seven others in 1976–77, Berkowitz has little resemblance to the image the world saw of a crazed-looking suspect handcuffed in the back of an NYPD squad car.

Today, living out his days at Sullivan Correctional Center in Fallsburg, New York, Berkowitz serves as a prison chaplain and even maintains a website where he shares his testimony and other spiritual writings (ariseand-

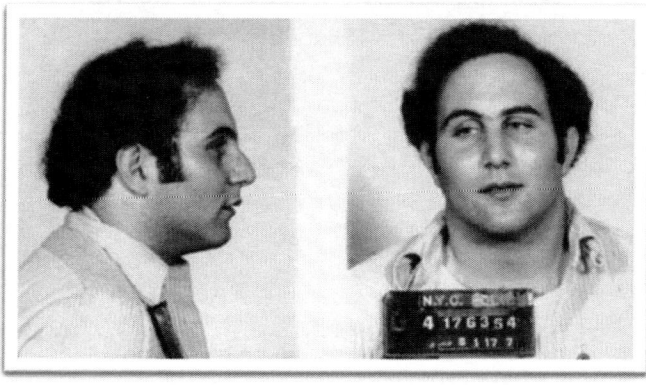

Figure 7.1. David Berkowitz.

shine.org). On the website, he professes to have been transformed through his faith from the *Son of Sam* to the *Son of Hope,* a change that took place in his prison cell nearly 25 years ago. He has done many interviews, and his demeanor is always that of a friendly and sincere man who shows no trace of the brutal killer he once was.

But is it really possible that Berkowitz has been rehabilitated? It is an easy question for a born-again Christian to answer. After all, to deny that possibility is to deny the power of God. But many in the secular community have argued against the proposition. Besen (2010) has suggested that what Berkowitz has somehow accomplished is to manipulate a group of gullible Christian evangelicals into playing a leading role in the rehabilitation of his public image. He likens it to nothing more than a public relations stunt by Berkowitz designed to benefit no one but himself. Joseph Coffey, the police sergeant who took Berkowitz's initial confession called his purported conversion and rehabilitation "a total charade to promote himself" (Kovaleski, 2010).

And the scientific community has been relatively quiet on the issue, perhaps because to admit that Berkowitz is rehabilitated would be difficult to assimilate into the consensus opinion among those who study this population of evildoers that they are measurably different from the general population on any number of psychological and/or biological variables.

Figure 7.2. David Berkowitz today.

CRIMINAL BACKGROUND

During the latter part of 1976, and into the following year, few stories garnered more media attention throughout the U.S. than the brutal crimes being committed by David Berkowitz in New York City. The man who, prior to his identification and capture, would be given the infamous moniker, *.44 caliber killer,* was causing an entire city to succumb to its collective fear and come to a virtual standstill. The shootings continued for over a year, and resulted in the deaths of six individuals, with seven others wounded. Adding to the public's fear, Berkowitz left a letter at the scene of one of his shootings indicating his plans to continue his killing spree. A month later he sent a second letter to *Daily News* columnist Jimmy Breslin indicating the same. One of the most intense manhunts in NYPD history ensued.

Although Berkowitz admitted to attacking two teenage girls with a knife on Christmas Eve, 1975, killing neither, his use of a firearm began on July 29, 1976, when he approached a parked car in the Pelham Bay area of the Bronx and fired three quick rounds in the direction of the vehicle's two occupants. Donna Lauria, 18, was killed instantly. Her friend, 19-year-old Jody Valenti, was seriously wounded but would survive the attack (NYTimes, July 30, 1976). Valenti told police that the assailant approached their vehicle with a paper sack in his hands, and when confronted by Lauria, pulled a gun from the bag, entered a crouched position, and began firing without saying a word. When he finished, he turned and quickly walked away. It was after this first shooting when police determined the weapon to be a .44 caliber.

The police speculated that the Lauria-Valenti shooting was either a case of mistaken identity, someone obsessed with one of the girls—there was speculation that perhaps the shooter had been spurned by Lauria—or even possibly related to mob activity, since Lauria's father was active in the Teamsters Union (Terry, 1987). No one at that point was speculating that a serial killer might be on the loose and beginning his deadly cycle of murder.

Nearly three months later, on October 23, 1976, Berkowitz zeroed in on his next victims, this time in a residential neighborhood in Queens. Carl Denaro, 25, and Rosemary Keenan, 38, were sitting in Keenan's parked car when the windows suddenly exploded from gunshots. Keenan quickly started her car and sped off, not realizing

Denaro had been shot in the head. He would survive the attack. Keenan had not been hit at all, and neither had seen the shooter. Investigators recovered a number of the bullets from Keenan's vehicle, and while they were able to identify them as .44 caliber, no connection was made to the earlier Lauria-Valenti shooting (Terry, 1987).

Berkowitz did not remain quiet for long. On November 27, 1976, he fired upon two teenage girls sitting on a porch in Bellerose, Queens. Donna DeMasi, 16, and Joanne Lomino, 18, both survived the attack, and reported that their assailant, dressed in military fatigues, approached the porch where they sat and began to ask for directions, but in mid-sentence pulled the gun from his pocket and began firing. This time the victims were able to provide a good description of the assailant, and a sketch was created (NYTimes, November 28, 1976). And once again, the bullets recovered from the scene were determined to be .44 caliber; however, they were too damaged to conduct any ballistic comparisons. Even after six victims, one of whom died from their wounds, the police still had not made a linkage between the shootings.

In the early morning hours of January 30, 1977, while sitting together in a parked car in Queens, Christine Freund, 26, and her fiancé John Diel, 30, became Berkowitz's next victims. Diel received only minor injuries from exploding glass as the bullets passed through, but Freund was shot twice in the head, becoming the second person to die from Berkowitz's attacks. It was after this shooting when the police finally pronounced publicly that the Freund-Diel shootings were possibly connected to other similar shootings. Suddenly the idea of an active serial killer, the *.44 caliber killer,* began to elicit the fear of an entire city.

The police began to construct an early profile of the killer, whom they speculated was focusing on young women with long, dark hair. They even theorized that when Carl Denaro was shot, a young man with long dark hair, that the killer had mistaken him for a girl. Their tentative profile was reinforced on March 8, 1977, when Columbia University student Virginia Voskerichian, 19, was shot and killed only a block from where Christine Freund was shot. A person walking close by reported that a husky, clean shaven boy had nearly bumped into them as he ran from the scene. As he passed by, he pulled his cap down over his face and said "Oh, Jesus!" (Terry, 1987).

Two days after the Voskerichian shooting, the NYPD and Mayor Abe Beame held a press conference and declared that at least two of the three individuals who had died to that point in the string of shootings, Lauria and Voskerichian, were shot by the same .44 caliber revolver. Now there was no doubting that a serial killer was on the loose. That same day, the NYPD announced the creation of a task force consisting of nearly 300 officers tasked with tracking down and bringing to justice the shooter. News of the *.44 Caliber Killer* spread rapidly across the country and around the world. In New York City, the collective mood was one of fear and apprehension. People began staying inside their homes at night. Businesses closed early to allow their employees to get home before dark. Women with long hair cut it short, while others with dark hair either dyed it blonde or began wearing light-colored wigs. It was a collective hysteria that years later would become the subject of books and Hollywood movies.

Unfortunately, the NYPD's highly-publicized manhunt didn't dissuade Berkowitz from continuing his murderous rampage. On April 17, 1977, in the early morning hours, Alexander Esau, 20, and Valentina Suriani, 18, were each shot twice as they sat in Suriani's car just a few blocks from where the Lauria-Valenti shootings took place the previous July. This time, for the first time, Berkowitz managed to kill both of his targets. His nine-month campaign of terror had now resulted in 11 people shot, with five of them dead. Near the bodies of these latest victims, police found a letter addressed to NYPD Captain Joseph Borrelli that read:

> I am deeply hurt by your calling me a wemon hater. I am not. But I am a monster. I am the "Son of Sam." I am a little "brat". When father Sam gets drunk he gets mean. He beats his family. Sometimes he ties me up to the back of the house. Other times he locks me in the garage. Sam loves to drink blood. "Go out and kill" commands father Sam. Behind our house some rest. Mostly young–raped and slaughtered–their blood drained–just bones now. Papa Sam keeps me locked in the attic, too. I can't get out but I look out the attic window and watch the world go by. I feel like an outsider. I am on a different wave length then everybody else–programmed to kill. However, to stop me you must kill me. Attention all police: Shoot me first–shoot to kill or else. Keep out of my way or you will die! Papa Sam is old now. He needs some blood to preserve his youth. He has

had too many heart attacks. Too many heart attacks. "Ugh, me hoot it hurts sonny boy." I miss my pretty princess most of all. She's resting in our ladies house but I'll see her soon. I am the "Monster"–"Beelzebub"–the "Chubby Behemouth." I love to hunt. Prowling the streets looking for fair game–tasty meat. The wemon of Queens are z prettyist of all. I must be the water they drink. I live for the hunt–my life. Blood for papa. Mr. Borrelli, sir, I dont want to kill anymore no sir, no more but I must, "honour thy father." I want to make love to the world. I love people. I don't belong on Earth. Return me to yahoos. To the people of Queens, I love you. And I want to wish all of you a happy Easter. May God bless you in this life and in the next and for now I say goodbye and goodnight. Police–Let me haunt you with these words; I'll be back! I'll be back! To be interrpreted as– bang, bang, bang, bank, bang - ugh!! Yours in murder Mr. Monster. (Gibson, 2004)

This was Berkowitz's first communication, and it received widespread attention. In it, Berkowitz assigned to himself the moniker by which he would forever come to be known . . . the *Son of Sam*. The letter was analyzed by practically every expert and profiler in the country for clues to the killer's identity. A group of psychiatrists working the case profiled Berkowitz as a paranoid schizophrenic who believed he was demon-possessed. With this information, investigators questioned all registered .44 caliber gun owners in New York City. They also set up traps with police officers posing as young lovers. Unfortunately, no suspects were immediately developed. Slightly over a month after the most recent shootings, Berkowitz sent a second letter, this one to *Daily News* columnist Jimmy Breslin. It read:

Hello from the gutters of N.Y.C. which are filled with dog manure, vomit, stale wine, urine and blood. Hello from the sewers of N.Y.C. which swallow up these delicacies when they are washed away by the sweeper trucks. Hello from the cracks in the sidewalks of N.Y.C. and from the ants that dwell in these cracks and feed in the dried blood of the dead that has settled into the cracks. J.B., I'm just dropping you a line to let you know that I appreciate your interest in those recent and horrendous .44 killings. I also want to tell you that I read your column daily and I find it quite informative. Tell me Jim, what will you have for July twenty-ninth? You can forget about me if you like because I don't care for publicity. However you must not forget

Donna Lauria and you cannot let the people forget her either. She was a very, very sweet girl but Sam's a thirsty lad and he won't let me stop killing until he gets his fill of blood. Mr. Breslin, sir, don't think that because you haven't heard from me for a while that I went to sleep. No, rather, I am still here. Like a spirit roaming the night. Thirsty, hungry, seldom stopping to rest; anxious to please Sam. I love my work. Now, the void has been filled. Perhaps we shall meet face to face someday or perhaps I will be blown away by cops with smoking .38's. Whatever, if I shall be fortunate enough to meet you I will tell you all about Sam if you like and I will introduce you to him. His name is "Sam the terrible." Not knowing the what the future holds I shall say farewell and I will see you at the next job. Or should I say you will see my handiwork at the next job? Remember Ms. Lauria. Thank you. In their blood and from the gutter "Sam's creation" .44 Here are some names to help you along. Forward them to the inspector for use by N.C.I.C: [sic] "The Duke of Death" "The Wicked King Wicker" "The Twenty Two Disciples of Hell" "John 'Wheaties'–Rapist and Suffocator of Young Girls. PS: Please inform all the detectives working the slaying to remain. P.S: [sic] JB, Please inform all the detectives working the case that I wish them the best of luck. "Keep 'em digging, drive on, think positive, get off your butts, knock on coffins, etc." Upon my capture I promise to buy all the guys working the case a new pair of shoes if I can get up the money. Son of Sam. (Terry, 1987)

Only three weeks after the world became aware of the letter to Jimmy Breslin, Berkowitz struck again, this time on June 26, 1977. Keeping with his usual method, Berkowitz approached a parked car in a neighborhood in Queens at 3 a.m. The car was occupied by Sal Lupo, 20, and Judy Placido, 17. Like the other shootings, Berkowitz fired rapidly through the vehicle's windows, causing the glass to explode from the force of the .44 caliber bullet. Both were hit, but both would survive the attack.

The following month, on July 31, 1977, Berkowitz carried out his final attack, and this time, fearing the intense police dragnet covering Queens, decided to seek out his next victims in Brooklyn instead. In the early morning hours, he happened upon Robert Violante and Stacy Moskowitz, both aged 20, kissing in a parked car. Berkowitz approached to within just a few feet and fired four shots from his .44 caliber revolver through the passenger side window. Both of his young victims were shot in the head. Moskowitz would later die from her wounds and Violante would be permanently blinded (Abrahamsen, 1985).

Like before, there were witnesses who had seen Berkowitz before and after the shooting, but this time there someone who could potentially identify him. A local resident had been walking her dog when she noticed a police officer ticketing an unoccupied car, a yellow Ford Galaxy, parked illegally by a fire hydrant. Immediately after the officer departed, the witness reported that a man walked past her from the area of the vehicle clutching a dark object in his hand. A few minutes later, from her home, she heard the shots that killed and wounded Stacy Moskowitz and Robert Violante. A few days later she decided to call the task force and report what she had witnessed the night of the shootings. Investigators checked every parking ticket issued that night and identified the owner of the Ford Galaxy. For the first time, they had the name of David Berkowitz, a resident of Yonkers. But initially, the police considered him a possible witness rather than a suspect. That changed when they contacted the Yonkers Police Department for help locating Berkowitz. Investigators there advised that their suspicions had already been raised when they read in the Son of Sam letters what seemed to be references to Yonkers-area crimes that Berkowitz was already suspected of committing. Now suddenly, task force investigators began to think they possibly had their killer.

On August 10, 1977, police officers approached Berkowitz's parked Ford Galaxy outside his apartment in Yonkers. Inside they found a rifle, ammunition, and maps of his various crime scenes. They also found a threatening letter addressed to task force commander Timothy Dowd. Investigators were certain now they had the killer, and to avoid a potential shootout, set up surveillance on the vehicle to swoop in and arrest Berkowitz when he left his apartment. At around 10:00 p.m., that night, carrying the .44 caliber revolver in a paper bag, he walked out of his apartment and was arrested without a shot fired. As police handcuffed him, his only words were, "Well, you got me. How come it took you such a long time?" (Scott, 2007). Berkowitz's year-long string of murders, all of which he eventually confessed to, had reached its end, and with it, an entire city let out a collective sigh of relief.

PERSONAL BACKGROUND

David Berkowitz was born on June 1, 1953. He was the son of Betty Broder Falco and a man with whom she was having an extramarital affair. Berkowitz was born Richard David Falco, and was put up for adoption immediately after birth. He was adopted by a Jewish couple from the Bronx, Nathan and Pearl Berkowitz. Not much is really known about Berkowitz during the earliest years of his development. He was an only child of loving parents. He was a bright young boy with a vivid imagination but, by his own account, was tormented throughout his childhood years. He describes how he would have fits of rage so bad that his father would be forced to pin him to the ground until he calmed down. His violent nature became apparent in school as well. One of his teachers described him as a bit moody at times. He became so violent during one outbreak that a male teacher removed him from the classroom in a headlock. Physically, he was overweight, which caused him to be teased by the kids in his neighborhood and at school (Berkowitz, 1999).

Eventually, school officials forced Berkowitz's parents to take him to see a child psychologist to avoid being expelled from school. He met with the psychologist on a weekly basis for nearly two years; however, the therapy had little impact on his behavior. It was during this period when he first reported bouts of severe depression. When he felt depressed, he would hide for hours under a bed or in a closet, and would avoid interacting with other people. He would sneak out of his apartment in the middle of the night, wander the dark streets of the city, and then sneak back in through the fire escape by morning. Even at his young age, he began to have thoughts of suicide. He would fantasize about stepping in front of moving cars, and would sit on the ledge of his window, six floors up, with his legs dangling over the edge.

During his early to mid-adolescent years, his life began to unravel even more. In 1967, his mother died of breast cancer. He was devastated by her death, and almost immediately more severe behavioral problems began to emerge. In addition to committing routine vandalism, he also began setting fires and torturing animals. He was a loner, with very few friends. He was filled with anger over the death of his mother, and he reported that following her death, his depression became even more severe.

As bad as things were for Berkowitz at this age, he still participated in some positive activities. He became an auxiliary fireman, as well as an auxiliary policeman at the NYPD's 45th precinct. He also considered for the first time the idea of joining the military. In 1971, after his father remarried, a circumstance he was not entirely accepting of, Berkowitz enlisted in the U.S. Army. It was at the tail-end of the Vietnam conflict, and Berkowitz was "fanatically patriotic," as he later described himself during this period. He liked the idea of being a soldier, and welcomed the opportunity for combat (Berkowitz, 1999).

Berkowitz served in the U.S. Army from June, 1971 to June, 1974. He never got the opportunity to see combat, but instead was stationed in Korea at an outpost near the 38th Parallel, the line separating North and South Korea. His military occupational specialty (MOS) was *11-Bravo*, an infantryman. This meant he was well trained in the use of firearms. His military years were both good and bad. In one respect, the military forced him to quickly grow into a man, and allowed him to make friends with many other soldiers. But during this period of his life, he also began experimenting with different types of drugs, especially marijuana and LSD, and began frequenting prostitutes. This lifestyle caused his military discipline, as well as any desire to remain in the military, to quickly fade.

In January, 1973, Berkowitz returned with his unit to Fort Knox, Kentucky, where he would serve out the remaining days of his enlistment. While there, he began attending a Baptist Church in Louisville, and was eventually baptized there as a member of the congregation. He later said that his time at the Church was the first time in his life he felt like he actually belonged somewhere. Unfortunately though, his membership was short-lived. Only a month following his baptism, he was honorably discharged from the Army, and returned to his father's apartment in New York City. Once there, his life began to fall apart. His use of drugs escalated, tensions between he and his step-mother developed, and he again engaged in setting fires, just as he had done during his adolescent years before the Army. He even kept detailed records of the fires, including their locations, dates and times, and even the fire department codes assigned to them. By his own account, and supported by the journals he kept, Berkowitz was responsible for well over a thousand arson fires between his return from the Army and his eventual arrest.

Making matters worse during this period, Berkowitz's father and step-mother moved to Florida. He had lost his last source of support and encouragement. He moved into an apartment on Barnes Avenue in the Bronx, took a job as a taxi driver, and enrolled at Bronx Community College. During this time, he also made the decision to seek out his birth parents. His father had told him the truth about his parents, and that he was a mistake and unwanted by them. He began his search by looking for a Betty Falco in an old phonebook. He found the address, called the operator, and to his surprise, she still lived there, but with an unlisted phone number. On Mother's Day, 1975, he left a card in her mailbox. Inside he wrote:

So, as once before
We've been destined to meet once more
And I guess the time is now
I should say hello—but how?
Happy Mother's Day
You were my mother in a very special way

He signed the card and provided his phone number (Abrahamsen, 1985). A couple days later, his phone rang. It was Betty Falco, and she wanted to meet him. At this time, he was working as a security guard at JFK Airport, and later reported that it was during his employment there when he began hearing voices. Berkowitz did in fact meet with his mother, and also with his new half-sister, Roslyn. It was a good meeting, and his mother reassured him that she never considered him a mistake. He visited his mother almost weekly for the next year, but then fell out of contact with her. During this time, he also learned that his birth father was deceased. Leyton (2003) describes the knowledge of his adoption, and the circumstances surrounding it, as the primary crisis of his life, and that it ultimately shattered his sense of identity. Within weeks of meeting his birth family, he once again turned to starting arson fires.

In November, 1975, Berkowitz wrote a letter to his father in Florida. In it he wrote how miserable he was, and how people just seemed to hate him, even people he didn't know. He described how guys always laughed at him, and even worse, how girls routinely called him ugly. He wrote that this latter circumstance was what bothered him the most. He had never had an intimate relationship with a woman to this point. With his father gone to Florida, he felt totally alone in the world (Abrahamsen, 1985).

One other factor that is important to an understanding of David Berkowitz is his interest in the occult. He claims to have met some guys at a party in 1975 who were heavily involved in the occult. Following this introduction, he began reading the Satanic Bible, and claims to have begun practicing various satanic rituals. By this time, he had moved to a new apartment on Barnes Avenue in Yonkers, his last apartment prior to his arrest. Alone, and suffering from loneliness, depression, and schizophrenic-like symptoms, and now living in a new area with even fewer lines of support, the conditions were right for Berkowitz to graduate from setting arson fires to a more deadly type of crime.

ANALYSIS AND CLASSIFICATION

Preidentification Inputs

We begin our analysis of David Berkowitz by looking at various factors that became apparent prior to his identification and arrest. Typically, these factors, or *inputs,* relate to victim selection, method, and postoffense behavior. Regarding his method, the following are most telling:

- Berkowitz killed from a distance, and did so quickly.
- He did not stick around to see if his victims were actually hit, nor did he execute his wounded victims with another shot at close range.
- At least one witness who observed him leaving the scene of one of his shootings described him as appearing nervous and stressed.

These inputs indicate a couple things. First of all, Berkowitz did not appear to enjoy the act of killing, nor was there ever a sexual component to his attacks. In most cases, he didn't even clearly see the faces of his victims. His MO was to shoot and run. This tells us that Berkowitz likely was not an opportunistic killer. This type of killer commits their crimes for the thrill and excitement of killing. They may torture or sexually assault their victims, and may engage in cannibalism and necrophilia. An opportunistic killer would likely never just shoot from a distance and run, not even knowing if their targeted victim was wounded or dead. For them, the thrill is in knowing they are dead, and experiencing as much of their victim's agony as possible. The desire for power and control that is almost always present in their crimes was absent in Berkowitz's.

His method was also not indicative of a symbolic killer. These killers commit their crimes out of rage, and choose victims who will serve as psychological surrogates for object of their rage, typically a parent. Evidence of rage was not apparent in Berkowitz's attacks. We will look at a moment at any postidentification inputs that may either support or refute this possibility. But in the crimes themselves, there appears to be none. There were no angry or hateful words spoken by Berkowitz during his attacks, no *coup de grace* shots, and no attempts to torture or mutilate. Also, here, too, it is significant that Berkowitz made no effort to determine if his intended victims were even wounded or killed. The fact is, the symbolic serial killer only quiets their rage, albeit temporarily, by symbolically killing the target of their rage. To leave the surrogate alive only symbolically leaves the target alive, and thus brings no psychological benefit. We can conclude that Berkowitz was not a symbolic offender.

Finally, it is significant that he appeared nervous and stressed during his egress from the crime scene. The opportunistic killer would likely be in a state of heightened excitement, even ecstasy, following their crimes. And the symbolic killer would likely feel a sense of power and control, even an emotional high, after having symbolically killed the object of their rage and hatred. The fact that Berkowitz appeared nervous and stressed indicates that he didn't necessarily enjoy committing his crimes, and was more concerned with getting away than with the condition of his victims. The idea that he didn't enjoy his crimes is also supported by the fact that he shot through car windows and from a distance. There is every possibility that he simply couldn't handle looking at the bloody aftermath of his crimes. It would have been just as easy for him to open the car door and shoot his victims at point blank range. Or in the case of the two girls on the porch, to simply walk up on the porch before shooting them, again at point blank range. He did neither.

Regarding Berkowitz's victim selection, the following inputs are apparent:

- He targeted primarily young women. Men were only shot when they were sitting in a parked car with a woman. An opportunistic killer would likely not have targeted multiple victims. Their desire would be to engage a single victim for the purpose of sexual assault or torture before killing them. For them, the thrill comes from engaging the victim and actually seeing and hearing their fear and agony.
- He did not stalk his victims, but was opportunistic in their selection. He went to a particular area, and if potential victims were present, he took advantage of it.
- He focused on younger female victims if he could actually see them. Otherwise, he focused on a particular profile; cars parked late at night in areas where young lovers frequented, and with two occupants inside. His approach to the vehicle was always on the passenger side, so it seems plausible to presume that he was targeting in each case whom he believed to be a female occupant. Also, it is interesting that on at least one occasion, as he walked toward the parked vehicle where Stacy Moskowitz and Robert Violante sat talking, he passed by an older female witness walking her dog and chose not to shoot her, an easy target indeed.

Finally, Berkowitz's postoffense behavior is classic of an ego-directed offender, especially writing letters and essentially trying to create his own storyline. It was obvious from his letters, especially the one addressed to Jimmy Breslin, that he was watching the media accounts of his crimes. An opportunistic offender tends not to write letters and taunt the very people who are tracking them down. They want to continue their killing, and will typically do nothing to draw unwanted attention to them and their crimes when it isn't necessary. And symbolic offenders, too, tend not to interact with the police or media. For them, killing is a need, a way of calming their torment and rage. There is little to be gained psychologically from writing letters or taunting the police. For ego-directed offenders, however, the more attention they get, the more it feeds their deficient ego and empowers them to continue their crimes.

Postidentification Inputs

When we look at those things we have learned about Berkowitz since his arrest, it becomes quickly apparent that he was a perfect storm for identity-related problems during the adolescent years of his development. The most meaningful aspects of his background include the following:

- Difficult temperament
- Social awkwardness
- Depression
- Desire for affiliation
- Fire-starter
- Adoption

Berkowitz was a child with a difficult temperament. Whether this was genetically-based, or perhaps the result of some toxin being introduced during the prenatal period of his development, we simply don't know. But the fact is, he was a difficult child. And a difficult temperament can lead to problems in two areas: the parent-child attachment process, and the formation of social relationships.

By all accounts, including Berkowitz's own, his adoptive parents were loving and tolerant people who did their best to adapt to their son's difficulties. There is no indication that his parents were authoritarian, abusive, or neglectful, nor is there any evidence of a dysfunctional or insecure attachment having formed with his parents. His behavior, however, could have impacted the quality of his relationship he had with them. Nonetheless, the death of his mother was a devastating event. A symbolic offender typically suffers from an insecure attachment, and their rage typically begins with an authoritarian, abusive, or neglectful parent. This does not appear to have been the case with Berkowitz.

We know that Berkowitz had serious problems in the area of developing friendships, and later, intimate relationships. Children with difficult temperaments typically have problems making friends. In Berkowitz's case, he had the additional problem of being an overweight child who was socially-awkward. Other kids made fun of him and physically harassed him. This can be a devastating circumstance for a developing child. How well they make same-sex friends in early to middle childhood will directly impact their ability to form intimate relationships beginning in adolescence. There is no indication that Berkowitz ever successfully developed an intimate relationship with a female. Even during his military years, he reports frequenting prostitutes, but again, no indication of a stable relationship with a woman.

The combination of his temperament and his social awkwardness was only compounded by the presence of some level of depression. He has talked about how he would hide under his bed or in a closet for hours when these feelings would overcome him. The depression no doubt only magnified his developing self-loathing, a common outcome for a young person who views their appearance or demeanor as the blame for their lack of friends. All adolescents go through periods of not liking certain aspects of who they are. Most are able to overcome these insecurities by focusing on other aspects of their self-identity. But some hold such a deep-seeded sense of self-contempt that they are simply unable to counterbalance those negative thoughts and emotions with anything positive. This can both result in, and exacerbate depressive feelings, and will typically derail an adolescent's efforts at developing a healthy sense of identity and purpose.

Berkowitz's efforts at identity-formation can clearly be seen in his desire for affiliation and purpose. It is a natural developmental course for an adolescent to desire a sense of *belongingness*. They desire to be part of a group, and they seek purpose in their affiliation with a group. Affiliation is a critical part of identity-formation. Our affiliations bolster the strength and confidence of our chosen gender role (sexual self); allow us to adopt and develop a system of beliefs that help to define us (ideological self); and provide a forum for social interaction and the development of a sense of self-efficacy (social self).

In Berkowitz's case, we see definite attempts at affiliation. As an adolescent, he became both a cadet fireman and a cadet police officer. These were positive steps seldom seen in the background of symbolic or opportunistic offenders. Symbolic offenders typically shy away from affiliation due to an insecure attachment and a fear of social interaction. Opportunistic offenders are typically too egocentric to affiliate with any group sentiment. If they do, it is typically for entirely egocentric reasons. Berkowitz appears to have made a positive and healthy attempt at affiliation. This is also seen in the fact that he joined the military at age 18, and actually completed his enlistment. Even his purported occult activities, though not typically viewed in a positive light by American society, was an attempt at affiliation.

Much has been made of Berkowitz's arson activities. He is reported to have set well over a thousand fires in and around New York City, both before and after his Army career. He kept detailed records of each fire, including which fire department units responded. Each of the three types of offenders will start fires for different reasons. The symbolic offender does so out of displaced rage and hatred. The building or vehicle they are torching becomes the surrogate for the object of their negative emotions. It is a way for them to gain some sense of power and control when an insecure attachment brought on by an authoritarian, abusive, or neglectful parent has left them void of such feelings. In short, they displace their desire to destroy the object of their rage and hatred, typically a parent, onto the object they setting fire to.

An opportunistic offender will engage in arson for one of two reasons. First, they simply get a thrill out of destroying things. The act of setting fire to something, watching it burn, and then watching the fire department respond, is an exciting thing for them. The second reason is for sexual pleasure. This typically results from a classical conditioning process that pairs a previously neutral stimulus (fire) with a response-eliciting stimulus, typically masturbation. Once this conditioning process takes hold, then suddenly the individual will experience the same effect (sexual gratification) when the conditioned stimulus (fire) is introduced.

In the case of the ego-directed offender, the arsonist is typically neither motivated by rage or sexual gratification. What they lack, and what they seek in a perverse way is purpose. For Berkowitz, starting fires gave him that purpose, however fleeting. He was able to control elements of the New York City Fire Department by simply starting fires. It is significant that he appears not to have harmed anyone with his arson activities, notwithstanding the fact that a fireman could have been harmed in any one of them. It indicates perhaps some level of moral reasoning on his part, a quality that is typically absent in an opportunistic offender. The fact that he kept such detailed records indicates that his focus was less on the fire itself, and more on the response to that fire. It was perhaps the only way he was able to feel any sense of purpose, and likely contributed to his cadet affiliation with the fire department.

The final postidentification input to be discussed is his adoption. This was no doubt a significant issue in his life, as evidenced by his eventual search for his birth-mother. A great deal of research has been conducted on the issue of identity formation in adopted children. Goebel and Lott (1986) point out that adolescence is a period of integrating past with future. It is a transitional stage between the dependence of childhood and the independence of adulthood. The adopted child, however, has two pasts to integrate, one of which is likely a mystery in large part. In essence, the adopted child must reconcile the loss of part of themselves (Brodzinsky, 1987). Adoption unavoidably creates inherent complications for the adolescent as they attempt to search for a sense of self-identity (Frisk, 1964).

Berkowitz, of course, did find his birth mother, as well as a half-sister he was unaware of. Very little is known about the relationship they developed, or the reasons why he fell out of contact with his mother after a short period of time. Abrahamsen (1985) has reported that he felt rejected by his birth mother, and even had thoughts of wanting to kill her at one point. Perhaps he came to realize that the bond he truly wanted just wasn't possible for any number of reasons. It is likely that whatever ultimately happened only reinforced his self-contempt and identity confusion.

Classification

David Berkowitz represents a classic *ego-directed* serial killer, one driven most by a deficient sexual self. Many factors came together to inhibit his social development at a young age; adoption, being an only child, his difficult temperament, and his appearance and self-image. During adolescence, having never been successful at making friends, he lacked the necessary skills and emotional stability to develop a healthy self-concept and identity. He attempted to compensate by affiliating with positive groups like the fire and police cadets, but at the same time, he struggled with depression, and had begun acting out his turmoil by starting fires. When he hid for hours under his bed or in a closet, he in effect was hiding from the world. He hated who he was, and he hated the world for making him like that.

When Berkowitz got out of the Army, he was right back in the same dysfunctional set of circumstances he had left three years earlier, only now the one constant in his life, his father, made the decision to move with his new wife to Florida, leaving David alone in New York City to fend for himself. And alone he remained. Once again, he attempted to compensate through affiliation, and this is when he purportedly turned to the occult. But the one thing he truly desired, intimacy, escaped him. When he finally reached his emotional breaking point, he decided to kill what he couldn't have (a young woman), especially one enjoying the very thing that eluded him (an intimate moment with another person).

So what about the David Berkowitz of today? The debate continues as to whether he truly has been rehabilitated. But the argument can be made that perhaps he has. At the heart of the ego-directed killer is the void that exists in their self-identity. An important component of that identity, and perhaps the most important, is sexuality. The argument can be made that if David Berkowitz were released from prison today, and was able to establish an intimate relationship with a loving and caring woman, then the chances of him returning to his prior life of crime would be minimal. In prison, sexuality is redefined, and in fact becomes of lesser importance in defining oneself than the social and ideological components of identity. Because of this reality, Berkowitz appears to have successfully filled the void in his identity with religion. It now defines him and gives him purpose. Would it do so if he were released? Perhaps, but the human biological need for intimacy would no doubt return in full measure. Assuming that particular void in his identity could be filled with a sincere relationship, Berkowitz would then likely enjoy a sense of purpose on all levels, and at that point his rehabilitation could perhaps be viewed as successful after a period of time.

Chapter 8

CHARLES MANSON
An Ego-Directed Killer, Subtype: Deficient Social Self

INTRODUCTION

No one has served as the face of evil in America more than Charles Manson. His was the most highly publicized murder case in American history up to that point, partly because one of his victims, Sharon Tate, was a beautiful and famous actress. But it was also the cold and seemingly purposeless nature of the killings that shocked people. No one was robbed or raped, there was no vengeance being sought, and both he and his band of followers seemed anything but mentally ill. There just seemed no reason for what they did. In a sense, the Manson murders brought to an end a

Figure 8.1. Charles Manson.

period of turmoil that arguably began with the assassination of John F. Kennedy in 1963. It was a period during which Americans endured an unpopular war, widespread domestic terrorism, political assassinations, and numerous riots. In a sense, the Manson murders represented the last gasp of an anomaly in history called the 1960s.

Charles Manson never personally killed anyone, and arguably lacked the courage to do so, although it is alleged that prior to what are commonly called the "Manson murders," he personally shot a drug dealer who survived. But when faced with the opportunity to kill Leno LaBianca and his wife after tying them up in their own home, he ordered three of his followers to do it and then left the house before they began their bloody assault. His followers killed on his instructions, and thus his complicity allows us to view him as a serial killer no differently than had he thrust the knife himself. Some have debated whether Manson should be viewed as such, but the fact is the same personality characteristics that can compel someone to kill can also compel them to direct others to kill. The motivation is the same, the lack of internal deterrence is the same, and the result is the same.

CRIMINAL BACKGROUND

The Manson story really begins in 1967 when Manson established himself as sort of an itinerant guru in San Francisco's Haight-Ashbury District. According to Bugliosi and Gentry (1974), the former being the district attorney who prosecuted Manson, he eventually moved in with a librarian from the University of California, Berkeley, and almost immediately began bringing other women home to live with them. In a short amount of time, Manson had 18 women living with him. It was the beginning of what eventually would come to rather infamously be known as the "Manson Family."

Manson had a charismatic way about him, and expounded a philosophy that mixed elements of Scientology with Satanism. During the summer of 1967, he and eight of his followers began touring the west coast in an old school bus, and eventually settled down in Topanga Canyon north of downtown Los Angeles on an old Hollywood movie set called Spahn Ranch. The ranch, now abandoned, had previously been used in the filming of westerns, including *Bonanza* and *The Lone Ranger.*

Manson fashioned himself a rock star. At one point, he even befriended Dennis Wilson of the Beach Boys, who allowed Manson and his followers to stay at his house for a short period of time. During this time, Wilson actually paid for studio time to record a series of songs written by Manson. Wilson introduced Manson to other entertainment executives, including Terry Melcher, The Beach Boys' producer and son of actress Doris Day. At the time, Melcher and his girlfriend, actress Candice Bergen, lived in a house at 10050 Cielo Drive in Los Angeles. While Melcher initially expressed some interest in signing Manson to a recording contract, he eventually turned him down after witnessing his erratic behavior. This angered Manson, and set in motion a chain of events that would soon lead to one of America's bloodiest crime sprees.

In December, 1968, Manson and one of his few male followers, Tex Watson, visited a friend who played the Beatles' *White Album* for them. Manson very quickly became obsessed with the album, particularly the song *Helter Skelter*. In his mind, the Beatles were referring to a coming race war in America between blacks and whites. He began telling his followers that the Beatles had released the White Album in order to send coded messages to a small group of righteous people—the Manson family themselves—who were especially chosen to survive the coming apocalypse, an event he referred to as Helter Skelter after the Beatles song. Manson's plan was to initiate the apocalypse by recording his own album of coded messages that once released, would somehow cause inner-city blacks to begin annihilating whites. He believed that whites would retaliate, but that racist and nonracist whites would ultimately turn against each other, assuring their mutual annihilation. In the end, blacks would reign victorious, but only to be ruled by Manson and his followers.

During this time, Manson returned to the house at 10050 Cielo Drive in search of Melcher to again seek a recording contract. This time he was advised by someone at the house that Melcher no longer lived there. By now the house had been rented to Sharon Tate and her husband, film director Roman Polanski.

In their book *Helter Skelter—The True Story of the Manson Murders,* Vincent Bugliosi and Curt Gentry (1974) provide a timeline of the crimes perpetrated by Manson Family members, and Manson himself, beginning in July, 1969. By this time it had become apparent to Manson that no recording contract was forthcoming, and he began telling his followers that Helter Skelter was at hand, and that it was up to them to initiate the apocalyptic war. The crime spree began with Manson himself shooting a black drug dealer named Bernard "Lotsapoppa" Crowe in his Hollywood apartment. Crowe had threatened to kill Manson's followers after one of them, Tex Watson, stole drug money from him. Manson mistakenly believed he had killed Crowe—he was only wounded—and that the Black Panthers would retaliate by attacking them at Spahn Ranch. In reality, Crowe was never a member of the Black Panthers.

On July 25, 1969, Manson sent three of his followers, including Bobby Beausoleil, to the house of Gary Hinman, an acquaintance whom Manson believed had recently inherited a significant amount of money. Beausoleil and two female followers, Mary Brunner and Susan Atkins, were sent to steal the money. The trio held Hinman hostage for two days attempting to force him to give up the money. When it became apparent that Hinman was not going to hand over the money, Manson eventually showed up at the residence and slashed his ear with a sword, after which he purportedly instructed Beausoleil to kill him. Beausoleil complied, and stabbed Hinman to death, after which the three wrote "political piggy" on a wall with Hinman's blood (Atkins & Slosser, 1977).

On August 6, 1969, Beausoleil was arrested while driving Hinman's vehicle. Police discovered the murder weapon inside the vehicle. Following the arrest, Manson called together his followers and announced, "Now is the time for Helter Skelter" (Bugliosi & Gentry, 1974). Two days later, Manson directed four of his followers—Tex Watson, Susan Atkins, Linda Kasabian, and Patricia Krenwinkel—to drive to the house where Terry Melcher had previously lived, and to kill everyone inside. Present at the house on the night of the murders was Tate, who was eight and a half months pregnant, hair stylist Jay Sebring, screenwriter Wojciech Frykowski, and Frykowski's lover Abigail Folger, heiress to the Folger's Coffee fortune. Polanski was out of the country at the time of the murders.

When Watson and the three women arrived at the residence, Watson first climbed a telephone pole and cut the line leading into the house. The four then jumped over an embankment and began walking up the driveway toward the house. They were met by 18-year-old

Steven Parent in his vehicle, who was just leaving after visiting with the house's caretaker in an adjacent cottage. Watson flagged the young man down and abruptly shot him four times in the chest and abdomen, killing him. The four then approached the house, and while Kasabian remained outside as a lookout, the other three entered through an open window.

Once inside the house, the threesome immediately began their gruesome killing spree. Sebring was the first to be shot by Watson after protesting the rough treatment of the pregnant Tate. Watson had tied the two of them together by their necks with a rope slung over a ceiling beam. Frykowski was next. While attempting to escape the house, he was stabbed repeatedly by both Atkins and Watson, and finally shot dead by Watson on the front porch. Abigail Folger fled through a back door to the pool area, but was eventually tackled and stabbed repeatedly by Krenwinkel. It was later determined that she had been stabbed 28 times, and Frykowski 51 times (Bugliosi & Gentry, 1974). That left only Sharon Tate. She pleaded with the assailants to spare her life and the life of her baby, and even offered to accompany them as a hostage until a ransom could be paid. Unfortunately for Tate, money was not their motivation. Watson and Atkins began stabbing her repeatedly until she was dead. Before leaving the grisly murder scene, Atkins dipped a towel in Tate's blood and wrote "PIG" on the front door. Watson would later testify that Manson instructed them to leave a message in blood on the wall (Watson, n.d.).

The very next night following the murders at the Tate residence, Manson again sent a group of followers out to commit murder. This time he accompanied the group, purportedly to show his followers how to complete the task without the type of chaos that had occurred the night before. After a few hours driving around L.A., Manson instructed Linda Kasabian, the driver of the vehicle, to proceed to a house Manson and some of his followers had partied at the year before. Once there, it was the house next door, at 3301 Waverly Drive, which Manson decided to target. The house was occupied by supermarket executive Leno LaBianca and his wife Rosemary (Bugliosi & Gentry, 1974).

Manson and Watson approached the LaBianca residence while the others remained in the vehicle. Through a window they could see Leno LaBianca asleep on the couch. The two found the back door to the house unlocked and entered from there. Once inside, Manson awakened Leno LaBianca at gunpoint and directed Watson to bind his hands together. They next awakened Rosemary LaBianca and bound her hands as well. Both had pillow cases placed over their heads and tied in place with lamp cords. At that point Manson left the residence and sent Krenwinkel and Leslie Van Houten inside with instructions to assist Watson in carrying out the murders. Both leno and Rosemary LaBianca were stabbed multiple times with a bayonet Watson had brought with them, as well as a knife one of the women had taken from the LaBiancas' own kitchen. After both were dead, Watson carved "WAR" into Leno LaBianca's abdomen. Krenwinkel wrote "RISE" and "Death to pigs" on the walls with the victims' blood, as well as "Helter Skelter" on the refrigerator door. As a final gruesome gesture, Krenwinkel stuck a carving fork in Leno LaBianca's stomach and a steak knife in his throat before leaving the house (Bugliosi & Gentry, 1974).

While the LaBianca killers carried out their gruesome crimes, Manson drover three other members of his group, one of them Linda Kasabian, to the apartment of an actor-acquaintance of Kasabian's. Their instructions were to kill the individual and then return to Spahn Ranch. Kasabian herself thwarted the attack by purposely knocking on the wrong apartment door. The group left and hitchhiked back to the ranch, where they met back up with the LaBianca killers.

The LaBianca killings would be the last for the group. Two circumstances made their eventual identification and capture inevitable. First, there was a large amount of physical evidence left at the crime scenes, something the killers made very little effort to clean up. And second, those involved in the killings were quick to brag about their murderous exploits. Both the LAPD and the LA County Sheriff's Department were actively investigating the murders. Eventually connections were made between the Hinman and Tate-LaBianca murders, and then the pieces began to quickly come together. Additionally, Bobby Beausoleil's girlfriend began cooperating with detectives, telling them that Manson had sent Beausoleil and Susan Atkins to Hinman's house to kill him. Atkins confessed to the murder, and while awaiting trial, she began telling jail inmates about the Tate-LaBianca murders. She told them that Manson was Jesus Christ, and that he was going to lead his followers down a hole in the earth in Death Valley to a place where a new civilization existed. She also told them that others were targeted for murder, including Richard Burton, Elizabeth Taylor, Frank Sinatra, Steve McQueen, and Tom Jones (Bugliosi & Gentry, 1974).

Beginning in December, 1969, arrest warrants were issued for Atkins, Leslie Van Houten, Patricia Krenwinkle, Linda Kasabian, Charles "Tex" Watson, and Charles Manson. All were charged with first-degree murder; however, since Kasabian had not actively participated in the murders, she was granted immunity in exchange for her testimony. The trial of Manson, Atkins, Van Houten, and Krenwinkle began on July 24, 1970, and ended on January 25, 1971 with all four defendants being found guilty of first degree murder. All were given the death penalty. Watson was tried separately, and in October, 1971, he, too, was found guilty of first-degree murder and sentenced to death. All five defendants would eventually have their death sentences commuted to life in prison after the U.S. Supreme Court ruled in 1972 that the death penalty was unconstitutional. All of the defendants except for Susan Atkins remain incarcerated in California prisons. Atkins died in prison in 2009 after battling brain cancer.

PERSONAL BACKGROUND

One thing we know for certain is that Charles Manson did not have a normal upbringing. He was born on November 12, 1934 to an unwed teenager named Kathleen Maddox in Cincinnati, Ohio. It is unlikely he ever knew his biological father, although he is alleged to have been a transient laborer named Colonel Walker Scott who was working on a local dam project when Manson's mother became pregnant (Emmons, 1986). He was initially given the name Charles Milles Maddox, but his surname was changed to "Manson" after his mother married a laborer named William Manson.

From the young age of 12, Manson was institutionalized almost continuously until reaching adulthood. According to biographer John Gilmore (1996), Manson began stealing at a very young age, and became quite good at it. In 1947, at the age of 12, he was caught and subsequently sent to the Gibault School for Boys in Terre Haute, Indiana. He ran away from the school less than a year after arriving, and was subsequently caught and ordered by the court to Father Flanagan's "Boys Town" in Nebraska. Prior to being caught, Manson attempted to reunite with his mother, but she purportedly rejected him.

Manson's stay at Boys Town was short-lived. Within days of his arrival, he and another boy committed two robberies. Now only 13-years-old, he was sent to the Indiana School for Boys for a three-year period of incarceration. He and two other boys eventually escaped and made their way to California, but made it only as far as Utah before they were recaptured. This time, Manson was sent to the National Training School for Boys in Washington, D.C., his fourth institutional confinement. A psychiatrist who examined him at the facility described him as an "extremely sensitive boy who has not yet given up in terms of securing some kind of love and affection from the world" (Gilmore, 1996). More than anything, the young Manson wanted status among the other boys. He wanted to be popular and held in high esteem, and he used his manipulative ways to secure both.

Eventually Manson began acting out sexually. After holding a razor blade to another boy's throat while the boy sodomized him, he was transferred to the Federal Reformatory at Petersburg, Virginia. There he was described as "homosexual, dangerous, and safe only under supervision" (Gilmore, 1996). Considered unsuitable for an open reformatory-type institution because of his dangerous behavior, Manson was next transferred to a secure facility in Chillicothe, Ohio, and from there was finally paroled in 1954 at the age of 19, having spent essentially his entire adolescence incarcerated.

Once back out on the street, Manson quickly returned to a life of crime. He reunited with his mother and married a waitress, who became pregnant shortly after their marriage. By this time, Manson was stealing cars to earn money. In 1955, he and his young pregnant wife headed to Los Angeles in one of the stolen vehicles. There a son was born, Charles Manson Jr. Manson continued stealing cars and committing other petty crimes for financial gain, but eventually was caught and convicted of the crimes. He would spend the next three years incarcerated at Terminal Island in San Pedro, California. By the time he was paroled in 1958, his wife had divorced him.

As was his pattern, once paroled, Manson immediately returned to a life of crime, earning money through a combination of pimping and stealing. In less than a year, he had been arrested on federal charges of stealing checks from mailboxes. By this time, he was also using stolen credit cards and continuing his usual practice of stealing cars. The judge in the case sentenced Manson to ten years in federal prison, but then ordered that it be served as probation after a young woman testified she was pregnant by Manson—a ruse on her part after Manson convinced her to do so—and pleaded to the judge to keep him out of prison (Gilmore, 1996). Within weeks of being placed on probation, Manson conned a young woman out of $700 and raped her roommate. He fled to Texas, but was quickly captured and sent to the U.S. Penitentiary at McNeil Island in Washington to serve out his ten-year sentence in the prior case.

At McNeil Island, Manson became obsessed with playing the guitar and writing songs. He also developed an obsession with the Beatles, and felt that he could be even bigger than them if given the opportunity. He learned to play the drums as well, and indicated to prison officials his desire to seek employment either as a guitar player or drummer once released from prison. He was finally paroled on March 21, 1967, and provided transportation to San Francisco. Manson protested his release, and argued to prison officials that he was no longer capable of surviving on the outside. He was happy in prison, having spent nearly half of his young life incarcerated to that point. But his protests went unheeded, and he was released back to the street with no education, no skills, no support systems, and no real plans for transitioning back into a mainstream society he had never really been part of to begin with. In a short amount of time, Manson would graduate from his status as a petty thief and pimp to become the very face of evil in America for decades to come.

ANALYSIS AND CLASSIFICATION

Preidentification Inputs

A number of things are apparent simply from the nature of the crimes the Manson family committed, especially the murders at the home of Sharon Tate. For starters, it was obvious that multiple assailants were involved. Given that five people were murdered, and all of them scattered throughout the house and premises, it would have taken multiple assailants to control the situation enough to commit the murders. This fact tends to rule out the idea of a symbolic killer. Symbolic killers tend to target certain types of victims: those who can serve as surrogates for the object of their rage and hatred, typically a parent. They tend not to work in groups, and they also tend not to leave messages behind, such as the messages in blood the Manson family members left on the walls. A symbolic killer makes no point with their killings. They endeavor only to quiet the inner turmoil they feel, and killing is the only way they can do it, however perverse it may seem.

Another important consideration was the absence of any evidence indicating that some type of sexual assault took place, either at the Tate house, or later at the LaBianca house. Nor was robbery involved. While this does not totally rule out the possibility that the killings were opportunistically motivated, it does lessen the odds of that being the case. Opportunistic killers are almost always sexually motivated. In some cases, they may be motivated by material gain; however, not only was there no evidence of a robbery in either the Tate or LaBianca murders, but the manner in which the victims were killed is inconsistent with this type of killer. Had robbery been the primary motivation, then the victims would have been killed quickly, likely execution style with the handgun that was known to have been used. The victims in this case were overkilled, including the presence of postmortem wounds. In some cases, multiple weapons were used on the same victim, indicating that more than one person took part. None of these circumstances are consistent with robbery being the motivation.

Opportunistic killers are also at times motivated by a desire to torture their victims. But these types of killers almost always kidnap and bind their victims to torture them in a slow and methodical way. The Tate-LaBianca victims were killed quickly and violently. There were no noticeable signs of any methodical torture, especially dismemberment or mutilation. For this type of opportunistic killer, the murder itself is secondary. The thrill for them is in eliciting extreme fear and agony in their victims. They tend to kill when that thrill begins to diminish. The killing itself is only a necessary end to the event.

The presence of messages left behind—Manson had instructed them to leave behind something "witchy" (Bugliosi & Gentry, 1974)—certainly would indicate that the killings were motivated by a desire to make a point of some kind. This would have been even more apparent once the Tate and LaBianca murders were connected. And given that multiple people had to participate, police at that time were no doubt looking at a cult or commune of people as the likely suspects, at least initially. Both were common in 1969, especially in southern California. From the preidentification evidence, it would have been difficult to develop a single profile of a group leader, or to determine if the group even had a single leader. The fact that the killers seemed unconcerned about leaving behind physical evidence, a circumstance that would have pointed to the presence of mental illness in the case of a single killer, would indicate in this case the possible influence of drugs.

Postidentification Inputs

Once Charles Manson was identified and his background uncovered, there were a number of factors that could be connected to his criminal conduct. First of all, and most importantly, was his complete lack of a normal childhood and adolescence. He had no father, and his mother, though not abusive, was certainly neglectful. And on top of that was the fact that he had been institutionalized from the age of 12 to adulthood, precluding any possibility of a normal psychosocial development.

Manson also had a history of manipulative behaviors. In essentially every institutional record this characteristic is indicated. This pattern began at a very early age. He was very egocentric, and schemed constantly to increase his own lot at anyone's expense. He also endeavored to increase his status among the boys with whom he was institutionalized. He was small in stature, a characteristic he attempted to overcome through cunning and fearlessness. He acted out sexually, typically with other boys, and as previously indicated, even forced one boy to perform fellatio by holding a knife to his throat. As an adult out on the street, he was accused of raping a woman on at least one occasion.

Eventually Manson discovered the guitar, and developed a keen interest in music and songwriting. He wanted desperately to secure a recording contract once in California, and made efforts to meet the right people who could facilitate that goal, including Dennis Wilson of the Beach Boys. Manson appeared to get a great deal of satisfaction and self-esteem from his songwriting; however, when rejected each time he attempted to secure a recording contract, that rejection turned to rage.

Throughout his institutional history, Manson had a history of dealing with failure and rejection in violent ways.

Finally, the fact that Manson had developed a following of people prior to the crimes, especially young women, certainly pointed to his ability to manipulate and influence others. This circumstance only continued the pattern of behavior he had developed and repeatedly demonstrated in the various juvenile facilities and prisons where he was incarcerated. Manson felt a sense of power and self-worth in controlling the thoughts and actions of others.

Classification

Charles Manson was an ego-directed killer with a deficient social self. We can rule out that he was either an opportunistic or symbolic killer based on one fact–Manson himself did not participate. The thrill for him was not in killing, but in having the power to get others to kill for him. Much has been said of his desire to start a race war; however, Manson had no ideological foundation. Such talk was only his way of manipulating his followers by providing them a justification for their criminal acts. Manson's only belief was in himself. While incarcerated at McNeil Island Federal Penitentiary, the following notation was made by a prison psychologist:

> A tremendous drive to call attention to himself. Generally he is unable to succeed in positive acts, therefore he often resorts to negative behavior to satisfy his drive. In his efforts to "find himself", Manson pursues different religious philosophies, e.g. Scientology and Buddhism, however he never remains long enough with any given teachings to reap meaningful benefits.

This notation is reflective of someone searching for self-identity. Identity-formation is the primary developmental task of adolescence, but in Manson's case, the typical routes by which an adolescent seeks identity were foreclosed by his institutionalization. The only identity he was able to develop was an institutional identity based on institutional values–things like power, control, and self-protection. These values also influenced his developing sexuality, and thus he was devoid of intimacy, or even the desire to experience it. In this way, he differed from David Berkowitz. For Manson, sex was for pleasure, nothing else. If he was denied the opportunity, then he resorted to violence or psychological manipulations. His methods worked well, as evidenced by the fact that he eventually lived with multiple women, having sex with any of them as he desired.

Manson was motivated entirely by his own wants and desires, and the one thing he craved most was status. He wanted to be seen as powerful and important among his peers. Eventually, when he discovered songwriting, Manson found a possible avenue to becoming both. He had witnessed the public's reaction to the Beatles, and he wanted the same reaction. He wanted to be on a stage with a crowd of screaming fans idolizing him. In music, the short little man who as a young boy had practically nothing he didn't steal, who had never accomplished anything of value, and who was characterized as a failure by all who encountered him during his many incarcerations, found purpose and self-worth. But his desire to be a rock star was not motivated by any sense of creative expression or self-actualization. Those qualities were unknown to him. Instead, it was all about gaining more power and control, not just over his own life, but over the lives of others as well. These were the institutional values he had internalized at a young age.

By the time of the Tate-LaBianca murders, it had become obvious to Manson that a recording contract would not be forthcoming. Always the schemer and manipulator, he had successfully become a rock star of a different kind; with his own family of loyal followers. And now, as a way of lashing out at the world, and at the same time experiencing the euphoric pleasure of wielding the ultimate power over his followers—the power to convince them to kill at his direction—seven innocent people were about to die for no reason, none of them at the hands of Manson himself. The young boy who had coldly held a knife to the throat of another young boy while he forced him to perform oral sex, was now about to symbolically hold a knife to the throat of an entire city.

Because of neglectful parenting and his institutionalization at an early age, Manson never had the opportunity to develop a healthy superego. And because of his lack of identity formation, he also never developed the ego-strength to effectively moderate the desires of ID. It can be said that he had a very fragile ego that manifest itself in the form of insecurity and a craving for status and power. With an underdeveloped ego and superego, he was at the whim and mercy of ID. He was thus undeterred by any sense of guilt or remorse (superego), and his judgment was such that he simply could not adequately weigh the rightness or wrongness of his actions or conform them to societal standards (ego).

In terms of deterrence, there is no question that Manson was devoid of any *social* or *self* deterrence. With no sense of identity, and certainly no secure attachment to anyone, those deterrence mechanisms were either underdeveloped or not developed at all. As far as *moral* deterrence, this is an unknown. Manson had no prior history of murder, or even of violent crime for the most part. He was a thief more than anything else. There is a possibility that some semblance of moral deterrence kept him from engaging in serial rape or murder, but with the other two deterrence mechanisms absent, he could still be described as having a criminal personality type.

Chapter 9

ERIC RUDOLPH: GOD'S CRUSADER
An Ego-Directed Killer, Subtype: Hyper-Ideological Self

INTRODUCTION

In the early morning hours of May 31, 2003, a rookie police officer in Murphy, North Carolina happened onto a man digging through a dumpster behind a Save-A-Lot grocery store. Suspecting a possible burglary, the officer placed the man in handcuffs and asked him his name. To his surprise, the man he had just detained eventually identified himself as Eric Robert Rudolph, who for over five years had been one of the FBI's most wanted fugitives, and for whom a $1 million reward had been offered for information leading to his arrest (Schuster & Stone, 2005). Described by many, in-

Figure 9.1. Eric Robert Rudolph.

cluding the FBI, as a domestic terrorist, Rudolph had set off bombs at various locations in Georgia and Alabama between 1996 and 1998, killing two and injuring as many as 150 others, some critically. His motivation for the violent attacks was to end the practice of abortion in America by instilling fear in doctors and other medical professionals involved in performing such procedures. His attacks were carried out during a period of heightened activism by prolife groups around the country, including violent actions by some. It can be argued that such actions did have an impact. From 1991 to 2013, nearly 70% of the abortion clinics in America, over 1,500 in number, closed their doors (Wysong, 2013).

One of the circumstances that set Rudolph apart from other serial killers was the fact that a significant group of law-abiding citizens, as well as some who were not, supported him, and some may even have helped him evade police during the period of time he was a fugitive. One radical prolife group, the *Army of God,* is an underground network of Christian terrorists who advocate the use of violence to bring an end to abortion in America. The organization has been known to harbor and fund abortion activists suspected of violent crimes, including murder and arson (Terrorist Organization Profile, 2010). Not only did the Army of God take credit for Rudolph's actions, but Rudolph himself has admitted to his past affiliation with the group (Schuster & Stone, 2005). Rudolph eventually pled guilty to all the charges against him in order to avoid the death penalty. He is incarcerated for the remainder of his life at the ADX Florence Supermax prison in Florence, Colorado.

CRIMINAL BACKGROUND

Rudolph began his killing spree on July 27, 1996, when he set off a bomb in Atlanta's Centennial Olympic Park during the Atlanta Olympic Games. At the time of the explosion, the park was filled with thousands of people attending Olympic events. At approximately 1:00 a.m., an anonymous caller dialed 911 from a payphone near the park and stated "there is a bomb in Centennial Park . . . you have 30 minutes" (CNN, Olympic Park Bombing, 2013). Sometime around midnight, Rudolph had planted an Army field pack containing three pipe bombs near a tower filled with P.A. speakers. The pipe bombs contained dynamite, and were wrapped in nails, a device that was sure to kill anyone standing in close proximity (Vollers, 2009). Police immediately swarmed the area and attempted to evacuate as many as possible.

Two things prevented the attack from becoming a much larger catastrophe. First, someone had bumped the backpack at some point, changing its position. Rudolph had included a metal plate inside the backpack that would direct the nails in a particular direction. When the backpack was bumped, the blast field was directed away from the crowd (Vollers, 2009). The other thing that helped prevent more death and injury were the heroic actions of a security guard named Richard Jewell, who had spotted the backpack and began moving people away from it. His actions are now credited with saving many lives that day.

Approximately 22 minutes after Rudolph's anonymous call, short of the promised 30 minutes, the bombs exploded together in one powerful explosion. Alice Hawthorne, 44, of Albany, Georgia was killed instantly by the blast. Over 100 others, including Hawthorne's daughter, were injured by the flying nails and shrapnel. Almost immediately, the FBI considered Richard Jewell a suspect after their Behavioral Sciences Unit confirmed that he fit the profile of a "lone wolf" terrorist (Brenner, 1997). That information was leaked to the Atlanta Journal-Constitution three days after the bombing. Jewell remained a suspect until October 26, 1996, when the FBI officially announced that he was no longer considered a person of interest (Olympic Park Bombing, 2013).

It would be nearly two years before the FBI would finally connect the dots and name Eric Rudolph as a suspect in the Olympic Park bombing, a crime he would eventually plead guilty to. On April 13, 2005, he issued the following public statement from his prison cell about the crime, a statement that was posted on the Army of God website:

> In the summer of 1996, the world converged upon Atlanta for the Olympic Games. Under the protection and auspices of the regime in Washington millions of people came to celebrate the ideals of global socialism. Multinational corporations spent billions of dollars, and Washington organized an army of security to protect these best of all games. Even though the conception and purpose of the so-called Olympic movement is to promote the values of global socialism, as perfectly expressed in the song IMAGINE by John Lennon, which

was the theme of the 1996 Games—even though the purpose of the Olympics is to promote these ideals, the purpose of the attack on July 27 was to confound, anger, and embarrass the Washington government in the eyes of the world for its abominable sanctioning of abortion on demand.

The plan was to force the cancellation of the Games, or at least create a state of insecurity to empty the streets around the venues and thereby eat into the vast amounts of money invested. (Rudolph, 2005)

One of the most important circumstances contributing to Rudolph' eventual indictment was that the FBI was able to connect the Olympic Park bombing to Rudolph's other bombings. His next one would occur on January 16, 1997, at an abortion clinic in Sandy Springs, Georgia, an Atlanta suburb. If there was any doubt about Rudolph's intentions to kill, that doubt was washed away in Sandy Springs. The first bomb detonated at approximately 9:30 a.m., destroying part of the building, but hurting no one. Fortunately, it was a day when very few people were present in the clinic. As police and firemen responded to the scene, a second bomb, set to explode an hour later when emergency personnel would be present and vulnerable to such an attack, detonated in a nearby garbage dumpster, injuring a number of people. That explosion was caught on live television, as local news crews broadcast from the scene (Bragg, 1997).

Rudolph's next attack came a month later, on February 21, 1997, when he detonated a bomb outside the Otherside Lounge, a gay and lesbian bar in Atlanta, injuring five patrons, but killing none. Like before, Rudolph planted a second "sucker" bomb on the side of the building where he anticipated emergency personnel would respond; however, the device was found and safely detonated by law enforcement authorities with no injuries (historycommons.org, n.d.). Now the FBI knew they had a serial bomber on their hands, given the similarities between the nightclub and Sandy Springs bombs, and that whoever was responsible was willing to kill even emergency personnel responding to assist the wounded. It was truly a dangerous situation.

Following the nightclub bombing, a handwritten unsigned letter was sent to the Reuters News Agency claiming that a unit of the "Army of God" had been responsible for both the nightclub and Sandy Springs attacks. The letter warned that anyone involved in performing abortions would become victims of retribution, and that gays and lesbians would also now be targeted. The letter stated, "We will target sodomites, their organizations, and all those who push their agenda" (The Otherside Lounge, n.d.). Now the authorities had an even bigger problem—a serial offender who was targeting two completely unrelated groups of people. It was clear from the letter that he had no intentions of stopping. In it, Rudolph provided a code—the date 4/19/93—he would use in the future so the police would know it was him and not a copycat offender. As it turned out, the date was the anniversary of the fire at the Branch Davidian compound in Waco, Texas, in 1993 that killed 76 men, women, and children while the FBI attempted to negotiate their surrender. It was also a reference to the bombing of the Murrah Federal Building in Oklahoma City on 04/19/95.

A short time following the nightclub bombing, a taskforce established to investigate the attacks, through an analysis of the materials used in the bombs, made a connection between the previous two and the Olympic Park bombing. Unfortunately though, no suspect had yet been developed, not even the name of a person of interest. That would finally change nearly a year later following a deadly bombing in Birmingham, Alabama.

On January 29, 1998, Rudolph planted a bomb in some bushes outside the "New Woman All Women Healthcare Clinic" at 1001 17th Street South in Birmingham. It was the same type of bomb he had used in the previous three bombings—dynamite surrounded by nails—but this time he employed a remote controlled detonator he could activate at will from a short distance away. At approximately 7:30 a.m., Birmingham police officer Robert Sanderson, who was working off-duty as a security guard at the clinic, noticed the device in the bushes and approached. When it became apparent to Rudolph that the bomb had been spotted, he detonated it, killing Sanderson instantly, and critically injuring Emily Lyons, a nurse who had just arrived to work. This time, however, Rudolph wasn't so lucky. Two eyewitnesses spotted him removing a blond wig and getting into a Nissan pickup truck. They were able to record the license plate number. The truck was registered to Eric Robert Rudolph (Schuster & Stone, 2005).

Police now had a suspect, and it didn't take long to connect the Alabama bombing to the three in Atlanta. A week after the bombing, on February 8th, hunters near Murphy, North Carolina, found

Rudolph's abandoned Nissan pickup. He was publicly identified on February 14, 1998 as the suspect in the Alabama bombing, and on May 5, 1998 he was added to the FBI's Ten Most Wanted list. He was described as armed and extremely dangerous, and a $1 million reward was offered for his capture. When Rudolph walked into the North Carolina woods that day, he would begin an elusive existence that would somehow evade a nationwide police dragnet until a rookie police officer happened onto him five years later digging through a dumpster for food.

There is little doubt that Rudolph would have continued his deadly attacks had he not been identified by eyewitnesses in Birmingham. The fact that he would detonate the bomb that killed Officer Sanderson, knowing full well the blast would kill him almost instantly, indicates that he was becoming more violent and brazen in his attacks. If he couldn't kill the abortion doctors, he was willing to kill anyone associated with an abortion clinic. His bombings were so well publicized that he no doubt knew the FBI had not yet developed his name as a suspect. He also was likely getting supportive messages from other Army of God members, either directly or indirectly. This emboldened him even more, and by now he had no doubt convinced himself that his actions were having an impact. This made him an extremely dangerous force to contend with–a serial killer who believed he was on the side of right; a crusader in service to God. But for the two eyewitnesses who recorded his license number as he sped away from the clinic in Birmingham, it is unimaginable the amount of death and destruction he may have perpetrated before being caught or killed.

PERSONAL BACKGROUND

Eric Rudolph was born in Florida on September 19, 1966 to Robert and Patricia Rudolph. By all accounts, he was very close to his parents and five siblings. According to Michael Ross (2005), they were a self-sufficient family who eventually relocated to a small house on one of the highest peaks in North Carolina. They were a religious family who harbored a general distrust of the federal government, even distilling their own water to avoid drinking public tap water. Everything was a government conspiracy, including the fluoride being added to drinking water.

A defining moment for Rudolph came in 1981 when his father died of cancer. It devastated the young teenager. According to Charles Stone, a former special agent with the Georgia Bureau of Investigations, Rudolph was extremely angry with the U.S. food and Drug Administration for not approving the drug "Laetrile" for use with cancer patients. Rudolph believed the drug could have saved his father's life (Ross, 2005). This only intensified his antigovernment feelings. It was during this time when he began to spend significant amounts of time in the woods camping, a practice that would equip him well with the skills necessary to evade law enforcement for five years. Some speculated that during his time on the run, he was living somewhere in a bunker he had built years earlier in the Nantahala National Forest near his home in Murphy, North Carolina. It was during this time when he also began using and selling marijuana.

When Rudolph turned 18, his mother took him and two of his younger siblings to Schell City, Missouri to become part of the Church of Israel, a local congregation headed by Pastor Dan Gayman that catered to isolationists and survivalists living in the Missouri hills. The church was known to have ties to the "Christian Identity" movement, an organization that espouses the radical belief that only white Anglo-Saxons will be allowed in Heaven. The movement is vehemently anti-government, and has maintained ties with white supremacist groups such as the Ku Klux Klan and various neo-Nazi groups. The Jewish Anti-Defamation League includes the Church of Israel in its list of anti-Semitic extremist groups (Extremism in America, n.d.).

Gayman became a surrogate father to Rudolph. Still suffering the trauma of losing his father, Rudolph welcomed Gayman's attention, and he reciprocated by becoming a passionate adherent to his radical teachings. He became extremely anti-Semitic, and blamed many of the Nation's ills on Jews. After a year in Missouri, he dropped out of high school, returned to North Carolina where he earned a GED, and eventually enrolled at Western Carolina University. By this time, he was continuing to smoke marijuana heavily, and was making a healthy income selling it. According to his sister-in-law, Deborah Rudolph, at one point he was making $60,000 annually selling marijuana (Ross, 2005).

Rudolph dropped out of college after only two semesters, and in 1987, joined the U.S. Army. He attended basic training at Fort Benning, Georgia, and later Air Assault School at Fort Campbell, Kentucky. He served as a member of the elite 101st Airborne Division, attaining the rank of "Specialist E-4." Rudolph's experience in the forests of North Carolina served him well in the Army. He was adept at using weapons, as well as navigating through rough terrain with a map and compass. He was perfectly suited for a combat role, but for one circumstance—his continued use of marijuana. Only 18 months after joining the Army he was discharged as a result of his drug use (Ross, 2005).

Back in civilian life, Rudolph returned to North Carolina where he made money selling marijuana and working construction. He earned a reputation as a skilled craftsman, and did work throughout North Carolina and Tennessee. During this time he also began to change. He began using aliases, and became more vehement in his anti-Semitic, antigay, and racist beliefs. These views became entangled in his distrust and hatred for the government, and then at some point the issue of abortion, cloaked in his radical religious beliefs, found its way into the mix. Rudolph was primed for violence. In December, 1977, a former girlfriend bumped into him in a grocery store. He had by that time carried out three of his bombings, and the deadly attack in Birmingham would happen just a month later. She later recounted that Rudolph acted very odd, staring at her strangely and telling her that he had been in the western states fighting forest fires (Pederson et al., 1998). Little did she know at the time that she was looking into the eyes of a serial killer; one who had reached the point of no return, and who was willing now to continue his deadly attacks for as long as possible before slipping into the North Carolina mountains and disappearing from sight.

ANALYSIS AND CLASSIFICATION

Preidentification Inputs

The fact that the killer used a bomb as his preferred killing method, and did so in public places, allows us to rule out the idea that the victims were being specifically targeted. Bombs kill indiscriminately, and most of the bombs he used were planted and timed to explode after he departed the area. This is significant in determining the type of killer he was. An opportunistic killer is motivated by the act of killing. To truly satisfy their need to kill, they must do so in close proximity to their victims, and in a way that allows them to actually feel the act of killing. The use of bombs timed to detonate after their departure would likely not satisfy this need. Also, a symbolic offender typically targets specific types of victims who can relieve their emotional turmoil by serving as surrogates for the object of their rage and hatred. With the use of a timed bomb, and not being able to select specific victims with any degree of certainty, it is not likely a symbolic serial killer would kill in this manner.

The fact that the killer tipped off police prior to the Olympic bombing indicates that they were not focused on the act of killing, but rather on the underlying message they wanted to convey. An opportunistic killer would have allowed the bomb to explode in the midst of the crowd and kill many. The killer did in fact attempt to do this with the bombings that followed; however, he likely made the decision that anyone who was at an abortion clinic or a gay nightclub was a guilty party, and thus in the killer's mind, the type of "collateral" damage that would have been possible at Centennial Park was no longer a consideration.

Also, it is an obvious clue that the killer was targeting abortion clinics and gay nightclubs. This certainly points to a particular ideology as the motivating factor behind the bombings. The fact that the two obvious issues were abortion and the gay lifestyle almost certainly pointed to a religious ideology. Also, the bomber was quiet following the Olympic bombing and the Sandy Springs, Georgia bombing. Even when Richard Jewell was identified as a possible suspect, there was no communiqué from the killer taking credit for the attacks. This would point to a single perpetrator rather than a religious terrorist group. Such a group would want to maximize the impact of their message by publicizing their identity and future intentions. The fact that there was no communiqué instead pointed to a "lone wolf" bomber, and one who truly espoused the ideology motivating his crimes. It was not someone simply seeking notoriety. Had that been the case, then they most certainly would have communicated with the police or press following the Olympic bombing. Also, the seriousness of the killer's "mission" was apparent in the fact that they planted bombs timed to detonate when first responders–police, firemen, EMTs–were present and in harm's way.

When the killer finally did communicate with the police following the nightclub bombing, he provided them a code that he would use in the future so they would know it was him and not a "copycat." The code was a date that related to both the FBI siege at Waco in 1993 and the bombing of the Murrah Federal Building in Oklahoma City in 1995. This would indicate a couple things. First, the killer was likely a white American, and very antigovernment. They also likely had a history of affiliation with right-wing extremist groups, as well as military experience. Building bombs with timing devices is a dangerous task, and not one typically taken on by someone with little or no experience handling munitions and weaponry.

Postidentification Inputs

After identifying Eric Rudolph as the killer, it became quite easy to construct a solid profile to account for his actions. Investigators determined quickly that Rudolph did in fact have a history of affiliating with groups, including religious groups, which espoused an extremist ideology based in racism, anti-Semitism, and religious fundamentalism. Rudolph believed his actions were morally-justified in order to save unborn babies from abortion, the sanctity of marriage and family from the influence of the gay agenda, and America from what he perceived to be a Jewish effort to control the world's finances.

Investigators would also have confirmed Rudolph's extreme distrust and hatred for the federal government, which he believed protected and actively promoted the very political agendas he wanted to eradicate. He also accused the federal government, especially the U.S. Food and Drug Administration, of contributing to the death of his father by not approving the cancer drug *Laetrile*. The fact that Rudolph lost his father during his adolescent years when he would have been immersed in the developmental throes of identity-formation is significant. It is likely he entered early adulthood identity-diffused to some extent, having lost his primary identity-model at such a critical point in his life.

Classification

Eric Rudolph was an ego-directed serial killer, spurred on by a hyper ideological self. He killed not for the sake of killing, but to feel a sense of purpose and meaning in his life. His adopted ideology gave his life meaning, and the bombs he detonated gave it purpose. When his father died, he likely lost the primary influence on his developing self-efficacy and identification. From that point on, his efforts at building a meaningful self-concept failed. It is likely that joining an elite unit of the U.S. Army was his attempt to gain purpose and a sense of identity. When that effort failed, having been kicked out for drug use, he turned to his extremist ideology. His hatred for the government likely intensified as a result of his less-than-honorable departure from the military, and the impact on his self-image was no doubt devastating.

There is every possibility that Eric Rudolph's crimes were motivated by a number of things that came together to form the perfect storm for the birth of an ideologically-based serial killer. First was his hatred of the government over his father's death and his discharge from the military. Second was his need to project his self-contempt, so common in an identity-diffused adult, onto someone or something else. In Rudolph's case, the hatred he subconsciously felt toward himself was projected onto gays, Jews, and anyone involved in the abortion industry. This displacement of anger and hatred was justified and reinforced by his extremist ideology. And third, there is no doubt that the publicity the Centennial Park bombing received gave his self-identity a "shot-in-the-arm," however fleeting. This was only intensified by the positive strokes he received later from other extremist religious groups, some of whom considered him a hero.

Rudolph had not only found a way to act out his anger and hatred toward the government, but also a way to finally feel good about himself. He had found purpose and meaning for his life, and he was able with his ideology to easily justify his actions and convince himself he was holding the moral high ground. Arguably, he was only deterred morally (MDM), and thus met the CTT definition of a criminal personality type. This moral deterrence is evident in his efforts to avoid senseless murder in Centennial Park by tipping off the police, and the fact that he had no history of violent crime prior to the bombings. But he was neither deterred socially (SDM) nor internally (SeDM). And thus when his moral deterrence was weakened by the ideology that justified his deadly actions, he had no other internal deterrence mechanisms to fall back on.

Chapter 10

THEODORE "TED" BUNDY: THE FACE OF EVIL
An Opportunistic Killer

INTRODUCTION

No killer in American history has demonstrated a more insatiable desire to kidnap, torture, and kill than Theodore "Ted" Bundy. Many have described him as America's worst modern-day serial killer. Certainly he was one of the most evil and indiscriminate. While many serial killers are forced to rely on more violent methods to overpower their potential victims, Bundy did it with charm. He was handsome and charismatic, and was a master at manipulating people, especially young women. At times, he would impersonate a police officer to gain control over a victim. Other times he would feign an injury, always in a public place, to gain a victim's unknowing compliance. And then still at other times he would simply break into a house or apartment and blud-

Figure 10.1. Theodore Bundy.

geon his victims to death while they slept. By the time he was finally executed in Florida's electric chair on January 24, 1989, he had confessed to 30 murders across seven states between 1974 and 1978. However, that number remains an open question to this day.

Bundy's crimes were especially horrific. It was not enough to simply kill his victims, all young women, and even very young girls. He beat them, raped them—many times penetrating them with sharp objects that caused massive internal injuries while they were still conscious—and then most of the time committed postmortem sex acts with their bodies. He decapitated many of his victims, and even kept some of the heads in his apartment as trophies (Sullivan, 2009). Bundy described himself as "... the most cold-hearted son of a bitch you'll ever meet" (Michaud & Aynesworth, 1989), and one of his own defense attorneys called him "... the very definition of heartless evil" (Nelson, 1994). Had Bundy not been caught when he was, it is frightening to think how many victims he would have left behind on his trail of death across the country.

CRIMINAL BACKGROUND

No one knows for certain when Bundy began killing. There is some consensus that he began in 1961 as a young teenager, when he killed eight-year-old Ann Marie Burr of Tacoma, Washington, an allegation he denied throughout his many confessions (Keppel, 2005). His first confirmed attack occurred on January 4, 1974, when he entered the basement apartment of 18-year-old University of Washington student Karen Sparks. It was a brutal attack. As she awakened, Bundy bludgeoned her with a metal rod. He then sexually assaulted her with a metal speculum, a device used by physicians for inspecting body cavities, including the vagina, and then left her for dead. Sparks would survive the attack, but with severe internal injuries and permanent brain damage (Michaud & Aynesworth, 1989). A month later, using the same method of attack, Bundy murdered Lynda Ann Healy, also a UW student. He first beat her unconscious in her basement apartment, and then carried her to his car. From there he took her to a remote location in the mountains where he sexually assaulted and murdered her. Only a few of her bones were ever found (Nelson, 1994).

Following the Healy murder, Bundy began killing at the rate of about once every 30 days. On March 12, 1974, he kidnapped and murdered 19-year-old Donna Gail Manson, a student at Evergreen State College in Olympia, Washington. On April 17, Susan Elaine Rancourt disappeared after attending a meeting at Central Washington State College in Ellensburg, Washington. On May 6, Roberta Parks, a student at Oregon State University in Corvallis, disappeared on her way to meet up with friends at the student union. Bundy would confess to all three of these killings prior to his execution, and the bones of two of them, Rancourt and Parks, would eventually be found at his remote killing site on Taylor Mountain near Seattle (Michaud & Aynesworth, 1989).

By the summer of that year, detectives from both the King County Sheriff's Department and the Seattle Police Department were beginning to look into the rash of disappearances. Unfortunately, Bundy was just beginning his campaign of terror. On June 1, Brenda Carol Ball, 22, disappeared after leaving a Seattle nightclub. A witness saw her in the parking lot of the club talking to a dark-haired man with his arm in a sling. On June 11, Georgeann Hawkins, a UW student disappeared while walking at night from her boyfriend's dorm to her sorority house. A witness reported seeing a man in the alley behind the dormitory that night walking with crutches and struggling to carry a briefcase. Another witness recalled that the man was driving a light-brown Volkswagen (Sullivan, 2009). Like the others, Bundy would eventually confess to abducting the two women, sexually assaulting them, and then brutally killing them.

Bundy's final two Seattle-area killings took place on July 14 when he abducted two women four hours apart and in broad daylight from a crowded beach 20 miles east of the city. Once again, Bundy has his arm in a sling, and was asking young women on the beach for help unloading his sailboat from atop his car. Unbelievably, he introduced himself as "Ted," his real name. He first approached a group of five young women. One of them agreed to help, but when they approached his vehicle and she could see there was no sailboat, she fled. Bundy next asked Janice Anne Ott, 23, a caseworker for the King County Juvenile Court. Ott agreed to help, and walked with Bundy toward his vehicle. She was never seen again. Four hours later Denise Naslund, 18, left a picnic at the same park to use the restroom. She too was never seen again. Both of their skeletal remains would later be found at one of Bundy's killing sites just a few miles from the park (Sullivan, 2009).

Police now had a number of clues to go on, including a good description of Bundy and his vehicle, the name "Ted," and the presence of either an arm sling or a foot cast. Once the information was published, two people almost immediately recognized Bundy and called the police. One was Elizabeth Kloepfer, a woman Bundy was dating, and the other was Ann Rule, with whom Bundy worked at the Washington State Department of Emergency Services (DES), one of the agencies involved in the search for the missing women. Rule would go on to author a number of crime-related books, including *The Stranger Beside Me* (1989), a book about her relationship with Bundy. Both called the police to report that Bundy not only fit the description, but also drove a light-colored Volkswagen. Unfortunately the tips were among hundreds the police were receiving, and because Bundy fit no particular profile—by now he was a well-liked and charismatic law school student who had no criminal record—his name faded into the hundreds of others with no particular focus by the police.

In August, 1974, Bundy relocated to Salt Lake City after being accepted into Law School at the University of Utah. He had previously been attending the University of Puget Sound's law school. Almost immediately he again began raping and murdering women. On September 2, he raped and murdered a hitchhiker in Idaho who remains unidentified to this day. On October 2, he abducted 16-year-old Nancy Wilcox from a suburb of Salt Lake City, dragged her into a wooded area, and then raped and strangled her. On October 18, Melissa Smith, 18, and the daughter of the Midvale, Utah Chief of Police, disappeared after leaving a restaurant. Her nude body was discovered days later in a mountainous area. She had been beaten severely and raped. On October 31, 17-year-old Laura Ann Aime disappeared after leaving a restaurant in Lehi, Utah. Her body was discovered by hikers in a remote canyon location. She, too, had been beaten and raped (Sullivan, 2009).

On the evening of November 8, Carol DaRonch, 18, became one of the very few Bundy victims to escape. He approached her at a mall posing as a police investigator, informing the girl that someone had broken into her car, and that she would have to accompany him to the police station. DaRonch complied, but objected when she realized Bundy was driving in the wrong direction. Bundy pulled the car over to the side of the road and attempted to handcuff DaRonch, but during the struggle inadvertently placed both handcuffs on the same hand without realizing it. This allowed DaRonch to open the door and escape. Angered, Bundy quickly sought out another victim. That evening, 17-year-old Debra Kent disappeared after leaving a theater production at her high school in Bountiful, Utah. Witnesses later recounted that a stranger had asked them to accompany him to the parking lot to identify a vehicle. Other witnesses recalled seeing the man pacing in the back of the auditorium during the play. Outside in the parking lot, investigators found a handcuff key. The key fit the handcuffs that had been put on DaRonch during her struggle with Bundy. Kent's skeletal remains were eventually found nearly 100 miles from the school where she was abducted (Michaud & Aynesworth, 1989).

By the time of the Kent murder, Bundy was becoming a more credible suspect in the Seattle murders. Unfortunately physical evidence linking him to any of the crimes was lacking, and witnesses from the beach abductions had failed to pick him out of photo lineup. Also by the time, news had reached Elizabeth Kloepfer back in Seattle of the disappearances in the Salt Lake City area. She called the police in Salt Lake City and passed along her suspicions. Bundy's name was added to the suspect list, but again, no physical evidence existed linking him to any of the disappearances (Sullivan, 2009).

As 1975 rolled around, Bundy extended his killing field across the border into Colorado. On January 12, 23-year-old Caryn Campbell, a registered nurse, disappeared from her hotel in Snowmass Village, Colorado. Her badly beaten nude body was discovered a month later next to a nearby dirt road. On March 15, Julie Cunningham, 26, a ski instructor in Vail, Colorado, disappeared while walking from her apartment to meet a dinner date. On April 6, 25-year-old Denise Oliverson disappeared from Grand Junction, and a month later, 12-year-old Lynette Culver disappeared from Pocatello, Idaho. Bundy would later confess to all of the murders. In the case of Lynette Culver, Bundy admitted taking her to his hotel room, drowning her, and then sexually assaulting her postmortem. He disposed of her body in a nearby river (Sullivan, 2009).

On June 28, 1975, Bundy claimed his 18th victim in as many months when he abducted 28-year-old Susan Curtis from the campus of Brigham Young University in Provo, Utah. Though Bundy eventually confessed to her murder, her body was never found. Curtis would be his final murder prior to his first capture. In October, 1975, Bundy was arrested and charged with the aggravated kidnapping and attempted criminal assault of Carol DeRonch. Although he was now a strong suspect in both the Utah and Washington murders, there still was insufficient evidence linking him to any of them. Bundy finally went to trial on the charges in February, 1976, and after a four-day trial was found guilty. He was sentenced to one to 15 years in the Utah State Prison. Later that same month, Colorado authorities completed their investigation and Bundy was charged with the murder of Caryn Campbell. He waived extradition and was transferred to a jail in Aspen to await trial.

Bundy elected to serve as his own lawyer, and following a preliminary hearing on June 7, 1977, while being allowed to use the courthouse's law library without handcuffs or shackles, he slipped out a second-story window and escaped. He remained in the area hiding out for the next six days before being spotted and recaptured by Aspen police. Back in jail, Bundy immediately began hatching a new escape plan. He had secured a small hacksaw blade from another inmate, as well as $500 cash that had been smuggled in by visitors over the previous six months. He spent a number of weeks sawing a hole in the ceiling of his jail cell, and once through, spent a number of additional weeks climbing through the hole and into the upper crawl space late at night to look for an escape route. Back in his cell, he would put the sawed piece back in its place, making it barely noticeable from outside the cell.

On December 30, 1977, with only a skeleton crew of jail staff on duty, and most of the short-term prisoners allowed to be home for the holidays, Bundy made his move. He crawled through the hole in the ceiling, and knowing that the Chief Jailer and his wife, who lived in an upstairs apartment, were out for the evening, broke through the floor of their apartment and climbed out of the crawl space. He quickly changed into some street clothes he found in a bedroom closet, and then quietly walked out the door and into the darkness. This time the police would not be so lucky in finding him. An unsuspecting motorist gave him a ride to Vail, and from there he caught a bus to Denver where he boarded a flight to Chicago. By the time jail staff found him missing–he had stacked books under a blanket to make it look like he was in bed sleeping–he had already landed in Chicago.

From Chicago, Bundy took a circuitous route to Tallahassee, Florida. He first traveled by train to Ann Arbor, Michigan, and from there drove a stolen car to Atlanta where he boarded a bus for Tallahassee. He rented a boarding room near the campus of Florida State University under an alias name. He later told investigators that his intent in going to Florida was to discontinue killing and settle into a normal life under a new name (Rule, 2009). Unfortunately though, within a week of his arrival in Florida, his hunger for killing young women once again became too powerful to ignore. On the night of January 15, 1978 at approximately 2:45 a.m., with a nationwide manhunt by state and federal law enforcement now underway, Bundy entered the Chi Omega sorority house on the FSU campus through an unlocked door and began his hunt. He first bludgeoned 21-year-old Margaret Bowman with a piece of firewood, and then strangled her. Next he entered the room of Lisa Levy, 20, beat her unconscious, and then sexually assaulted her with a bottle. He then strangled her, leaving a deep bite mark on her left buttock, evidence that would be used against him at trial.

Before leaving, Bundy attacked two other young women–Kathy Kleiner and Karen Chandler–however both would survive, but with severe head injuries. In less than 15 minutes, he had brutally attacked four women, killing two of them. But even that wasn't enough. Only eight blocks from the sorority house, Bundy broke into yet another basement apartment and attacked FSU student Cheryl Thomas. She, too, survived the attack, but with permanent disabling injuries. On her bed police found semen stains and a pantyhose mask containing hairs that would later be matched to Bundy's (Sullivan, 2009).

Bundy knew his reign of terror was reaching its end. He knew the police dragnet was tightening, and that the sorority house murders would only intensify their search. On February 8, he drove east to Jacksonville in a stolen van. After unsuccessfully attempting to abduct a 14-year-old girl there, the daughter of the Jacksonville Police Department's Chief of Detectives, he drove back toward Tallahassee, stopping in Lake City, Florida. The next morning he abducted his last victim, 12-year-old Kimberly Diane Leach from her school. Weeks later her remains were found nearly 40 miles from the school (Rule, 2009).

After returning to Tallahassee, Bundy stole a car and headed west across the Florida panhandle. Near the Alabama border he was stopped by a Pensacola police officer after the officer determined that the car he was driving was stolen. Bundy made one last effort to escape by exiting the vehicle and attacking the approaching officer. After kicking the officer's legs out from under him, Bundy ran for it. The officer quickly pursued him, and within a short distance was able to tackle and handcuff him. It was the last breath of freedom Bundy would ever take. One of the most violent crime sprees in U.S. history had finally come to an end.

PERSONAL BACKGROUND

A number of biographers have provided accounts of Bundy's upbringing (Rule, 2009; Michaud & Aynesworth, 1989). All describe a fairly normal upbringing with loving parents and grandparents. Bundy was born Theodore Robert Crowell at the Elizabeth Lund Home for Unwed Mothers in Burlington, Vermont on November 24, 1946, to Louise Cowell, an unwed teenager. It was never certain who his father was. There was a discrepancy between what his birth certificate indicated and the man his mother would later identify as his father. Bundy never met either man. There was some speculation that Bundy's mother became pregnant by her own father; however, that was never confirmed, even by Louise Cowell in her later years (Michaud & Ayneworth, 1989).

For the first three years of his life, Bundy was raised by his grandparents in Philadelphia, believing them to be his parents and his young mother his older sister. Bundy described his grandfather as a loving man with whom he identified and clung to (Rule, 2009). Others have described him as a racist bully who abused his wife. There is no indication that Bundy's grandfather was abusive toward him. At the age of four, he and his mother moved west to Tacoma, Washington to live with one of Louise Cowell's cousins, a move that saddened the young boy, who did not want to leave his grandfather.

In Tacoma, Louise Cowell met a hospital cook named Johnny Bundy, and within a year they were married. Bundy legally adopted

Ted, and four siblings were eventually born. By all accounts, Johnny Bundy was a good father who attempted to form a close relationship with young Ted. Bundy described his childhood home just hours before his execution in an interview with Dr. James Dobson (Ted Bundy, personal communication, January 23, 1989):

> I grew up in a wonderful home with two dedicated and loving parents, as one of 5 brothers and sisters. We, as children, were the focus of my parent's lives. We regularly attended church. My parents did not drink or smoke or gamble. There was no physical abuse or fighting in the home. I'm not saying it was "Leave it to Beaver", but it was a fine, solid Christian home.

Much of Bundy's life in Tacoma remains a mystery, mostly because Bundy himself was never consistent in describing his upbringing there. One circumstance he did discuss on multiple occasions prior to his execution was his fascination at an early age, a fascination bordering on obsession, with pornography and true crime magazines containing graphic depictions of rape, murder, and sexual mutilation (Michaud & Aynesworth, 1989). He would dig through people's garbage looking for pictures and magazines that satisfied his craving for such images. He also began looking in people's windows at night attempting to catch a glimpse of a woman undressing. During this time, he also started stealing, and would eventually be arrested twice for suspicion of burglary and auto theft. Despite these transgressions, he seemed to have no significant problems in school, and his classmates later described him as a well-liked kid who was fairly well known among the school body (Rule, 2009). Bundy himself, however, would tell interviewers prior to his execution that he had no real friends, and that he chose to be alone (Michaud & Aynesworth, 1989).

After graduating from high school in 1965, Bundy entered college at the University of Puget Sound. After just a year, he transferred to the University of Washington, where he studied Chinese for two years before dropping out. During this time he also began a relationship with a UW classmate named Stephanie Brooks. By all accounts Bundy was quite taken by Brooks; however, the relationship would be short-lived. Frustrated by his lack of maturity and the fact that he was now working mostly minimum-wage jobs, Brooks broke off the relationship after graduating from UW and returning to her home in California.

Although some have suggested that the breakup devastated Bundy (Nelson, 1994), he would later re-establish his relationship with Brooks and break it off himself, even after the two began discussing marriage.

In a strange twist, after dropping out of UW, Bundy developed an interest in politics, and began working as a volunteer in the Seattle office of Nelson Rockefeller's 1968 presidential campaign. He even attended the Republican National Convention in Miami that year as a Rockefeller delegate. Bundy seemed to be finding purpose in his life, and he re-enrolled at UW, this time as a psychology major. At the same time he met and began his relationship with Elizabeth Kloepfer, who later would provide one of the critical tips leading to his identification as a suspect, both in Washington and Utah.

This time around, Bundy did quite well in college. He was well respected by his professors and became an honor student. In 1971, to gain experience in an area related to his studies, he became a volunteer at Seattle's Suicide Hotline Crisis Center. Fellow employees later described him as kind and empathic (Rule, 2009). He remained there until graduating from UW in 1972. Upon graduating he joined the re-election campaign of Governor Daniel J. Evans, and later took a job with the Washington State Republican Party. In 1973, Bundy was accepted into law school at UPS, but almost immediately began having problems keeping up with the tough academic regimen. When his grades began to suffer, he started skipping classes. This only exacerbated the problem; by the end of his first semester in law school, he simply quit attending at all. At the same time, young women in the area began disappearing, and one of the most brutal killing sprees in U.S. history had begun.

ANALYSIS AND CLASSIFICATION

Preidentification Inputs

Unfortunately, at the time of Bundy's crimes, the law enforcement community in America did not yet have a fully integrated computer infrastructure. Consequently, it was difficult for departments to share information about missing persons and unsolved homicides. In Bundy's case, had they made the connection, they would've seen obvious evidence of the type of killer he was. The best evidence of course comes from witnesses, especially the victims who survived his attacks. Consider the following inputs that could have been, and in some cases were connected early on.

• Almost all of the missing women were college students. Some have made much of the fact that Bundy's victims all resembled a former fiancé, but even Bundy himself discounted that theory. The fact is, the college campuses were Bundy's hunting grounds. This type of evidence would indicate a predatory killer, one who methodically searched for, stalked, and abducted his victims. His killing became his avocation. His selection of mostly attractive victims indicates a killer who had a preferential taste. This would point to an opportunistic killer. It would support the idea that for such a killer the act of killing is the primary focus. A symbolic offender, too, may choose a particular type of victim, but they are less concerned about where they find them. For them, the goal is to calm the internal rage and hatred that tends to build until they take steps to reduce those emotions. They are more opportunistic in their victim selection, and once they set out to kill, they will take any opportunity that presents itself, including the easiest opportunity—the street-level prostitute.

• It is also important to consider that Bundy was actually breaking into people's apartments to carry out his attacks. This truly indicates an opportunistic killer, someone for whom the method of attack is a critical component. The opportunistic killer has a proven routine, one that is sure to satisfy their needs and desires. A symbolic or ego-directed killer simply needs to kill, and in most cases to do it quickly. If there is a sexual component, then a rape typically occurs, followed by the murder. In both cases, they tend to take the easiest route to selecting a victim, since the specificity of the victim is of little consequence. For the opportunistic killer, however, the victim is everything, as is the method of killing.

• Eighteen-year-old Karen Sparks was his first confirmed attack. Bundy bludgeoned her with a metal rod, and then sexually assaulted her with a metal speculum, a device used by physicians to inspect body cavities. This, too, indicates an opportunistic killer, one for whom the method is important. While a symbolic killer may out of rage assault a female victim with an object, the use of speculum, which was known to police since Sparks survived the attack, indicates a fantasy component to the killing, again indicative of an opportunistic offender.

• There were numerous eyewitness accounts of Bundy approaching women either walking with crutches or with his arm in a sling. Once again, this circumstance would point to an opportunistic killer who was using a particular method for stalking and abducting his victims. It points to a killer who is "act-focused," unlike either the symbolic or ego-directed killer. Also, the frequency of confirmed sightings and missing women would indicate that the killer was not experiencing a "cycle of violence," or alternating periods of calm and tension so often experienced by both the symbolic and ego-directed killers. In this case, the killer was preoccupied with stalking, abducting, torturing, and killing young women, even to the extent of becoming psychologically addicted to the act. There was no "cooling off" period and returning to a normal life until the tension again began to build. In looking at the timing and method of the killings, assuming investigators could have connected them, it should have been obvious not only that the killer would continue killing, but would likely increase their rate of murder as their appetite for such cruelty intensified.

• Bundy's crime scenes had all the tell-tale signs of an opportunistic killer, especially his killing site on Taylor Mountain near Seattle. Had investigators found the location prior to Bundy's capture, they would have found evidence of torture, dismemberment, postmortem sexual activity, and even the application of makeup to some of the victim's corpses. There was evidence that the killer periodically returned to the site to again perform sex acts on the bodies, which Bundy later admitted to. This type of evidence would point either to a mentally ill killer, or to a completely sane but psychopathic-opportunistic killer. When evaluated along with the other evidence from surviving victims and eyewitnesses, they would have known they were most certainly dealing with the latter.

• One final important preidentification input was the fact that Bundy also abducted and killed young girls. This indicates that he was focused on the act of killing rather than the specific victim. It also indicates a pedophilic component to the killer's motivation, which typically rules out a symbolic offender. In the case of an ego-directed killer, the question is whether killing children can somehow fill the void in their sense of self. Given our cultural beliefs about pedophilia, and the utter disdain society holds for those who harm children, it is unlikely, though not entirely out of the question, that an ego-directed killer will resort to killing innocent children as a way of calming their self-directed contempt. If they do, then it is likely that all of their victims will be children, not just a few occasionally mixed in with adult victims. In almost all cases of serial murder involving child victims, there is an opportunistic or mentally ill offender at work.

From the preidentification inputs, it was obvious that Bundy was a psychotic, predatory killer who selected his victims and murdered them in ways that satisfied his sadistic needs and desires. There were specific types of victims he selected, as well as opportunistic abductions, such as children, and specific ways of killing them. Investigators could have ruled out a mentally ill offender based on the eyewitness accounts of Bundy. He was handsome, well kempt and well-spoken, drove a vehicle, and took well-planned steps to manipulate and deceive his victims into a position where he could complete his attack and abduction.

Postidentification Inputs

The best evidence we have pointing to the type of offender Bundy was are his own words. While it can be argued that even some serial killers have fragments of an internal deterrence system, Bundy had none. He was completely egocentric and felt no sympathetic arousal at all for his victims. On the eve of his execution, Bundy granted an interview to Christian broadcaster Dr. James Dobson on January 23, 1989. The interview allows us to peer into the mind of a sadistic psychopath who did everything for self-pleasure, and whose entire adult life was a series of manipulations designed to protect the fragile façade he projected to the world.

Like all psychopaths, Bundy was egocentric to the extreme. He felt no emotional connection to anyone, and even when he purported to, it was yet another manipulation designed to shroud the monster within. He endeavored to project to the outward world a certain image of *self* because, like all psychopaths, there really was no real *self* to express naturally. Psychopaths live in fear of being exposed for what they really are. Consider the following response to Dobson's question about killing 12-year-old Kimberly Leach:

> I can't really talk about that right now. It's too painful. I would like to be able to convey to you what that experience is like, but I won't be able to talk about that.

The fact is, there is nothing about recalling the brutal murder of a young child that is "too painful" for Bundy. In fact, he probably replayed the murder over and over in his mind with a great amount of personal satisfaction. What was too painful for Bundy was the possibility of being labeled a "pedophile," a characteristic entirely inconsistent with the image of self he attempted to portray. Psychopaths are narcissistic to the extreme. Bundy projected an image of being intelligent, handsome, and well-liked by people. Being labeled a pedophile was simply something he could not handle.

In response to that same question by Dobson, Bundy states the following:

> I can't begin to understand the pain that the parents of these children and young women that I have harmed feel.

Throughout his exchange with Dobson, Bundy portrays himself as a victim. In his case, a victim of violent pornography. Even on the eve of his execution, he has difficulty facing the reality of what he did, not because of the brutality of his acts, but because it exposes him as the psychopathic fraud he knows he is. He did not "harm" these children and young women. He brutally tortured, raped, and murdered them. We see this emotional denial throughout the interview. Later he says:

> During the past few days, myself and a number of investigators have been talking about unsolved cases–murders I was involved in.

Bundy wasn't just "involved" in the murders, he committed them! By saying it this way he is depersonalizing the acts, and thus keeping the spotlight of responsibility again from shining brightly on no one but him. He attempts throughout this entire interview to portray himself as but one cog in the wheel. In his formulation, again, one designed to protect his very fragile façade, the murders involved a cast of players; not just him, but the victims, their families, pornography, society, and his childhood conditioning. He presents an emotionless summary of events almost in an academic manner, as if there is something to be learned from his experiences. In almost every statement he makes he is deflecting the reality he cannot face, that he has been found out to be nothing more than a cold-blooded, and at times pedophilic murderer.

Bundy also presents an idealized version of his upbringing and home life. He states:

> I grew up in a wonderful home with two dedicated and loving parents, as one of 5 brothers and sisters. We, as children, were the focus of my parent's lives. We regularly attended church. My parents did not drink or smoke or gamble. There was no physical abuse or fighting in the home. I'm not saying it was "Leave it to Beaver", but it was a fine, solid Christian home.

His version of his upbringing, which evidence suggests is not entirely true, is designed to lend credence to his assertion that violent pornography is what compelled his brutal acts. After all, the effects of violent pornography must be powerful if it can do this to a normal Christian boy who was the focus of his parents' lives. Once again he employs manipulative devices to avoid taking emotional responsibility for what he did. He does so even more blatantly when he discusses the aftermath of his killings:

> There is no way to describe the brutal urge to do that, and once it has been satisfied, or spent, and that energy level recedes, I became myself again. Basically, I was a normal person. Ted: I wasn't some guy hanging out in bars, or a bum. I wasn't a pervert in the sense that people look at somebody and say, "I know there's something wrong with him." I was a normal person. I had good friends. I led a normal life, except for this one, small but very potent and destructive segment that I kept very secret and close to myself. Those of us who have been so influenced by violence in the media, particularly pornographic violence, are not some kind of inherent monsters.

Now Bundy protects his fragile *self* by disconnecting it in a sense from the murderous acts he committed. There was nothing normal about Bundy, neither before, during, or after his murders. Bundy was a Psychology undergrad in college. He knew about the "cycle of violence" some offenders experience—serial rapists, domestic abusers, some serial killers. But he felt no such emotional cycle. By claiming he did, he was able to compartmentalize his murders and cast blame on the "other" Ted Bundy, the one outside his control. Once again, even on the eve of his execution, he could not face being exposed for what he really was.

Classification

Ted Bundy was an opportunistic killer, perhaps America's worst. He killed to satisfy his sadistic sexual desires, which included torture and postmortem dismemberment and sexual activity. He selected victims who were most satisfying to him—attractive young women—but when an opportunity to abduct and kill a victim not fitting that profile presented itself, such as an unattended child on a playground, he took advantage of the situation. For him, it was the act of killing that motivated him, not any internal rage (symbolic) or self-contempt (ego-directed). He simply killed because he enjoyed it.

In Bundy's last narcissistic attempt to protect his psychopathic sense of *self*, he blamed his actions on an addiction to violent pornography. It was an effort on his part to separate the "normal" Ted, who presumably would never commit such heinous acts, from the Ted who because of his addiction to pornography had no control over his own behavior. Either way, he was avoiding any sense of responsibility for what he had done. It wasn't the pornography that had led to his offending, but rather a complete lack of any internal deterrence system, typical of a psychopath. He felt no sympathy for his victims, nor for anyone else. He was entirely egocentric, and what even normal people sometimes fantasize about, but then for reasons of morality quickly send to the far reaches of their mind to be forgotten or repressed, Bundy overtly acted out. He lacked any degree of morality to deter him, and thus sought to fulfill his sexual desires with absolutely no internal controls on his behavior. If ever a criminal offender deserved the descriptor "evil incarnate," it was certainly Ted Bundy.

Chapter 11

EDMUND KEMPER: THE CO-ED KILLER
A Symbolic Killer

INTRODUCTION

Edmund Kemper is often identified by the infamous moniker, "Coed Butcher." Now living out his years in a California prison for killing multiple women in the 1970s, he is among the worst of America's serial killers. But Kemper didn't become a brutal serial killer overnight, and certainly not without the help of an abusive mother who derailed his psychosocial development at an early age. He is a classic example of the symbolic killer, one whose victims serve as surrogates for the true object of their rage and hatred, typically a parent. In Kemper's case it was the oppressive mother who

Figure 11.1. Edmund Kemper.

viewed her son as an unattractive sexual deviant—even forcing him at a young age to sleep in a cold basement out of fear that he might rape his own sister—who had no hope of ever developing friendships or intimate relationships, an assertion she repeated often.

It is during the critical periods of childhood and adolescence when the developing personality is at risk of taking a wrong turn; one that is extremely difficult, if not impossible, to correct once those attitudes and values have been internalized.

CRIMINAL BACKGROUND

Following his release at age 21 from the Atascadero State Hospital for the Criminally Insane in 1969, having been sent there as a juvenile after murdering his own grandparents, Kemper made efforts to return to a normal life. He first moved in with his mother, who by now was living in Santa Cruz, California, where she had taken a job at the University of California at Santa Cruz. According to Cheney (1992), he was released to the care and custody of his mother against the wishes of several of his doctors at Atascadero who were well aware of the volatility of their relationship. It was a decision that would have disastrous consequences.

By early 1972, Kemper was employed by the California Highway Department, and had even applied for a job as a California Highway patrolman. At 6'9", and over 300 pounds, his application was rejected because of his size. During this time, he had befriended a number of police officers in an around Santa Cruz, and routinely drank with them at a local bar the police frequented. These friendships, which he actively sought, would ultimately allow him to stay one step ahead of investigators when his killing spree finally began. The officers would freely discuss Kemper's murders in his presence, having no suspicion at all that the killer was in their midst.

Kemper's murders began in May, 1972. He had been practicing for months picking up and dropping off hitchhikers (Cheney, 1992). It was a prelude to his planned crimes. He reached a point finally on May 7th when he felt mentally prepared to escalate his activities to the next brutal level. On that day, driving his 1969 Ford in Berkeley,

California, Kemper picked up two 18-year-old Fresno State students—Mary Ann Pesce and Anita Luchessa—and agreed to give them a ride to Stanford University. They never reached their destination. Kemper drove to a secluded area near Alameda, California, stabbed both of the girls to death, and then transported their bodies back to his apartment in Santa Cruz in the trunk of his car (Stephens, 1973).

Back at home, Kemper took the two bodies inside, took a series of pornographic pictures, and then engaged in various sex acts. He then dismembered the bodies, placing the body parts in plastic bags, and set out to discard the remains in multiple locations near Loma Prieta Mountain. Both of the girls' heads were discarded in a nearby ravine, but not before Kemper performed oral sex with one of them (Ramsland, n.d.). It was a gruesome ending to his first foray into serial killing. On August 15, 1972, one of the heads, that of Mary Ann Pesce, was discovered by hikers. No other remains were ever found, but it was assumed that Luchessa, too, had been murdered. The police were now actively looking for a killer on the loose.

It would be four months before Kemper again decided to kill. The opportunity came on September 14, 1972, when we happened onto 15-year-old Aiko Koo, who was hitchhiking to her dance class from her home in Berkeley after missing the bus. Almost immediately after Koo got into the car, Kemper pulled out a gun and held her at bay until he was able to reach a more secluded spot outside of town. There he immediately strangled her to death and had sex with her corpse (Newton, 2006).

On January 7, 1973, Kemper came across 19-year-old Cindy Schall near the campus of Cabrillo College. Schall had stopped at a friend's house a short time earlier and told the friend she was hitchhiking to class at the college. The friend witnessed her getting in a vehicle moments after leaving the house. It was the last time anyone would see her alive. Kemper drove Schall to a wooded area where he immediately shot and killed her. He then placed her body in the trunk of his car and drove to his mother's house. There he dismembered Schall's body in the bathtub, and as a joke, buried her head in his mother's garden. He later quipped to investigators that his mother liked talking down to people, so he decided to give her someone to talk down to (Newton, 2006). Two days later Schall's arms and legs were found on a cliff overlooking the Pacific Ocean, and a short time later her torso and hand washed ashore. The body parts were quickly identified as belonging to Schall.

By now, the police knew they had a serial killer on their hands. Making matters worse, Kemper wasn't the only serial killer operating in the area. In late 1972 and early 1973, another series of brutal murders, 13 in all, occurred in the Santa Cruz area. The victims included men, women, children, and even the priest the killer eventually confessed to. The killer, 25-year-old Herbert Mullin, was quickly arrested after committing his final murder in broad daylight. He was later found to be severely schizophrenic, and believed his murders would somehow save California from a super-earthquake. Although mentally ill, Mullin was found to be legally sane, and was ultimately convicted of ten of the murders and sentenced to life in prison (Lunde & Morgan, 1980).

Unlike Mullin, Kemper was completely sane. He was very cunning, and by now, he was hanging out with local police as often as he could to stay abreast of the ongoing murder investigations. The police wanted to pin all the unsolved homicides on Mullin, but they were fairly certain after looking at the evidence that two killers were operating in the area. Kemper's crimes appeared to be well planned, and the dismemberment of his victims' bodies was clean and done with some amount of precision. Mullins, on the other hand, acted impulsively, and appeared to be unconcerned about leaving evidence behind. He, too, dismembered some of his victims' bodies, but his style was reckless and imprecise (Faraci, 2013). As police speculated on these issues, Kemper kept a close ear to the discussions. He was staying one step ahead of investigators by knowing their every move.

On February 5, 1973, the day before Mullin would murder four teenage boys camping in Henry Cowell Redwoods State Park, Kemper left his house in search of a victim after having an especially bad argument with his mother. While driving through the UC Santa Cruz campus, he came across 24-year-old Rosalind Thorpe and 23-year-old Alice Liu walking. He offered them a ride, and they both got in his car. Almost immediately after leaving the campus grounds Kemper drew his .22 caliber pistol hidden beside his door and shot and killed both of the girls. He then wrapped their bodies in blankets in his back seat and drove to a remote location where he sexually abused both of the corpses. The next morning he dumped their dismembered remains in a ravine near San Francisco. A week later they were found by hikers (Newton, 2006).

On April 20, 1973 (Good Friday), for reasons perhaps known only to Kemper, he decided to end his killing spree, but not before committing one final series of brutal acts. On that night, he was awakened by his mother as she returned from a party. A short time later, he entered her room to find her in bed and reading a book. According to Kemper, when his mother saw him enter the room she said, "I suppose you're going to want to sit up all night and talk now?" They would be her final words. Moments later, Kemper had beaten her to death with a claw hammer. He then decapitated her and used her head for oral sex. In a final symbolic act he removed her vocal cords and attempted to dispose of them in the garbage disposal, but they were ejected back out. Kemper later told investigators, "that seemed appropriate, as much as she'd bitched and screamed and yelled at me over the years" (Newton, 2006).

A short time after killing his mother, Kemper phoned her best friend, 59-year-old Sally Hallett, and invited her to the house. Once again, for reasons perhaps known only to Kemper, once she arrived, he immediately strangled her. Her murder would be his final act of violence. He left the house and drove eastward through Nevada and Utah. He finally stopped at a phone booth in Pueblo, Colorado and called the Santa Cruz Police Department. Surprisingly, when he attempted to confess to the dispatcher that he had killed his mother and her best friend, the dispatcher refused to take him seriously and told him to call back later. A short time later, he did call back, and this time demanded to speak to an officer he knew. When the officer got on the phone, he not only confessed to the murders of his mother and Sally Hallett, but also to the missing coeds the police were still investigating. The officer, too, was reluctant to believe Kemper, but agreed to go to his mother's house to confirm the murders. Kemper agreed to remain at the phone booth. Within an hour of making the call, Pueblo police had Kemper in custody, and his killing spree was thankfully brought to an end.

PERSONAL BACKGROUND

Edmund Kemper was born in Southern California on December 18, 1948, to Clarnell and Edmund Kemper, Sr. As a child, Edmund Jr. had a very good and close relationship with his father, but his mother was a violent alcoholic with whom he had a terrible relationship. She would often belittle and verbally abuse him, and routinely favored his two sisters. When he was nine years old, his parents divorced, mostly caused by his mother's alcoholism and mental illness. It has been reported that she suffered from *borderline personality disorder* (Lawson, 2002). Kemper remained with his mother and sisters after the divorce, moving with them to Helena, Montana, and the split only intensified tensions between the young boy and his mother.

Kemper began demonstrating behavioral problems almost immediately after arriving in Montana. He was extremely bright but had difficulties making and keeping friends. He also started abusing animals, and was becoming more and more violent toward his two sisters. He acted out bizarre sex acts with his sister's dolls and exhibited a dark and active fantasy life (Martingale, 1995). It was during this time when his mother began humiliating him by referring to Kemper as a sexual pervert she feared would rape his own sisters if precautions were not taken. She began making him sleep in a locked basement.

In the summer of 1963, Kemper ran away from home and located his father in Van Nuys, California. He learned that his father had remarried and had another son. He stayed with his father for a short time before being sent back to Montana. His mother, however, did not want him back, and forced him to move in with his paternal grandparents, Edmund and Maude Kemper, in North Fork, California. His relationship with them deteriorated almost immediately. Kemper described his grandfather as being senile, and his grandmother was in some ways as abusive toward him as his mother. He would later say that his grandmother constantly emasculated both him and his grandfather (Von Beroldingen, 1974). It wasn't long before the rage he felt toward his abusive mother was projected onto his grandmother. It wouldn't be long before that rage would boil over in a brutal and deadly way.

On August 27, 1964, after an especially bad argument with his grandmother, Kemper grabbed his grandfather's rifle, his course already decided. His grandmother saw him grab the gun, and warned him not to shoot the birds. Unfortunately it was not the birds he wanted to kill. With little thought or emotion, he turned the gun on his grandmother as she sat at the kitchen table and killed her with a single shot to the head. He then stabbed her repeatedly with a kitchen knife (Ramsland, n.d.). While he was dragging her body to the bedroom, he heard his grandfather's car pull up outside. Kemper grabbed the rifle and stepped onto the front porch as his grandfather got out of the vehicle. He took aim, and with a single shot, his grandfather, too, was dead. He would later tell investigators that he killed his grandfather because he knew he would be mad at him for killing his grandmother (Edmund Kemper, 2014). As Margaret Cheney (1992) would later write about the murders, "in his way, he had avenged the rejection of both his father and mother."

At the young age of 15, Edmund Kemper had now committed multiple murders. Because he was a juvenile, rather than being convicted and sentenced to a lengthy prison term, he was instead committed to Atascadero State Hospital for the remainder of his juvenile years. There his behavior was exemplary. He became an assistant to a staff psychiatrist, administering psychological tests and maintaining files. During this time, Kemper himself was tested and found to have an IQ of 136. As an adult, he reportedly would test as high as 145 (Russell, 2002). His time assisting the psychiatrist allowed him to watch, listen, and learn, and by the time he reached the age of 21, the point at which a decision would be made whether to release him or continue his commitment, he knew just what to say and how to act. Against the wishes of at least some of the doctors at the facility, Kemper was released back to the custody of his mother. He was no longer the young boy who had been committed nearly five years earlier. He was now 6'9" and weighed nearly 300 pounds. In a short amount of time, the internal rage that had at least temporarily been quieted during his commitment was now about to boil back to the surface in a deadly way.

ANALYSIS AND CLASSIFICATION

Preidentification Inputs

Investigators in the Kemper case had the unbelievable problem of a second serial killer being active in the same location and at the same time. Herbert Mullin was mentally ill, and his crime scenes reflected the disorganized and impulsive nature of his killings.

One important characteristic of Kemper's crimes was that he decapitated his victims. He also tended to discard the heads in areas apart from the bodies. Decapitation is common among the most brutal of serial killers, but their motivations may differ. There are three predominant reasons for committing such a heinous act:

• *Possession*–Some serial killers choose to keep their victims' heads. It allows them to maintain a perverse sense of attachment to them. They may continue to carry on conversations with the remains or even engage in sex acts. Some have kept the skulls once decomposition has had its effect. These killers tend either to be mentally ill or *ego-directed* offenders with a deficient sense of sexuality. They are typically loners who have never experienced intimacy or a normal relationship, and in a sense, by keeping their victims' heads, they are able to enjoy what in their minds is the most intimate type of relationship, and with someone who can never leave or reject them.

• *Sexual Sadism*–These killers decapitate their victims because they derive some sexual gratification from doing so. A classic example of this type of offender is Ted Bundy. They tend to be *opportunistic* offenders who get the ultimate thrill from the ultimate form of mutilation. With the sexual sadist, it is typical that other forms of mutilation will accompany the decapitation, especially genital mutilation. There may also be evidence of torture and mutilation while the victim is still alive, and there will always be evidence of sexual activity.

• *Dehumanization*–This type of killer will decapitate their victims as a form of dehumanization and humiliation. They commit their crimes out of anger, and will most likely fall in the category of *symbolic* offender. The decapitation may or may not be accompanied by other forms of mutilation or sexual activity. This type of decapitation may be difficult to distinguish from the sexual sadist; however, if efforts are made to manipulate the victim's appearance with make-up, clothes, or in other ways, then it is likely that the individual is carrying out their crimes for sexual gratification. This was the case with Ted Bundy.

In Kemper's case, investigators knew he was disposing of his victims' heads in locations apart from the bodies. There was also evidence that he had used some of the remains to perform oral sex on. Given the organized and well-planned nature of his crimes, it was evident they were not dealing with a mentally ill offender. His crimes had both symbolic and opportunistic characteristics. The frequency of his murders, with a number of months typically passing from one to the next, would point to a killer who was able to control his urges, and who perhaps lacked the insatiable desire to kill that serial killers like Bundy and Gary Ridgeway, the *Green River killer,* as well as H.H. Holmes a century earlier, all demonstrated. This circumstance would point more to a symbolic killer, one with enough restraint or internal deterrence to keep his murderous behavior in check until stressors in his life caused it to boil over.

As far as victim selection, Kemper chose primarily college students who were walking from one location to another. This would indicate a killer who was very methodical, and who picked his victims based on the level of risk. College students tend to be far from home, with fewer community contacts and involvement, and in many cases can go days without being seen before anyone notices or becomes suspicious. He was not opportunistic in his selection, but would hunt for a specific type of victim at a specific time and location. He also operated in a relatively small geographic area. This would point to an individual who was established in the Santa Cruz area.

From the preidentification inputs, it would have been apparent that Kemper was probably a sane, intelligent, and sociable individual who had the ability to manipulate young women to get into his vehicle; sometimes more than one woman at the same time. The fact that he used a handgun would indicate that he was not interested in torturing his victims, but rather, killing them quickly in order to engage in postmortem sexual activity. In the absence of torture and mutilation while his victims were alive, it would indicate that his practice of decapitating his victims was for the purpose of depersonalizing and humiliating them, thus pointing to a symbolic killer. The frequency of his killings, and the relatively consistent intervals between, would indicate a killer caught in a deadly cycle of violence; one able to abstain from further killing until tensions rose to compel him to seek out another victim in order to calm those tensions. This would point away from an opportunistic offender; one who kills more frequently and with no consistent time intervals in-between.

Postidentification Inputs

Within a short amount of time after identifying Kemper as the "Co-ed butcher," two important pieces of the puzzle came to light. First was the fact that in his final murderous act before turning himself in, he killed his own mother and her best friend. Even the murder of his mother's friend was a symbolic gesture directed at his mother. After committing those final brutal acts, Kemper's killing spree had reached its conclusion. He had no need to kill any longer because the object of his hatred was now dead. It is also quite telling that he decapitated his mother just like his victims, and even humiliated her further by performing oral sex with her head. This not only demonstrated the abject hatred he held for her, but also shed light on why he committed such acts with his other victims. In short, he decapitated his mother to depersonalize and humiliate her, not to enjoy any sense of sexual gratification. His reasons were the same when his victims were merely surrogates for the person he most wanted to kill.

During one jailhouse interview, one of many Kemper has granted over the years, he discusses the murder of his mother:

> One week before I murdered my mother I said, she's got to die, and I got to die . . . she said, for seven years I haven't had sex with a man because of you, my murderous son. So I killed her and humiliated her corpse . . . six young women dead because of the way she raises her son. (Irishredrose, 2010)

In this same interview, when the interviewer asks why he decided to give himself up after killing his mother, he responds, "It had to stop. Once my mother was dead it was almost a cathartic process." With this statement, Kemper demonstrates some degree of remorse for his actions, both at the time of the interview and during his killing spree. This clearly would not be the case with an opportunistic offender. Most in that category feel absolutely no sympathy for their victims or remorse following their crimes.

Classification

Edmund Kemper is a classic symbolic offender. After losing his father at a young age following divorce, he was raised by an abusive and alcoholic mother whose constant humiliation and verbal abuse of him led to an extremely dysfunctional relationship, and thus an insecure attachment. He likely blamed his mother for his parents' divorce, and when he eventually went to live with his grandparents, the hatred he felt toward his mother was projected onto his overbearing grandmother, the woman who would eventually become his first murder victim. His insecure attachment precluded him from developing normal friendships and relationships, and spending his later adolescent years confined to a psychiatric facility disrupted any normal identity-formation.

It can be argued that Kemper did develop some sense of morality, and thus did demonstrate to some degree of an internal deterrence system. There is no indication that he engaged in crime or violent behavior apart from his murders, and even aspired to being a police officer at one point. Also, he eventually turned himself in to stop the murders he believed he was incapable of stopping himself. Unlike opportunistic killers like Ted Bundy and John Wayne Gacy, Kemper has shown remorse for his actions.

Edmund Kemper provides a striking example of the power a parent has to shape their children through their words and actions. In his case, the abusive demeanor of his mother turned an innocent young boy into the monster he became. Do we place all the blame on his mother? The answer, of course, is no. Ultimately, Kemper had the cognitive ability to understand the difference between right and wrong. He knew the torment of his victims and their families. No one but Edmund Kemper made the decision to take an innocent person's life, and then to repeat that brutal act multiple times. But we can place a good amount of blame squarely on the back of his mother for shaping the type of personality in her young son, and long before he had the ability to shape his own personality, that would perceive the benefits of killing innocent young women as outweighing the potential consequences. In his case, the benefit he derived from each of his murders was the symbolic death of his mother, indeed a transitory benefit, but one that at least calmed the internal rage that was so negatively impacting his life. It was a rage that would only be quieted when the murder of his mother by his own hands was no longer a symbolic gesture.

Chapter 12

THE ZODIAC KILLER
A Lingering Mystery

INTRODUCTION

Since the 1990s, the phenomenon of the serial killer has been greatly overshadowed in the American press by the *mass killer*–the person who enters a school, theater, or post office and shoots as many people as they possibly can before the police kill them, or they kill themselves. Mass killers have never grabbed the public's fascination in the same way the serial killers of the 1960s–1980s did. The biggest reason is because very few of them survive their crimes. Those who do seem more often than not to be mentally ill. And because their murders all happen at the same time, neither the police nor the press ever gets the chance to assign some colorful moniker to know them by until that they are eventually identified and captured.

Figure 12.1. Artist's rendering of the Zodiac killer.

The era of the serial killer was also the era of the airline hijacker. The latter came to a close with an unsolved mystery still lingering in the collective mind of the public–the case of D. B. Cooper. The man who in 1971 came to be known by the alias used to purchase his plane ticket was never identified after parachuting from a Boeing 727 somewhere over the Pacific Northwest with a bag of money under his arm. The longer he went unidentified by the FBI, the larger his legend grew. Everyone had a theory about his identity, and as people oftentimes do, their speculation took them more in the direction of hero than villain. In a short amount of time, after a number of books, movies, and songs added to the growing myth, a man who deserved the reputation of a common criminal had somehow been transformed into a modern-day Robin Hood.

The era of the serial killer is not without its own lingering mystery, the case of the *Zodiac killer,* who operated in the San Francisco Bay area between December 1968 and October 1969. Still unidentified over 40 years after his crimes, Zodiac is believed to have attacked seven individuals, five of whom died from their wounds. The moniker "Zodiac" originated from a series of letters the killer sent to local newspapers that included mysterious cryptograms. Perhaps it is the mystery of the killer's methods, or simply the fact that he has never been identified, but Zodiac still fascinates the public decades later. Like D. B. Cooper, there have been books, songs, and movies about the killer, and also like Cooper, there have been a number of possible suspects identified by amateur investigators and profilers, none of whom have ever been identified as credible suspects by the police. Not only does the fascination with Zodiac continue to this day, but both the San Francisco Police Department and the California Department of Justice maintain open case files; files that were opened nearly 45 years ago following the first attack.

CRIMINAL BACKGROUND

Zodiac's killing spree began on the night of December 20, 1968 on Lake Herman Road in Benicia, California. Two high school students, Betty Lou Jensen and David Faraday, were on their first date, and around 10:15 p.m. pulled into a gravel turnout that was a well-known lover's lane. Approximately 30 minutes later, their bodies were found by a local resident. Both had been shot to death. Police determined from the available evidence that someone had pulled up in a car beside Faraday's car and apparently ordered the couple out of the car. Faraday was shot in the head as he exited the vehicle and died immediately. Jensen appeared to have run from the vehicle, probably after Faraday was shot. She was found laying dead approximately 30 feet away with five shots in her back. Tracks were visible where the killer then drove away from the scene (Graysmith, 2007).

By the time Zodiac struck again on July 4, 1969, the police still had not developed a credible lead in the Lake Herman Road murders. Just before midnight, Darlene Ferrin, 22, and Michael Mageau, 19, parked their car in Blue Rock Springs Park in Vallejo. The park was only four miles from Lake Herman Road. Mageau, who survived the attack, reported that a car pulled in beside theirs, but then quickly drove away. The car returned ten minutes later, but this time parked behind them. The driver got out and walked to the passenger side of Mageau's vehicle and shined a flashlight inside. Almost immediately shots rang out from a 9mm Luger. Both victims were hit multiple times. The shooter walked away, but then returned and shot each victim twice more when he heard sounds coming from inside the victims' vehicle. Now believing both to be dead, he returned to his car and drove away. Ferrin would later be pronounced dead at the hospital.

On August 1, 1969, three San Francisco newspapers received an identical letter from someone taking credit for both the Lake Herman Road and Blue Rock Springs murders. Each letter also contained one third of a 408-symbol cryptogram which the killer claimed would provide his identity. He demanded that each of the newspapers publish their third of the cryptogram or else he would murder 12 more people the following weekend.

Only one of the newspapers, the *San Francisco Chronicle,* published their third of the cryptogram at that time, along with an article in which Vallejo Police Chief Jack Stiltz challenged the killer to send a second letter with more details to prove that he was in fact the real killer. A week later the *San Francisco Examiner* received a second letter. This one began "Dear Editor, this is the Zodiac speaking" (Graysmith, 2007). This was the first time the name by which the killer would come to be known was publicly used. This second letter contained details of both murders the police had never released to the public. They were now certain the writer was in fact the killer.

At the same time the second letter was received, two people in

Salinas, California, cracked the cryptogram. It was a message containing numerous misspelled words that read as follows:

> I LIKE KILLING PEOPLE BECAUSE IT IS SO MUCH FUN IT IS MORE FUN THAN KILLING WILD GAME IN THE FORREST BECAUSE MAN IS THE MOST DANGEROUS ANAMAL OF ALL TO KILL SOMETHING GIVES ME THE MOST THRILLING EXPERIENCE IT IS EVEN BETTER THAN GETTING YOUR ROCKS OFF WITH A GIRL THE BEST PART OF IT IS THAE WHEN I DIE I WILL BE REBORN IN PARADICE AND THEI HAVE KILLED WILL BECOME MY SLAVES I WILL NOT GIVE YOU MY NAME BECAUSE YOU WILL TRY TO SLOI DOWN OR ATOP MY COLLECTIOG OF SLAVES FOR MY AFTERLIFE EBEORIETEMETHHPITI

Contrary to what Zodiac represented in his letter, the cryptogram did not provide his identity. Less than two months later, on September 27, 1969, he would strike again. College students Bryan Hartnell, 20, and Cecilia Shepard, 22, were picnicking at Lake Berryessa in Napa County when a man approached holding a gun and wearing a black executioner's hood with clip-on sunglasses covering the eye holes. He also was wearing a bib-like piece of clothing that had a symbol drawn on it—a circle with a cross through it. The man claimed to be an escaped prison inmate from Montana, and told them he needed their car and money to make his way to Mexico. He pulled out some clothesline and instructed Shepard to tie up Hartnell. After doing so, the mysterious man then did the same to Shepard. Then without warning he pulled out a knife and stabbed both of them repeatedly.

Before leaving the scene, the killer stopped at Hartnell's vehicle and drew the circle design from his bib on Hartnell's door. Beneath it he wrote:

Vallejo
12-20-68
7-4-69
Sept 27-69-6:30
by knife

The killer then left the area and telephoned the Napa County Sheriff's Office from a payphone only a few blocks from their station to report his latest crime, identifying himself as the Zodiac killer (Kelleher & Nuys, 2002). Police traced the call back to the payphone, where they were able to lift a wet palm print from the receiver. At the same time, park rangers at Lake Berryessa, as well as deputies from the Napa County Sheriff's Department, were responding to the scene of the crime after fishermen found Hartnell and Shepard both still alive but badly injured. Shepard was conscious when the deputies arrived, and was able to give a good description of the attacker. She would lapse into a coma in the ambulance and die two days later. Hartnell survived the attack, and was able to give additional details from his hospital bed.

Two weeks later, on October 11, 1969, Zodiac claimed his seventh victim. Paul Stine, 29, was a San Francisco cab driver. At 9:55 p.m., a teenager called the San Francisco Police Department to report that a cab driver had just been shot, and that the attacker was walking toward the Presidio of San Francisco, a U.S. Army installation a few blocks away. The teen also reported that the shooter wiped off the cab before walking away. Police responded and found Stine still in his cab, dead from a 9mm gunshot to the back of his head. They also discovered that his wallet and car keys had been taken, as well as a section of his blood-stained shirt tail (Graysmith, 2007).

On October 14, 1969, the *San Francisco Chronicle* received a letter from Zodiac that contained a piece of Paul Stine's bloody shirt. In the letter, he threatened to start killing school children by targeting a school bus. In describing his planned method, he wrote, "just shoot out the front tire and then pick off the kiddies as they come bouncing out." Although such an attack would never happen, it was clear that Zodiac was becoming more and more motivated by the amount of media attention he was getting. A few days later, he called the Oakland Police Department demanding that lawyers F. Lee Bailey and Melvin Belli, both quite famous, appear together on a local television show. Only Belli appeared, and during the show a caller purporting to be Zodiac called in and agreed to meet with Belli. During the call he identified himself as "Sam." The meeting would never take place.

In November and December, 1969, Zodiac continued to mail his communiqués to both the press and the police. On November 8th, he sent a 340-item cipher that has never been decoded. The next day he sent a letter claiming that within minutes following the Paul Stine murder, two police officers stopped and talked to him, but then let him go. And then on December 20th, he sent a letter to Melvin Belli that included another piece of Paul Stine's bloody shirt. In the letter he asked Belli to help him.

For the next two years, Zodiac continued to send communiqués, many of them containing more symbols and cryptograms. He continued to threaten further murders, and took credit for attacks the police believed then, and continue to believe today, were committed by someone else. Then in 1971, Zodiac went silent. He remained silent until January 29, 1974, when the *San Francisco Chronicle* received one final letter from Zodiac. In it, he discussed the movie *The Exorcist,* and included a passage from Gilbert and Sullivan's *The Mikado.* The letter ended with the line "Me = 37, SFPD = 0" (The Exorcist Letter, n.d.).

Following this final letter, the Zodiac killer was never heard from again. He simply disappeared from the public's eye. Some have speculated that he died or went to prison for other crimes. Others have suggested that he simply lost his nerve for killing. And still others have postulated that he found religion. We may never know the reason he abruptly stopped his crime spree, but it has now been 40 years since that final communiqué, and not so much as a whisper out of him.

ANALYSIS AND CLASSIFICATION

Certainly there are some interesting facts about the Zodiac killer that can help us form a picture of this mysterious individual's personality. While it can never be more than mere speculation, we will take a look at some of the known preidentification inputs in an effort to develop an opinion about the type of offender Zodiac was.

Preidentification Inputs

Each of the following circumstances of Zodiac's crimes is an important piece of evidence to consider:
 • *Costume.* There are a couple things to consider about Zodiac's use of a costume during the daylight attack at Lake Berryessa. First, there is no evidence that he had used the costume up to that point, his third

attack. Only one victim from the first two shootings, Michael Mageau, survived the attack. He made no mention of a costume in his statement to police. Also, the fact that the costume had a specific design, to include the display of a symbol, indicates that its intended use went beyond merely to hide the attacker's identity. He was making a statement with the costume, but one must wonder to whom? Obviously he intended to kill both of the victims at Lake Berryessa. It would indicate that the costume was part of the killer's fantasy play, and that it facilitated some internal psychological need he had to live out the particular fantasy that preoccupied him.

• *Use of symbols.* Just before Zodiac first donned the costume, we see him begin to use cryptic symbols and cryptograms. In addition, he began sending letters to the newspapers, a clear indication he was being driven by the media attention surrounding his attacks. This type of activity is almost always an indication of an ego-directed killer. In contrast, opportunistic offenders like Gacy and Bundy would never place their killing routine at risk by taunting the police before they were even identified as a suspect. For them, the thrill is in the killing, not the media attention. And symbolic offenders, those who kill out of displaced hatred and rage, kill to quiet the emotional torment they experience. Media attention does little, perhaps nothing, to bring about that desired end. The symbolic offender may even experience some level of shame and guilt following their crimes. Media attention only intensifies those negative emotions if felt.

When the killer sent the 408-symbol cryptogram, he had to know that such a simple "substitution" code would be easy to break. So why use it? He likely did so for the same reason he left the symbol on the Lake Berryessa vehicle. It was likely just fantasy play, reinforced by the media attention he was getting. In his mind, he wasn't just another serial killer. He was now a mythical figure who held the power of life and death in his hands. The 340-symbol cryptogram has never been decoded. Decades later, people all over the world are still trying. But what if this cryptogram was nothing more than random scribblings that contained no message at all? It would be the perfect set-up. First, give the public an easily decipherable message to sensitize them to the mystery of Zodiac's methods, and then follow that with a message they can never possibly decipher. As long as people continue their efforts to break the code, it only adds to the mystery and legend of the Zodiac killer, perhaps its intended purpose all along.

• *Poor spelling.* When we look at Zodiac's numerous communiqués, we see many misspelled words. We must assume that this is the result of one of two things. Either it is related to a low level of academic achievement, or Zodiac learned English as a second language and is making phonetic spelling errors in his letters. He also makes other basic mistakes. For example, he abbreviates "Friday" as "Fry." In terms of syntax, however, his letters do appear consistent with an English-speaking person. It would thus seem reasonable to conclude that Zodiac was lacking academically, and had possibly dropped out of high school. It could also be that during his formative academic years, he was confined to a juvenile detention or psychiatric facility.

• *Location and victim selection.* He chose a well-known lover's lane to commit his first murders. This was likely not a random selection. He knew the area, and no doubt knew that any car he came across at that location would have two young people inside. In fact, his first three attacks all involved young couples engaged in a moment of intimacy. This is highly relevant. It is also relevant that he made no efforts to sexually assault any of his female victims. His attacks were thus not sexually motivated.

• *Written statements.* There are a number of subtle clues contained in Zodiac's many communiqués. A couple stand out. First of all, in a letter dated March 13, 1971, and sent to the Los Angeles Times, he refers to the police as the "Blue Meannies," an obvious but misspelled reference to the Beatles' *Yellow Submarine*. This at least tells us he has some connection to pop culture, and may help determine an age range for the killer. A more important clue, however, is found in the 408-symbol cryptogram. In it he writes, ". . . to kill something gives me the most thrilling experience. It is even better than getting your rocks off with a girl." Here he provides a dichotomy–killing versus having sex with a girl. Perhaps he has inadvertently shown us in this passage the very conflict that is motivating him . . . the one thing he has absolute power over (taking life) versus the one thing he has no power over (intimacy). He is perhaps convincing himself that he does in fact enjoy killing as a way of minimizing the pain he likely feels in being unable to develop and maintain an intimate relationship.

- One of the most telling circumstances of Zodiac's crimes is that he just decided one day to quit. Very few serial killers have ever walked away from their killing routine. And but for the letter in 1974, he has never been heard from again. There have been no further killings, no taunting letters to the police or press, no deathbed confessions, and no adult children coming forward to expose their father as the killer. He simply disappeared.

Classification

The Zodiac killer can be classified as an ego-directed killer with a deficient sexuality. He was likely in his mid-20s, white, unemployed, and had probably spent his youth in foster homes or a juvenile facility of some sort. He was poorly educated, but had some level of "street smarts." He probably read comic books, and went to the movie theater as often as he could. He may even have been a special ed student in school. He likely never had a girlfriend, which was probably the one thing he wanted most.

Like David Berkowitz, the infamous *Son of Sam* killer, Zodiac chose initially to attack young people engaged in intimacy. He was in effect destroying what he himself could not enjoy. But there is one thing that sets an ego-directed offender apart from the other two types. For the ego-directed killer, it is not the killing itself that motivates them, but rather the effect the killing has in filling the void in their sense of self and identity. Most such killers are *identity-diffused,* meaning they have no clear sense of identity. Their crimes allow them in a perverse and distorted way to walk out of the crowd and become someone unique. And while Zodiac was no doubt lacking in the sexuality component of identity, the notoriety he received following his crimes tended to at least temporarily close the gaping void he experienced in his sense of self. He truly had become someone unique, almost mythical, in part because of the mystery surrounding his methods and communiqués.

So what happened to him? Where is he today? The truth is the notoriety probably did have only a transitory effect on his insecurities. Eventually it burned out, but so too did his will to take innocent lives because it was never the act of killing that was paramount. It is likely that his final letter in 1974 was a half-hearted attempt to test the waters, but by then he had been relegated to the cold case files. He was attempting to reinvigorate the myth without having to kill again. When he failed, he simply walked away from it all. It may also be the case that the void his crimes temporarily filled was eventually filled permanently by something else, either religion or having finally found intimacy.

The opportunistic killer arguably never loses their insatiable desire to kill, and is stopped only after finally being captured, dying, or *aging-out* of their ability to carry out their crimes. Similarly, the symbolic killer never loses the deep-seeded hatred and rage that compels their crimes. If not captured, they tend to turn themselves in, commit suicide, or eventually die from alcohol or drug abuse. In the case of the ego-directed killer, however, the dynamic is different. What is important is to fill the void. It is the primary developmental task of all adolescents. The void that compels deviance may be filled with positive things like religion, military service, education, and most of all, intimacy with another human being. When that happens, then there is a hope the deviance will never again bubble to the surface.

So today, Zodiac would likely be 65-70 year old. He may have married and had kids, but probably has never told any of them of his crimes. He likely found employment eventually as a maintenance worker or janitor, or perhaps in a factory. His crimes have no doubt continued to haunt him. He may have a long history of alcoholism and failed relationships, and may be alienated from his children as a result. If he eventually died, then he took his secret with him. If he is still alive, it is likely he will do so in the future. Either way, chances are we have heard the last of the Zodiac killer, a young man who murdered to feel better about himself, got way too wrapped up in the notoriety and media attention, and then simply lost his nerve to kill. Whether he did so out of fear of being caught, or because he did in fact have some level of morality, we will never know.

Chapter 13

INTERVENTION STRATEGIES
Changing a Killer's Course Before They Kill

INTRODUCTION

Is there a way to identify and intervene in the life of a potential serial killer before they ever kill? Is there something that could've been done early on that would've prevented people like Ted Bundy and Edmund Kemper from ever considering serial murder as a viable option? We have presented in this text a clear picture of the internal deterrence system that compels a person to turn away from crime and deviance in favor of more socially-appropriate behaviors. The question that must be asked is whether it is possible during a child's earliest stages of development to identify deficits in the individual components of the child's internal deterrence system and correct those deficits before they manifest themselves in the form of deviant behavior.

Any theory of criminality must point to preventative strategies. To draw an analogy, if we are tasked with easing the congested traffic in a particular part of town, we will have little success unless we have a thorough understanding of where the traffic is originating, and where it is heading. By first understanding that we can then take the necessary steps to reroute the traffic into more efficient patterns before it ever reaches the congested area. Some will no doubt take the less efficient routes regardless of our best efforts to prevent them from doing so, but our goal of reducing the congestion can certainly be met. Another option is to reduce the congestion by investing in more traffic wardens, better synchronized traffic lights, and by adopting a more aggressive stance toward those who violate traffic laws in the congested area. But these reactive strategies only address the symptoms, and not the underlying problem.

In terms of criminality, we tend to take a reactive stance in America. We throw enormous amounts of human and financial capital at reacting to crime by investigating, prosecuting, and incarcerating the offender, yet by comparison, we spend very little trying to prevent criminality by intervening in a potential offender's early development. There are two obstacles to doing this. First, we have a political system that is at times reluctant to fund programs where immediate and measurable results cannot be documented. Any early childhood intervention program focused on reducing future criminality is by design one where only long term results can be measured. It requires a longitudinal method carried out over 10–20 years, with continued funding to do so.

The second major obstacle is the conservative nature of our criminal justice system. It tends to have little interest in the developmental history of the criminal offender, and little sympathy for those who were subjected to adverse developmental factors that may have influenced their decision to engage in deviance. It is a system that demands adherence to the statutory rules society has deemed appropriate, and acceptance of responsibility and the applicable consequences for violating them. The philosophy that guides our system is that regardless of a person's upbringing, unless they are mentally ill, in which case concessions are made, the individual is assumed to possess the capacity to know right from wrong, and thus there are no acceptable excuses for engaging in premeditated and unprovoked criminal deviance. With this type of underlying philosophy, there is less of a perceived need to understand the psychosocial developmental factors that contribute to criminality.

In spite of these obstacles, however, there have been a number of important studies over the years that have attempted to intervene in the lives of at-risk children at an early point in their development. One such study, begun in 1962, was the High/Scope Perry Preschool Program in Ypsilanti, Michigan. This study involved 123 high-risk African American children ages three to four. The children were all from lower socioeconomic families and had IQ scores in the 70–85 range, and thus were considered at high risk of failing school. Fifty-eight of the children were assigned to the experimental program group, while the rest, 65, were assigned to a control group. The groups were matched according to age, gender, IQ, and socioeconomic status.

Participants in the program group attended the Perry Preschool daily for 2.5 hours over a two-year period. The preschool provided a very high quality learning environment with a low teacher-to-child ration. Special attention was paid to each child's intellectual and social development, and individualized education plans were tailored to the child's needs. Additionally, teachers were required to meet each week with each family in their home environment. Parents took an active role in their child's education, and further, participated in small group sessions with other parents to discuss their child's progress, their own issues as a parent, and to provide each other some level of support. The progress of the children, both intellectually and socially, was then measured at various points in their development over the next approximately 25 years.

While the study was not initially intended as a delinquency deterrence program, but rather an academic intervention strategy, the former was indeed achieved. It was found that far fewer children from the program group than the control group were eventually arrested or adjudicated delinquent minors (Schweinhart, Barnes, & Weikart, 1993). By age 19, only 31% of the program group had been arrested, as compared to 51% of the control group. The program group also demonstrated a lower incidence of fighting and general misconduct. This trend continued into adulthood. By age 27, the control group had accounted for a total of 98 felony arrests, as compared to 40 for the program group, with a much lower number considered habitual offenders. There also were significant differences in both scholastic and socioeconomic success.

The results certainly support the utility of early intervention, and point to the positive effects of a child-centered education program that involves the parents in the child's learning. The High/Scope project targeted a number of risk factors associated with delinquency. Most importantly, the project facilitated academic success, which in turn strengthens a sense of self-efficacy. This then impacts identity formation in a positive way during adolescence. A child who internalizes academic success as part of their identity is significantly less at risk for engaging in deviant behavior.

Another important component of the High/Scopes project was the involvement of the parents at various levels, and the teacher's home visits. Parental involvement was found to be critical to the success of the High/Scopes project (Seitz, 1990). It allowed for positive attachment behaviors on the part of the parents. They assisted their children in academic assignments and provided positive feedback in response to academic achievement. By allowing teachers into their homes, the parents were able to get feedback on their parenting skills and environmental factors that facilitate learning. And by participating in the group sessions, they were able to get feedback and support from other parents. The simple lesson to be learned from this project is that positive and responsive involvement by parents in their children's education, combined with an education plan designed to maximize a child's learning, will increase their academic success and self-efficacy, and in turn promote a more secure parent-child attachment. These are the critical components of personality that ultimately will deter the individual from engaging in criminal deviance.

Similar results have been achieved by the Chicago Parent-Child Center (CPC) program. Created in 1967, the CPCs were established to provide educational and family support services to at-risk children between the ages of three and nine in some of Chicago's most poverty-stricken neighborhoods. The centers require parent participation for at least half a day each week, and are staffed with parent-resource teachers to facilitate the parents' active involvement. Additionally, the centers employ community outreach representatives who proactively work to identify children in the neighborhood who qualify for the program, and who make home and school visits with enrolled participants and their families.

The curriculum offered by the centers is designed to promote language and reading skills, as well as appropriate socioemotional development. They follow a child-centered format, with individualized instruction and relatively small staff-to-student ratios. Educational field trips and opportunities for constructive learning are frequent, and always with volunteer parents involved. In fact, parents are involved in essentially every aspect of the child's school day. They read to students, supervise play activities, and assist with arts and crafts, among other things.

In one longitudinal study of a matched 1989 graduating cohort of 878 CPC and 286 comparison-group children (Reynolds, 1997), it was found that participation in the program was associated with positive school performance, and that the longer a child participated, the more positive the results. A second study (Reynolds et al., 2001), which tracked 989 program participants and 550 similar children over a 14-year period, concluded that the children who were not part of the program were 70% more likely to be arrested for a violent crime by age 18. The study also concluded that the rate of neglect and abuse of those children participating in the program was half that of nonprogram children.

These programs and others like them clearly illustrate the benefits of early childhood intervention for at-risk children. They increase self-esteem and a sense of self-efficacy in the child by promoting academic achievement, and a more secure-attachment by involving the parents in their learning experience. They also have a positive impact on the parents themselves. By including them in their child's education, it gives them a sense of accomplishment when the child shows progress. The more confident a parent is in their parenting abilities, the more sensitive they will be to the needs of the child. And the more success a parent and child can experience together, the deeper and more secure their attachment to each other.

One of the benefits of Criminal Triad Theory is that it identifies three very clear developmental entry points where an intervention in the life of an at-risk child can be attempted: *attachment, moral development,* and *identity-formation.* A dysfunctional developmental course can be disrupted, at least in terms of preventing criminality, at any one of these three stages with a proper intervention strategy. It requires the ability on the part of teachers, social workers, and criminal justice professionals to recognize a criminal personality type in its developmental stage, and to have access to proven programs that will strengthen a young person's ability to self-deter from criminality. Each of the three entry points will be discussed briefly.

ATTACHMENT

The difficulty with identifying an insecure attachment in early childhood is that it is typically before the time when the child can really articulate the problem themselves. It is also before the time when the child is observed at any length by other than family members. While there is some assessment that takes place, perhaps if the family is involved in social service programs for financial assistance, housing, or medical care, it is typically minimal unless there is some indication of abuse. It isn't until the child begins school when their attachment behaviors can truly be observed for extended periods of time, thus allowing knowledgeable teachers and school counselors to identify a child in need of intervention. Unfortunately, training and instruction in this critical area is typically minimal in most elementary education programs. Dealing with an insecurely-attached child in the classroom can be frustrating and demanding. These children tend to be either egocentric, controlling, and manipulative, or they retreat to the back of the class and refuse to participate. Without the proper training, teachers may be less prepared to identify a child in need of intervention, and may inadvertently reinforce in the child the problematic behavior by reacting in ways that are counterproductive, such as with an authoritarian demeanor.

The identification of an attachment problem in early childhood should begin with the completion of a behavior inventory by the child's teacher which identifies behaviors known to be associated with poor attachment. These behaviors may include the following:

- Abnormal eye contact
- Self-control problems
- Destructive
- Cruel to other children
- Hoarding and hiding food and toys
- Inability to connect cause with effect
- Lack of conscience
- Preoccupied with fire, blood, or gore
- Poor peer relationships
- Stiffens when touched
- Incessant chatter and nonsense questions
- Chronic lying
- Learning disorders
- Self-isolation and avoidance behaviors

This behavior inventory should be completed over a period of days to establish that the behaviors do in fact represent a pattern. The inventory should include information about when the various types of behaviors are displayed by the child, and how the child reacts to attempts by the teacher to correct them. Many of these behaviors are displayed from time to time in most children, regardless of their upbringing, but the insecurely-attached child will display many of them on a continuing basis. When it is obvious that the child's behavior is in fact an established pattern, then the teacher should refer the matter to the school counselor to begin the intervention process.

The second stage of the identification process should involve engaging the parents. The purpose is to gain an understanding of the child's family structure and history, and to get a clear picture of the parenting style to which the child is being subjected. It is important to consider such things as:

- How many parents are present in the home? If only one, why?
- The developmental history of older siblings
- Any history of mental illness or criminality in the family
- The presence of drugs and alcohol in the home
- The family's socioeconomic status
- The form of discipline used by the parent(s)
- The parents' level of cognitive functioning

During this evaluation, it also gives the school counselor an opportunity to observe how the parent(s) and child interact. An insecurely-attached child will give clear indications of such in almost any activity involving the participation of the parent(s). Chances are the child will appear disinterested and detached. There will likely be little touching between the parent(s) and child, except in an effort to keep the child still. The child will likely fight against the efforts of the parent(s) to physically control them, and may even hit one of the parents.

In the case of an authoritarian or abusive parent, the child will display much different behaviors in a parent-counselor meeting. Once again the child will make little eye contact with either the counselor or the parent. They will likely be very subdued, and may appear quietly preoccupied. They will seem emotionally flat, and will answer questions with bodily movements (i.e., shaking head, shrugging shoulders, etc.) rather than verbally doing so. They will immediately comply with the demands of the parent, and may even look frightened in the parent's presence. If the counselor asks the child for feedback, the child will typically look to the parent for some nonverbal approval before answering.

The behavior of an abusive parent can also be recognized by a trained counselor. Abusive parents need to avoid detection, and will attempt to hide their abusive nature behind a facade of concern and caring. They will go to great lengths to portray themselves as loving parents, and will have various theories about the causes of their child's classroom behavior, none of which will involve them personally. They may attribute it to the child's temperament, or to a difficult pregnancy, or even to toxins in food products. If the parents are still together, and only one is abusive, then chances are the abusive parent will not be in attendance, and the parent that is there (typically the mother), will attempt to portray the other in an overly positive light, even when such information is not solicited by the counselor.

There are innumerable indicators, both in the child and in the parent(s), of problems in the home that may be disrupting the child's development of a secure-attachment. The counselor must look at the totality of the information gathered through the evaluation process in order to make a decision regarding intervention. Obviously, if there is physical evidence of abuse, then the counselor or the teacher must act immediately by following the proper protocol established for that particular school. School personnel are mandated reporters of abuse, and are obligated under the law to contact the appropriate authorities without delay. Short of this type of evidence being presented, however, the counselor must make a decision whether to recommend some type of intervention based on the observable behavior and self-report of both the child and the parent(s), and must do so with the parent(s) full involvement. Obviously, if the goal is to foster the development of a secure-attachment in the child, then the parent(s) must be part of any intervention strategy.

The first step in the intervention process is to gain the parent's full cooperation. This can be a difficult thing in some cases. Parents are obviously very protective and territorial when it comes to their children. Some simply are not interested in being told there may be a problem in the family. Also, in the minds of some parents to admit that intervention is necessary is to admit their failure as a parent. But part of the job of the counselor is to deal with this problem as best they can when it presents itself. They can do this by explaining to the parent how attachment problems will ultimately create significant academic and achievement problems for their child. Most parents want their children to succeed. By keeping the discussion in this context even the most reticent parents should be more willing to allow some type of intervention to take place, and more importantly, to participate themselves.

There are numerous programs available in essentially every geographic region of the country designed to address these issues. The two programs mentioned at the beginning of this chapter are good examples of successful programs. If both parents are still involved in the child's life, then a program in which the parents and child participate together should be tried. These programs are designed to teach more effective parenting skills that promote secure parent-child attachment. At the same time, they are designed to promote the development of positive social skills in the child. In some programs, the parents are mentored by successful parent-volunteers while the children are given the opportunity to build friendships with other children in the program. Many of these programs offer support groups where parents can get help with any problems they may be experiencing, and just as importantly, encouragement from other parents struggling with the same issues. These programs may also include home visits that allow a trained professional to observe the family in their natural setting, referrals for medical care and other social services, and perhaps even academic tutoring for the child.

More often than not there is only one parent present in the home of a child in need of intervention, and in many cases, the other parent is not even involved at all in the child's life. In this case, especially for a young boy, then an effective intervention includes a combination of a parent-child program as described above, and a mentoring program that pairs the child with an older adolescent or an adult to interact socially. Mentoring programs come in many forms, with some being confined to the school setting where close supervision can be maintained. These are especially good for very young children and older adolescent mentors. The mentors are typically of the same sex as the child, and spend time with them a few times each week talking and participating in recreational activities together. It allows the child to form a relationship with a role model who provides positive feedback and reinforcement, and promotes in the child the development of positive social skills and a sense of self-efficacy.

A community-based mentoring program involving an adult mentor is also advantageous, and doesn't confine the child-mentor relationship to the school. There are a number of such programs; however, the *Big Brothers Big Sisters* program is one of the more successful. It pairs primarily single-parented children, ages five to 18, with adult mentors in a structured program designed to foster positive development. The program has been evaluated extensively. One often-cited study (Tierney, Grossman, & Resch, 1995) found it to be successful in promoting academic achievement and deterring the child from drug and alcohol use, thus closing two of the most powerful gateways into delinquency and criminality. The study looked at 959 10- to 16-year-olds from eight different cities who had applied to the program. Half of the youths were randomly assigned to a mentoring group and matched with a mentor. The other half were assigned to a waiting list. After 18 months, the two groups were compared, with the results being recorded and attributed to the child's relationship with their adult mentor and presented in Figure 13.1.

Essentially all well established and successful mentoring programs show positive outcomes in the young people who participate. They

OUTCOME	% CHANGE
Antisocial Activities	
Initiating drug use	-45.8%
Initiating alcohol use	-27.4%
Number of times hit someone	-31.7%
Academic Outcomes	
Grades	3.0%
Scholastic competence	4.3%
Skipped class	-36.7%
Skipped day of school	-52.2%
Family Relationships	
Improved parental relationship	2.1%
Trust in parent	2.7%
Lying to parent	-36.6%
Peer Relationships	
Emotional support	2.3%

Figure 13.1. Outcome comparison of Big Brothers-Big Sisters participants and nonprogram youth 18 months after applying to the program.

typically report an increase in academic achievement, with more positive attitudes toward school and better attendance. Perhaps the most important outcomes reported, at least in terms of deterring criminality at an early point in development, are less substance abuse and less contact with the juvenile justice system. Most mentoring programs also report increases in their participants' socioemotional development. These programs lead to stronger parent-child relationships, and because of the more positive social skills program participants tend to build, the kids also develop friendships that provide stronger social support and foster healthier identity formation.

MORAL DEVELOPMENT

Another entry point to the development of a criminal deterrence system in a young person is in the process of *moral development.* There was a time in America when moral/ethical training was commonplace in the public schools. Education was rooted in religion, and the Bible was considered the moral code by which children were to be raised and socialized. But near the end of the nineteenth-century, things started to change as science and rationalism began to replace religion as the primary source of society's guiding principles. Great thinkers like Darwin, Marx, Nietzsche, and Freud began to redefine society and its institutions without the involvement of God. This trend only intensified following the brutality of World War I, when it became apparent that a God-based morality had simply become insufficient as a means of maintaining peace among the diverse peoples of the world. The move toward secularism shifted into high gear.

The final blow to traditional moral training in the public schools occurred in the 1960s, when for the first time there was no longer a moral consensus. The moral-ethical standards of white America were no longer acceptable to black Americans. The male dominance that was built into our traditional moral code, originating in the Bible, was no longer acceptable to women struggling for equal opportunity. And the morality of a society that had willingly marched off to two world wars was simply no longer viable for young people across the land who were fed up with war, assassinations, and the prospect of nuclear annihilation. For many, it was a time to redefine our moral code, and to do so in secular terms without the influence of religion.

During this chaotic time in our social evolution, educators began to pull away from using the schools for moral training, leaving it instead to family and church. There was a renewed emphasis on separation of church and state, and with the public school system funded primarily by the government, it became inevitable that the courts would pressure public schools to rid themselves of any sign of God's influence. With this paradigm shift, they began to face criticism for teaching moral relativism and secular humanism, criticisms that to this day remain leveled against our educational system by significant segments of our society. The change also brought other unwanted outcomes that eventually set off alarms. Academic achievement scores dropped while disciplinary problems increased. This, coupled with an increase in school violence, eventually led two U.S. Presidents, Bill Clinton and George W. Bush, to once again make character development an important component of our educational paradigm, albeit still from a secular perspective.

Currently there are a number of different programs being carried out in our public and private schools that are aimed at character development. Superka et al. (1976) have identified five basic approaches to character development in the schools:

• *Inculcation:* This approach views moral and ethical values as socially and culturally determined. They therefore endeavor to shape a child's moral development by getting them to accept and internalize the values of the dominant culture. They do this through positive and negative reinforcement, role playing activities, and by presenting positive role models who demonstrate the desired values. These role models are typically famous individuals, both contemporary and historical, in whose lives the children are immersed. They are taught about their value-oriented acts in the hope that the young person will emulate those behaviors in their own lives. Stories such as George Washington cutting down his father's cherry tree, or Abe Lincoln walking miles to return a borrowed book have been used by teachers for years as lessons in honesty and virtue. The young person is a passive participant in this type of moral education. They are expected to simply internalize the values they are presented, and to act in ways consistent with those values. When they do, they are reinforced. When they act in ways that are inconsistent with those values, they are punished.

The downside to this type of education is that it devalues individual moral reasoning. Moral and ethical values become a template the child is expected to use to shape their behavior. It also tends to devalue the diversity found in American culture, and fails to fully recognize that moral and ethical values are not universal across cultures. When educators attempt to teach alternative values through the thoughts and actions of such thinkers as Malcolm X, Cesar Chavez, and Saul Alinsky, they invariably meet with resistance from parents and administrators alike. Ultimately schools require funding, and when educators are perceived to be breaking from the values of the dominant culture, a fear invariably arises that such teaching may jeopardize the money they need to operate. This has been seen time and again, even in our present day. Depending on the geographic area, when schools are found to be teaching such things as the rights of gays and lesbians, the unscientific nature of Intelligent Design, or the economic sense of opening the U.S. border to Mexico, school boards and parent organizations often step in to bring a halt such teaching. In 2008, a bill was presented in the Illinois State Senate that would have discontinued funding for any university in Illinois that hired former radicals to serve in faculty positions. Many of these individuals, now in the later years of their careers, were radicalized on moral-ethical grounds. To suppress such teaching greatly devalues diversity in moral-ethical thought, and ultimately acts to suppress the student's own moral development by limiting their access to ideas.

- *Moral development:* This approach is based on Lawrence Kohlberg's theory of moral development, discussed previously. It is a cognitive approach that attempts to influence a young person's moral reasoning skills in an effort to lead them to a higher stage of moral thought. Kohlberg himself proposed the establishment of *Just communities* within schools that would facilitate a young person's moral development by engaging them in the operation of the school. He developed this concept after visiting an Israeli *kibbutz* in 1969. A kibbutz is a communal settlement with shared responsibilities, even among the children. Kohlberg was shocked by how advanced the children were in terms of their moral development, and attributed it to their participation in the daily affairs of the kibbutz. He believed that by infusing in them a sense of responsibility for the success of the kibbutz, this increased their ability and desire to think and act in more moral and ethical ways for the good of the group.

Kohlberg's concept of a Just community in an educational setting involved establishing a democratic relationship between teacher and students. The students would participate in such activities as choosing curricula, scheduling school activities, and even setting and enforcing conduct standards. As a cognitive theorist, Kohlberg believed that if young people were to begin thinking in moral-ethical ways, then their behavior would follow. For example, he believed that if young people were partly responsible for enforcing a disciplinary code, even to the extent of ruling on the type of disciplinary action to be taken against another student, then the chances of them violating the conduct standards would be less likely.

In reality, Kohlberg's conception has seldom been attempted in a school setting. For the most part, such an idea is easily thwarted by large class sizes, government-mandated curricula, school boards that are reluctant to deviate from traditional methods, and overworked teachers who simply haven't the time to dedicate to such a program. There are, however, schools that attempt to incorporate programs based on Kohlberg's theory. Such programs make use of moral dilemmas, role-playing, and group discussions of moral-ethical issues. They are primarily cognitive-based programs that attempt to influence a young person's behavior by influencing how they think about various moral-ethical issues. Unlike the *Inculcation* approach, this approach doesn't simply subsume a set of predominant values and then endeavor to get the student to internalize those values. Rather, its goal is to foster in the young person the ability to think critically about moral-ethical issues, and to confront those issues at an increasingly higher stage of moral reasoning.

• *Analysis:* This method takes a more scientific approach to values education. Its goal is to promote a reliance on rational thought and reason to decide moral-ethical questions. It tends to focus primarily on social values, and teaches a student to fully research an issue before taking a well-reasoned position based on the best available evidence. Methods used in the classroom may involve individual or group study projects, field study, and group discussions about the evidence for and against a particular moral-ethical position. It is essentially a critical thinking method that endeavors to "unpack" a problem, analyze it, study the available evidence, test hypotheses, and then take a position that can be supported.

A good example of an issue that can easily be addressed in this manner is that of abortion. To come to an informed decision, students might do a number of things. First, they may research the medical literature to find a consensus on the issue of when a fertilized human egg—a *zygote*—becomes a living human being. Then they might review the church's teachings on the issue. Perhaps they might research the statistical data on the prevalence of abortion among various socioeconomic classes and age groups. Certainly at some point, the students will gather in a group to discuss their evidence and findings. Hopefully, they will reach their own consensus on the rightness or wrongness of the practice based on their research, and not grounded in emotion or purely religious beliefs.

This, too, is a cognitive approach that attempts to influence behavior by promoting critical thinking skills. This method is quite amenable to the demands and limitations of our modern education system. It can be done is a very structured way, and because it is based somewhat on a scientific methodology and the students' active involvement, it tends to avoid the emotional debate that inevitably follows when a teacher simply addresses a controversial moral-ethical issue, a circumstance that may easily be misinterpreted by the public as the teacher, or even the school for that matter, taking a particular stand on the issue; usually one that goes against the dominant values of that particular geopolitical region.

The downside to this approach is that it assumes the student will be actively engaged, and that they have the cognitive tools necessary to research and understand abstract moral-ethical issues. Neither, of course, is the case in all situations. The paradox is that the kids who most need moral-ethical guidance may be the least able to participate in this type of instruction. Also, such an approach will do little for the student suffering from extreme deficits in self-esteem and self-efficacy, or those forced to endure an abusive or authoritarian parent. On the one hand, they are presented new expectations relating to their own moral-ethical behavior, but then they are forced to return to a home where they are treated in ways that are inconsistent with those expectations. It leads to a cognitive dissonance in the young person that is both confusing and self-defeating. A purely cognitive approach may have some value as a proactive measure, but as a reactive measure applied to a young person already experiencing character deficits, it may have limited utility.

• *Values clarification:* With its foundation in humanistic psychology, this approach is focused on promoting self-awareness in the young person, and leading them to clarify their own personal values with the goal of actualizing those values. It is neither a purely cognitive approach, nor is it focused only on a culturally-accepted set of moral-ethical values. Instead, it teaches the student to use both reasoning and emotional awareness to evaluate behavior choices. Its goal, as is the goal of all humanistic approaches, is self-actualization, or the maximizing of one's potential and sense of self-fulfillment. It is an individualistic approach in that the student is free to define their own set of desired values. Once those values are clarified, then the student is encouraged to actualize them in their personal life, and to affirm or deny them by reflecting on the consequences of their actions, both positive and negative.

This approach is not unlike the humanistic awareness groups of the 1970s. What is important is that the student communicates with other students in an honest and transparent manner about what they think and how they feel. Group activities are a necessary part of this type of moral instruction; however, the teacher avoids influencing the students toward any particular set of values. Freedom of choice, even a choice of what values they will make their own, is a crucial element of this approach. The role of the teacher is to facilitate self-awareness, self-evaluation, and the exercise of free choice. It is believed that the more a student can feel free to make their own value choices, and to affirm or deny those choices by their own experience without fear of criticism or judgment, then the more likely it is they will make reasoned choices that promote self-actualization.

The downside to this approach is that it requires a great deal of openness and honesty on the part of the student. In fact, in many ways, it mirrors a humanistic therapeutic approach. The problem with such an approach is that it can potentially do as much harm as good if the teacher or group leader is not skilled in this area or prepared to deal with the emotionality of adolescent honesty. It is difficult for a young person to expose themselves to their peers, as this method requires. Their very identity is at stake. To pursue an honest self-evaluation of their own values before a group of students requires that the student search their own experience and feelings to understand why they believe as they do. Such searching can at times cause painful memories to surface that were previously repressed. The teacher or group leader must be prepared to de-escalate any emotional self-reporting or group interactions. To be effective, they must be part facilitator and part counselor.

In reality, most teachers are unwillingly to pursue honest self-awareness in a group setting. There is consensus within our educational system that schools are not the place for this type of activity. Some schools actually prohibit teachers from having any deep personal exchanges with students. This prevents a personal relationship from developing between the teacher and student that may continue outside the school setting. Teachers who target students for sexual exploitation tend to do so by first establishing rapport on an emotional level. Young people with attachment-based problems will quickly bond with a teacher who shows an interest in them and provides positive feedback. For this reason, and the potential liability associated with it, schools are less inclined to provide this type of instruction on more than a superficial level.

• *Action learning:* This experiential approach attempts to promote moral-ethical development by engaging the student in prosocial behaviors. A number of schools are now requiring students to participate in a predetermined number of hours of community service as part of their requirements for graduation. Students may volunteer their time at a local nursing home, a pet rescue and adoption center, meals on wheels for the sick and elderly, or perhaps even a program that plants trees in areas where fire or logging has depleted the foliage. Other schools take summer trips to depressed areas around the world where students can assist in building schools, tutoring their counterparts, installing clean water systems, and a host of other activities designed to improve the quality of life for the young people they visit.

The goal of these types of programs is to place the young person in a position where moral-ethical behavior becomes necessary in order to complete the task. The hope is that they will eventually internalize the values they are forced to demonstrate by their actions. Also, by participating in altruistic and socially-conscious behaviors, it will only strengthen the young person's sense of self-efficacy by allowing them to accomplish a task for the benefit of others, and increase their self-esteem by allowing them the opportunity to achieve successful outcomes. Many adolescents simply have no conception of their own potential for goodness. They may in fact believe that such potential simply doesn't exist, at least not in them personally. It is a belief that can very quickly become a self-fulfilling prophecy. The goal of action learning is to provide the circumstances for a young person to prove to themselves through their own behavior that their potential for goodness is in fact real. It is truly a powerful method that can have life-changing results.

In the context of Criminal Triad Theory then, the goal of moral intervention is to provide at-risk youth the opportunity to more fully develop a moral deterrence mechanism (MDM). Early identification is critical, and can possibly be achieved with a combination of psychometric testing and family history review. The personality characteristics that may indicate problems in the area of moral development include:

- Habitual fighting with other children
- Extreme Selfishness
- Verbally aggressive
- Few close friends
- Abusive toward animals
- Destructive with other students' property
- Inappropriate affect (for example, laughs during a sad movie or when a classmate skins their knee)
- An interest in blood and gore
- Routinely gets caught cheating or stealing

Once a young person is identified as *at-risk* by the school, it is then imperative to engage the parents and develop an intervention strategy. Cognitive approaches to moral education have not been found to be terribly successful. Therefore a combination of individual values clarification and experiential learning may serve as the best strategy. The school must engage the community in this endeavor to provide opportunities for this type of learning. Business owners, social services directors, and community outreach coordinators are all in a position to provide the school an ongoing conduit for placing at-risk youth. Additionally, membership in organizations such as the Boy and Girl Scouts of America, 4H, Civil Air Patrol, and Explorers should be highly encouraged. These programs all foster moral-ethical decision-making and behaviors. They also promote the development of positive social skills and personal self-efficacy. All encourage behaviors that benefit the goals of the group, and thus they act to reduce a young person's egocentricity. When a young person abandons their own self-interests in favor of those of the group they only strengthen their empathic awareness of the needs and feelings of others. This is a key component in the development of a moral self and its associated deterrence mechanism.

IDENTITY FORMATION

Intervention in the life of an adolescent experiencing identity diffusion is one of the toughest challenges our educational system faces. In our modern and complex society, the types of problems experienced by adolescents are themselves becoming increasingly more complex. With single-parent families now the majority in most economically depressed areas, children experimenting with drugs at increasingly younger ages, gang violence and child exploitation at all-time highs, and a juvenile justice system that has neither the time nor the funding to attack the problem in a proactive manner, it is little wonder why so many adolescents are at risk of succumbing to the temptation to engage in delinquent behavior. Most have significant identity problems caused by a combination of poor parenting, a lack of opportunity and hope, and the inevitable low self-esteem that accompanies poor academic performance and/or unachievable parental expectations. The end result of this toxic mix of circumstances is an adolescent lacking the necessary self deterrence mechanism (SeDM) that will compel them to turn away from criminality in favor of a course of conduct that is consistent with the core values of their ideal-self. In the most severe cases, the adolescent may even be void of an ideal-self.

Typically, adolescents with identity problems make themselves known either by engaging in deviant behavior or by failing to achieve academically. It is not difficult to identify them when you look at their overt actions together with their family history and home environment. It is likely the style of parenting which has been imposed on them will fall at either extreme of the parenting spectrum. Either the parents will be uninvolved in the adolescent's life to any significant degree due to some dysfunction such as substance abuse or alcoholism, or they will be authoritarian and overly involved in the life of the adolescent, such is often seen in a fundamentalist religious family. Either way, their ability to form a healthy and robust identity is greatly inhibited. Either they wander aimlessly in the fog of family dysfunction, never quite finding themselves, or they are denied the opportunity to even begin the search.

So how do we intervene in the life of an adolescent experiencing identity diffusion or foreclosure? We do so by providing them the opportunity to try out new and healthy components of identity in the hope that they will commit to them rather than to criminality or to some type of deviant group membership. In order to develop a positive identity, the adolescent needs to have a sense of purpose and the belief that they are capable of fulfilling that purpose. Simply put, they need to achieve something positive in their life, aspire to some future goal, and believe in something by which they can define themselves. If you ask an adolescent to define themselves, they will do so with their beliefs, their goals, and their achievements. An adolescent experiencing identity problems has likely not enjoyed the self-confidence and autonomy needed to venture out and experiment as adolescents who develop healthy identities do.

While cognitive approaches are an important component of any intervention strategy, they are not terribly successful as a singular strategy. Adolescents with identity problems need experience and the opportunity to succeed. Cognitive approaches should be utilized as a way of processing and reinforcing those successes when they are experienced. It is therefore imperative that an intervention strategy begin with some experiential opportunity. Wilderness programs have been used successfully for years. In these programs, at-risk adolescents are taken into the wilderness under the supervision of trained adult personnel and forced to survive for a period of time by working as a team to complete various survival-oriented tasks. These programs are designed to tap into the young person's potential, and to allow them to prove to themselves, perhaps for the very first time, that they are capable of succeeding. They are pushed to their physical and emotional limit in an effort to extricate them from the unhealthy and self-defeating thinking and behaviors that have prevented them from developing a positive identity.

Programs such as these employ a myriad of other experiential opportunities. "Project SOAR" (Skills Organization through Attitude Reconstruction) takes a group of at-risk adolescents and teaches them to fly a glider. Their training requires a great deal of discipline and focus, something that is new to many of these young people. The training culminates in their first solo flight, which serves also as a powerful metaphor for their first step into a new life with a new and positive identity. The great benefit of this program, along with others that actually teach a skill, is that the adolescent takes away from the experience something they can hang on to for the remainder of their lifetime. Whether it is flying a glider, scuba diving, rodeo riding, or sailing, the newly acquired skill has the potential for becoming such a strong component of their identity that it will become the centerpiece of who they are. And the inevitable spike in self-esteem will hopefully be accompanied by academic achievement, goal-setting, and even a healthier sense of their sexuality.

Unfortunately, a newly configured identity based on some type of experiential intervention is still a fragile thing. The adolescent still must return to the same home environment, the same neighborhood, and the same socioeconomic circumstances. The progress made can easily be wiped away with the first stressful encounter they experience. For this reason, it is imperative that an after-care plan be implemented that includes regular contact with an adult mentor and the opportunity to continue practicing the skill they have acquired. It is also important that the adolescent remain connected with the other adolescents from their intervention group. Ideally, regular awareness groups with the other adolescents should be held. One of the problems for an adolescent with identity problems is their lack of connectedness to others, which is the primary reason they so often end up affiliating with unhealthy peer groups. Maintaining the intervention group allows the adolescent to open up and share with other young people they can identify with, and with whom they share similar experiences. It instills a sense of connectedness in their lives, and provides a safe base of operations for self-exploration and sharing. It allows the adolescent to be transparent, and in doing so, provides an environment where continued growth can occur.

This after-care plan should have a graduated intensity level, with very close contact maintained in the weeks immediately following the intervention activity. Eventually, as the young person's personality continues to develop with these newly acquired values now internalized, the amount of contact can be reduced, with the goal of eventually discontinuing it altogether, at least on an intervention level. It is hoped that the adolescent will continue their acquired skill well into adulthood, and maintain lifelong friendships from the intervention group. The combination of increased self-esteem, a heightened sense of self-efficacy, and the development of positive social relationships based on shared experience are powerful building blocks in the development of a self deterrence mechanism (SeDM).

SUMMARY

In terms of criminality, the great benefit to intervening in the life of an at-risk child is that it can lead to the development and strengthening of their *social, moral,* and *self* deterrence mechanisms. Intervention strategies can be focused during early childhood on attachment issues, hopefully with the parents involved. The quality of their early attachment will determine the quality of their later social and intimate relationships, and the more successful they are at building and maintaining positive relationships, the less likely they are to engage in deviant behavior.

Intervention can be focused on moral development throughout childhood. The goal is to increase their capacity to empathize, and with it, their ability to feel sympathy in response to another's distress. The more they are able to do this, the more likely their behavior will be altruistically-motivated rather than criminally so. Feeling both a concern for other people and a temptation to victimize them creates a cognitive dissonance in the individual. One or the other will win the day depending on the strength of the young person's internal deterrence system, and more specifically, their moral deterrence mechanism (MDM). The strength of a young person's MDM will only increase over time the more they practice prosocial behaviors and become more sensitive to the distress and hardships of others.

And then we have interventions aimed at developing more fully an adolescent's identity, perhaps the last stop on the road to adult criminality. Strategies and activities focused on providing the adolescent opportunities for achievement, accomplishment, and self-acceptance can have a profound impact. Successful outcomes lead to self-efficacy, and an adolescent who sees themselves as capable of achieving something positive and worthwhile will move forward in a goal-oriented manner, all the while defining their identity by the goals that empower them and the accomplishments they experience. Each successful outcome closes the identity gap a little bit more. Few adolescents will claim criminality as a desired component of their ideal-self. Consequently, the more narrow the gap between their perceived and ideal-self, the less likely it is that the temptation to engage in criminality will see the light of day.

And that concludes our journey through the mind of the serial killer. Some would argue that the age of the serial killer has now passed. It is true that as investigative technologies have advanced, the likelihood of a serial offender, regardless of the nature of their crimes, has been greatly reduced. But there will no doubt always be serial killers, as well as serial rapists, arsonists, and those who habitually commit essentially every other type of crime. Regardless of the crimes they commit, our three typologies—*symbolic, opportunistic,* and *ego-directed*—remain the same. Some will commit their crimes as a way of calming the emotional turmoil associated with an abusive or authoritarian parent. Others will do so because of the material or psychological gain they derive from the crime, having little ability to either empathize or sympathize with their victims. And still others will commit their crimes to fill the void in their sense of self. In short, serial offenders, regardless of their crimes, will continue to be *other-focused, act-focused,* or *self-focused.*

Any study of the serial killer to understand their crimes apart from their psychosocial development will yield few benefits. They are people with few, if any redeeming qualities. Those who have taken the time to meet with serial killers inside the walls of the prisons where they are confined have discovered that they are manipulative, self-protecting, and psychologically impenetrable. Some are in denial of their crimes, while others refuse to talk about them. Still others portray themselves as victims while they dehumanize their own. The deviant personality characteristics that compelled their crimes are typically magnified in prison where they have adaptive benefits.

As stated in Chapter 1, the real benefit to studying serial offenders, especially those who kill, is to work backwards from the onset of their criminal offending to determine what it was in their psychosocial development that led to their offending. What was it that precluded them from developing the necessary internal deterrence system that would have compelled them to turn away from the temptation to kill? By identifying those variables, then we are in a position to develop effective interventions to change the developmental course of what could potentially be a future serial killer. That, of course, is the real benefit to studying society's worst and most heinous offenders.

BIBLIOGRAPHY

Abrahamsen, D. (1985). *Confessions of Son of Sam.* New York: Columbia University Press.

Ainsworth, M. (1978). *Patterns of attachment: A psychological study of the strange situation.* Hillsdale, NJ: Lawrence Erlbaum.

American Extremism: Dan Gayman. (n.d.). Retrieved December 10, 2013, from http://archive.adl.org/learn/ext_us/gayman.html?xpicked=2.

Atkins, S., & Slosser, B. (1977). *Child of Satan, child of God.* Plainfield, NJ: Logos International.

Batson, C. D. (1991). *The altruism question: Toward a social psychological answer.* Hillsdale, NJ: Lawrence Erlbaum.

Baumrind, D. (1971). Current patterns of parental authority. *Developmental Psychology, 4*(1, Pt.2), 1–103. doi: 10.1037/h0030372.

Baumrind, D. (1991). The influence of parenting style on adolescent competence and substance use. *The Journal of Early Adolescence, 11*(1), 56–95. doi: 10.1177/0272431691111004.

Berkowitz, D. (1999, March). Son of hope: My story. Retrieved March, 2013, from http://www.inetworld.net/hutrcc/testimony.htm.

Besen, W. (2010, July 23). Jesus and the Son of Scam. Retrieved from http://www.huffingtonpost.com/wayne-besen/jesus-and-the-son-of-scam_b_645258.html.

Bothe, E. (2002, December 15). Facing the Beltway snipers, profilers were dead wrong. *The Baltimore Sun.*

Bowlby, J. (1973). *Attachment and loss.* London: Hogarth Press.

Bowlby, J. (1999). *Attachment and loss* (2nd ed., Vol. 1). New York: Basic Books.

Bragg, R. (1997, January 17). 2 bomb blasts rock abortion clinic at Atlanta; 6 are injured. *New York Times.*

Brenner, M. (1997, February). American nightmare: The ballad of Richard Jewell. *Vanity Fair.*

Brodzinsky, D. (1987). Adjustment to adoption: A psychosocial perspective. Clinical Psychology Review, 7, 25–47.

Bronx Woman Is Shot to Death As Shooting Outbreak Spreads; Vacation Plans. (1976, July 30). Retrieved from http://select.nytimes.com/gst/abstract.html?res=F40C16F7355E1A738DDDA90B94DF405B868BF1D3.

Bugliosi, V., & Gentry, C. (1974). *Helter skelter: The true story of the Manson murders.* New York: Norton.

Canter, D. V., & Wentink, N. (2004). An empirical test of Holmes and Holmes's Serial Murder Typology. *Criminal Justice and Behavior, 31*(4), 489–515. doi: 10.1177/0093854804265179.

Canter, D. V., Alison, L. J., Alison, E., & Wentink, N. (2004). The organized/disorganized typology of serial murder: Myth or model? *Psychology, Public Policy, and Law, 10*(3), 293–320. doi: 10.1037/1076-8971.10.3.293.

Cheney, M., & Cheney, M. (1992). *Why: The serial killer in America.* Saratoga, CA: R & E.

Cheney, M. (1992). *Why: The serial killer in America.* Saratoga, CA: R & E.

Douglas, J. E. (2006). *Crime classification manual: A standard system for investigating and classifying violent crimes.* San Francisco, CA: Jossey-Bass.

Douglas, J. E. (2006). *Crime classification manual: A standard system for investigating and classifying violent crimes.* San Francisco: Jossey-Bass.

Douglas, J. E., Ressler, R. K., Burgess, A. W., & Hartman, C. R. (1986). Criminal profiling from crime scene analysis. *Behavioral Sciences & the Law, 4*(4), 401–421. doi: 10.1002/bsl.2370040405

Duffy, J. (1974, April 18). Extreme measures in Zebra hunt—police to stop a lot of people. *San Francisco Chronicle.*

Edmund Kemper. (2014). The Biography Channel website. Retrieved 04:57, Mar 28, 2014, from http://www.biography.com/people/edmund-kemper-403254.

Emmons, N. (1986). *Manson in his own words.* New York: Grove Press.

Erikson, E. H. (1964). *Childhood and society.* New York: W. W. Norton.

Erikson, E. H. (1968). *Identity: Youth and crisis.* New York: W. W. Norton.

The Exorcist Letter. (n.d.). Retrieved April 6, 2014, from http://www .zodiackiller.com.

Faraci, D. (2013, July 28). The psychos who turned surf city into murder city. Retrieved March 24, 2014, from http://badassdigest.com/2013/07/28/the-psychos-who-turned-surf-city-into-murder-city/.

Festinger, L. (1957). *A theory of cognitive dissonance.* Stanford, CA: Stanford University Press.

Frisk, M. (1964). Identity problems and confused conceptions of the genetic ego in adopted children. *Acta Paedo Psychiatrica, 31,* 6–12.

Gibson, D. C. (2004). *Clues from killers: Serial murder and crime scene messages.* Westport, CT: Praeger.

Gilligan, C. (1982). *In a different voice: Psychological theory and women's development.* Cambridge, MA: Harvard University Press.

Gilmore, J., & Kenner, R. (1996). *The garbage people: The trip to helter-skelter and beyond with Charlie Manson and the family.* Los Angeles: Amok.

Godwin, M. (1998). Reliability, validity, and utility of extant serial murderer classifications. *Criminologist, 22*(4), 194–210.

Goebel, B. L., & Lott, S. L. (August, 1986). *Adoptees' resolution of the adolescent identity crisis: Where are the taproots?* Paper presented at annual meeting of the American Psychological Association, Washington, D.C.

Graysmith, R. (2007). *Zodiac.* New York: Berkley Books.

Guinn, J. (2013). *Manson: The life and times of Charles Manson.* Waterville: Thorndike Press large print biography.

Hazan, C., & Shaver, P. (1987). Romantic love conceptualized as an attachment process. *Journal of Personality and Social Psychology, 52*(3), 511–524. doi: 10.1037/0022-3514.52.3.511.

Hoffman, M. L. (2000). *Empathy and moral development: Implications for caring and justice.* Cambridge, U.K.: Cambridge University Press.

Holmes, R., & DeBurger, J. (1985). Profiles in terror: The serial murder. *Probation, 49,* 29–34.

Holmes, R. M., & DeBurger, J. J. (1988). *Serial murder.* Newbury Park, CA: Sage.

Holmes, R. M., & Holmes, S. T. (1998). *Contemporary perspectives on serial murder.* Thousand Oaks, CA: Sage.

Holmes, R. M., & Holmes, S. T. (1998). *Serial murder.* London: Sage.

Howard, C. (1979). *Zebra: The true account of the 179 days of terror in San Francisco.* New York: R. Marek.

Irishredrose (2010, October 29). *Edmund Kemper talks about killing his mother* (Video file). Retrieved from http://www.youtube.com/watch?v=MKK3XDI7wTE.

Kelleher, M. D., & Nuys, D. V. (2002). *"This is the Zodiac speaking": Into the mind of a serial killer.* Westport, CT: Praeger.

Kemper, E. (1974, March). I was the hunter and they were the victims [Interview by M. Von Beroldingen]. Retrieved March 26, 2014, from http://www.truecrime.net/kemper/interview.htm.

Keppel, R. (2005). *The riverman: Ted Bundy and I hunt for the Green River killer.* New York: Pocket Books.

Kohlberg, L. (1981). *Essays on moral development, vol. I: The philosophy of moral development.* San Francisco: Harper and Row.

Kohlberg, L. (1984). *The psychology of moral development: The nature and validity of moral stages.* San Francisco: Harper & Row.

Kovaleski, S. (2010, July 12). Backers give "Son of Sam" image makeover. *New York Times.*
Lawson, C. A. (2002). *Understanding the borderline mother: Helping her children transcend the intense, unpredictable, and volatile relationship.* Northvale, NJ: Jason Aronson.
Leyton, E. (2003). *Hunting humans: The rise of the modern multiple murderer.* New York: Carroll & Graf.
LiveLeak.com–flashback: Zebra Murders and the Cupertino killer–Shareef interviews Jackson–Sharia in Aceh province. (n.d.). Retrieved May 10, 2013, from http://www.liveleak.com/view?i=b5a_1318046668.
Lunde, D. T., & Morgan, J. (1980). *The die song: A journey into the mind of a mass murderer.* New York: W. W. Norton.
Main, M., & Solomon, J. (1990). Procedures for identifying disorganized-disoriented infants during the Ainsworth strange situation. In M. Greenberg, D. Cichetti, & M. Cummings (Eds.), *Attachment in the preschool years* (pp. 121–160). Chicago: University of Chicago Press.
Marcia, J. (1973). Ego-identity status. In M. Argyle (Ed.), *Social encounters.* New York: Penguin.
Marcia, J. E. (1966). Development and validation of ego-identity status. *Journal of Personality and Social Psychology, 3*(5), 551–558. doi: 10.1037/h0023281.
Martingale, M. (1995). *Cannibal killers: The impossible monsters.* New York: St. Martin's Press.
McCrary, G. (2004). Criminal profiling: The reality behind the myth. *Monitor on Psychology, 35*(7), 66.
Meltzhoff, A. N. (1982). Infant imitation and memory: Nine-month-olds in immediate and deferred tasks. *Child Development, 59,* 217–225.
Michaud, S. G., & Aynesworth, H. (1989). *Ted Bundy: Conversations with a killer.* New York: Signet.
Muhammad, E. (1965). *Message to the blackman in America.* Chicago: Muhammad Mosque of Islam No. 2.
Nelson, P. (1994). *Defending the devil: My story as Ted Bundy's last lawyer.* New York: W. Morrow.
Newton, M. (2006). *The encyclopedia of serial killers* (2nd ed.). New York: Checkmark Books.
O'Connor, T. (2012). Profiling Serial Killers. Retrieved March 29, 2013, from http://www.drtomoconnor.com/4050/4050lect04.htm.
One of two girls shot is in serious condition. (1976, November 28). Retrieved from http://select.nytimes.com/gst/abstract.html?res=FA081FFF355C107B93CAAB178AD95F428785F9.

The Otherside Lounge. (n.d.). Retrieved December 9, 2013, from http://www.historycommons.org/entity.jsp?entity=the_otherside_lounge_1.

Pederson, D., Klaidman, D., & Smith, V. (1998, July 27). A mountain manhunt. *Newsweek, 132*(4), 16.

Ramsland, K. (n.d.). Edmund Kemper: The coed butcher. Retrieved March 20, 2014, from http://www.crimelibrary.com/serial_killers/predators/kemper/edmund_1.html.

Reamer, F. G. (2003). *Criminal lessons: Case studies and commentary on crime and justice.* New York: Columbia University Press.

Ressler, R. K., Burgess, A. W., & Douglas, J. E. (1988). *Sexual homicide: Patterns and motives.* Lexington, MA: Lexington Books.

Reynolds, A. J. (1997). The Chicago child-parent centers: A longitudinal study of extended early childhood intervention. *Institute for Research on Poverty.* Retrieved June 1, 2009, from www.irp.wisc.edu.

Reynolds, A. J., Temple, J. A., Robertson, D. L., & Mann, E. A. (2001). Long-term effects of an early childhood intervention on educational achievement and juvenile arrest: A 15-year follow-up of low-income children in public schools. *Journal of the American Medial Association, 285*(18), 2339–2346.

Ross, M. (2005, April 13). Eric Rudolph's rage was a long time brewing. Retrieved December 9, 2013, from http://www.nbcnews.com/id/7398701/.

Rudolph, E. (2005, April 13). Eric Rudolph's Written Statement. Retrieved December 3, 2013, from http://www.armyofgod.com/EricRudolphStatement.html.

Rudolph, E. (2005, April 13). Eric Rudolph's Written Statement. Retrieved from http://www.armyofgod.com/EricRudolphStatement.html.

Rule, A. (2009). *The stranger beside me.* New York: Pocket Books.

Russell, S. (2002). *Lethal intent.* New York: Kensington.

Sack, K. (2007, August 30). Richard Jewell, 44, hero of Atlanta attack, dies. *New York Times.*

Sanders, P. E., & Cohen, B. (2011). *The zebra murders: A season of killing, racial madness, and civil rights.* New York: Arcade.

Schoenberg, C. (1964). Adoption: The created family. *The ANNALS of the American Academy of Political and Social Science, 355*(1), 69–74. doi: 10.1177/000271626435500109.

Schuster, H., & Stone, C. (2005). *Hunting Eric Rudolph.* New York: Berkley Books.

Schweinhart, L. J., Barnes, H. V., & Weikart, D. P. (1993). *Significant benefits: The High-Scope Perry preschool study through age 27.* Ypsilanti, MI: High/Scope Press.

Scott, G. G. (2007). *American murder.* Westport, CT: Praeger.

Seitz, V. (1990). Intervention programs for impoverished children: A comparison of educational and family support models. In R. Vasta (Ed.), *Annals of child development: A research annual* (Vol. 7, pp. 73–103). London: Jessica Kingsley.

Serial Murder. (n.d.). Retrieved November 3, 2012, from http://www.fbi.gov/stats-services/publications/serial-murder.

Snook, B., Eastwood, J., Gendreau, P., Goggin, C., & Cullen, R. M. (2007). Taking stock of criminal profiling: A narrative review and meta-analysis. *Criminal Justice and Behavior, 34*(4), 437–453. doi: 10.1177/0093854806296925.

Stephens, H. (1973, August). I'll show you where I buried the pieces of their bodies [Editorial]. *Inside Detective.* Retrieved March 20, 2014, from http://www.truecrime.net/kemper/article.htm.

Sullivan, K. M. (2009). *The Bundy murders: A comprehensive history.* Jefferson, NC: McFarland.

Superka, D. P. (1976). *Values education sourcebook: Conceptual approaches, materials analyses, and an annotated bibliography.* Boulder, CO: Social Science Education Consortium.

Terrorist Organization Profile. (2010). Retrieved December 7, 2013, from http://www.start.umd.edu/start/data_collections/tops/terrorist_organization_profile.asp?id=28.

Terry, M. (1987). *The ultimate evil: An investigation into America's most dangerous satanic cult.* Garden City, NY: Doubleday.

Thomas, A., & Chess, S. (1977). *Temperament and development.* New York: Brunner/Mazel.

Tierney, J. P., Grossman, J. B., & Resch, N. L. (1995). *Making a difference: An impact study of Big Brothers Big Sisters* (Rep). Philadelphia: Public/Private Ventures.

Vollers, M. (2006). *Lone wolf: Eric Rudolph : Murder, myth, and the pursuit of an American outlaw.* New York: HarperCollins.

Washington State Institute for Public Policy. (1996). *Juvenile offenders: How often do they become adult offenders in Washington State?* Retrieved June 6, 2009, from www.wsipp.wa.gov.

Watson, C. (n.d.). Helter Skelter I (August 8–9): Will you die for me? Retrieved October 4, 2013, from http://www.aboundinglove.org /sensational/wydfm/wydfm-014.php.

Wysong, P. (2013, January 21). Report: 1500 abortion clinics have closed since 1991. Retrieved December 9, 2013, from http://www.lifenews.com/2013/01/21/report-1500-abortion-clinics-have-closed-since-1991/. (n.d.). Retrieved from http://www.ariseandshine.org/.

INDEX

4H, 110, 245

A

Action learning, 252-253
ADX Florence Supermax Prison, 189
Aesthetic, 113-118
Aime, Laura Ann, 202
Ainsworth, Mary, 23-29, 43, 261, 264
Alexander's Disease, 32
Alinsky, Saul, 248
Altruistic motivation, 53, 63-65, 76-79, 82-84, 91
Anarchist, 116-118
Anti-defamation League, 194
Antisocial identity, 130-131
Antisocial personality disorder, 138-139, 142
Anxiety, 26-29, 36-37, 44-46, 61, 88, 96, 146-148
Anxious-ambivalent insecure attachment, 29, 43, 45
Anxious-avoidant insecure attachment, 29, 43, 46
Anxious-preoccupied insecure attachment, 44-45, 47-48
Army of God, 189-193
Assimilation phase, 20
Atascadero State Hospital, 216, 221
Atkins, Susan, 177-180
Attachment, 23-34, 38-40, 43-50, 85-88, 91, 93, 98-99, 102, 120, 124, 126-127, 134, 136-137, 141, 146, 152, 169-171, 187, 222, 225, 239, 240-241, 243-244, 252, 257, 261, 263, 264
Attention Deficit and Hyperactivity Disorder, 36
Authoritarian parenting, 25, 41-42, 45, 59-60, 69-71, 95, 110, 114, 127-128, 131-132, 145-152, 169, 171, 241-242, 250, 255, 258
Authoritative parenting, 40-42, 129
Avoidant Personality Disorder, 147, 149

B

Bailey, F. Lee, 230
Ball, Brenda Carol, 201
Batson, Daniel, 64-65
Baumrind, Diana, 39
Beach Boys (the), 176, 184
Beame, Abe, 159
Beat Movement, 121-122
Beatles (the), 176, 182, 186, 233
Beausoleil, Bobby, 177, 179
Behavioral sequence, 20
Belli, Melvin, 230-231
Belongingness, 51, 170
Benicia (CA), 227
Bergen, Candice, 176
Berkowitz, David, 6, 15, 155-157, 159, 160-173, 185, 234
Berkowitz, Nathan & Pearl, 163
Big Brothers Big Sisters, 246-245, 266
Bipolar disorder , 139
Black Panthers, 107, 177
Blue Meanies, 233
Blue Rock Springs Park, 228
Borderline Personality Disorder, 147, 220
Borrelli, Joseph, 159-160
Bowlby, John, 26-27, 33, 44, 261
Bowman, Margaret, 205
Boy and Girl Scouts of America, 253
Boys Town, 180
Branch Davidians, 192

Breslin, Jimmy, 157, 160-161, 168
Brigham Young University, 204
Bronx, 157, 163, 165, 262
Brooks, Stephanie, 207
Brunner, Mary, 177
Bugliosis, Vincent, 175-180, 183, 262
Bundy, Theodore, 137, 199-214, 222-225, 232, 236, 263-264, 266
Burr, Ann Marie , 200
Burton, Richard, 180
Bush, George W., 247

C

Cabrillo College, 217
California Department of Justice, 227
Campbell, Caryn, 203-204
Capone, Al, 52
Centennial Olympic Park, 17, 189, 196, 198
Central nervous system, 31
Central Washington University, 201
Chandler, Karen, 205
Chavez, Cesar, 248
Chess, Stella, 34
Chicago Parent-Child Center Program, 238
Christian Identity Movement, 194
Church of Israel, 194
Civil Air Patrol, 253
Classical Conditioning, 61, 81, 171
Clinton, Bill, 247
Coffey, Joseph, 156
Cognitive dissonance, 6, 250, 257, 262
Congruous identity, 130-131
Contagious crying, 55
Conventional morality, 69, 74
D.B. Cooper, 227
Criminal Personality Type, 23-34, 46-47, 53, 120, 133, 135, 154, 187, 198, 240
Criminal Triad Theory, 23, 53, 79-80, 104, 154, 240, 253
Crowe, Bernard, 177
Crowell, Theodore Robert, 206
Culver, Lynette, 203
Cunningham, Julie, 203
Curtis, Susan, 204

D

Darwin, Charles, 246

Day, Doris, 176
DaRonch, Carol, 204
Deficient identity, 130, 132, 145
Dehumanization, 222
Delinquency, 21, 43, 115, 120, 234, 245
Denaro, Carl, 157-158
Dendritic spreading, 31
DeMasi, Donna, 158
Diel, John, 158
Difficult child, 37-38, 41, 169
Discordant identity, 130-131
Dismissive-avoidant attachment pattern, 46
Disorganized-disoriented insecure attachment, 264
Disorganized killer, 10-11, 20
Dobson, James Dr., 207, 211
DSM-IV, 138, 142-143, 147-149

E

EGO, 96, 102, 124, 130, 136, 140, 144, 168, 186-187, 262, 264
Egocentric empathy, 55
Ego-directed offender, 139-140, 142, 144-145, 152, 168, 171, 234
Elizabeth Lund Home for Unwed Mothers, 206
Empathic awareness, 49, 53-60, 64, 79, 82-85, 115, 136, 143, 146, 254
Empathy, 54-58
Erikson, Erik, 23, 124
Esau, Alexander, 159
Ethics, 53, 75-81, 83
Evans, Daniel (Gov.), 208
Evergreen State College, 201
Exorcist (movie), 231, 262
Explorers, 253

F

Falco, Betty, 165
Faraday, David, 227
FBI, 7, 10, 12, 14, 16-17, 20, 189-193, 197, 227, 268
Fearful-avoidant attachment pattern, 46-49
Ferrin, Darlene, 228
Festinger, Leon, 6
Folger, Abigail, 177-178
Fort Benning (GA), 194

Fort Campbell (KY), 195
Freud, Anna, 87
Freud, Sigmund, 87, 246
Freund, Christine, 158
Frykowski, Wojciech, 177-178

G

Gacy, John Wayne, 137, 225
Gayman, Dan (pastor), 194-261
Georgia Bureau of Investigation, 194
Geographic profiling, 17
Gibault School for Boys, 180
Gilligan, Carol, 75-76, 79, 82, 263
Global empathy, 55
God, 104-107, 156, 160, 189-193, 246, 261
Goodness-of-fit, 38-41
Green River Killer, 223, 263
Guillain-Barre Syndrome, 32

H

Haight-Ashbury District, 175
Hallett, Sally, 219
Hartnell, Bryan, 229-230
Hawkins, Georgeann, 201
Hawthorne, Alice, 190
Healy, Lynda Ann, 200-201
Hedonist, 115-116
Hedonistic killer, 13-14
Heinz Dilemma, 66, 68, 73, 76
Helter Skelter, 176-179, 262-263, 266
Henry Cowell Redwoods State Park, 218
High/Scope Perry Preschool Program, 237-238, 265
Hinman, Gary, 177, 179
Histrionic Personality disorder, 142
Hoffman, Martin, 54-56
Holmes, H.H., 223
Holmes (Ronald and Stephen), 12-15, 262-263
Humanistic Psychology, 251
Humanity, 53, 73, 77, 79-82, 86
Hyper-ideological self, 4, 188

I

ID, 186
Ideal self, 123-124, 129-134, 145, 254, 258

Identity achievement, 128
Identity crisis, 124, 263
Identity diffusion, 126, 132, 147, 254-255
Identity foreclosure, 127
Identity-formation, 23-24, 50, 86-88, 99, 119-126, 130, 132, 134, 136-137, 145, 170, 172, 185-186, 197, 225, 238, 240, 246, 254
Identity gap, 123-132, 137, 140, 58
Identity moratorium, 126
Ideological self, 87-88, 122, 170
Illinois State Senate, 248
Inculcation, 247, 249
Indiana School for Boys, 181
Insanity, 8-9
Interest-oriented, 90
Intermittent Explosive Disorder, 147-151
Internal deterrence system, 23-25, 46, 152, 154, 211, 214, 225, 236, 257, 259

J

Jensen, Betty Lou, 227-228
Jewel, Richard, 190, 196, 261, 265
Jones, Tom, 180
Justice, 9, 16, 53, 71, 75-83, 85, 116, 135, 142, 159, 227, 237, 240, 246, 254, 262-263, 265-266

K

Kaczynski, Ted ("Unabomber"), 5
Kasabian, Linda, 177-180
Keenan, Rosemary, 157-158
Kemper Clarnell, 220
Kemper, Edmund, 102, 215-225, 236, 262-266
Kemper, Edmund Sr., 220
Kemper, Edmund (grandfather), 220
Kemper, Maude, 220
Kennedy, John F., 175
Kent, Debra, 203
Kibbutz (Israel), 248
King County Sheriff's Dept, 201
Kleiner, Kathy, 205
Kloepfer, Elizabeth, 202-203, 208
Kohlberg, Lawrence, 23, 65-69, 72-74, 76, 78, 83, 248-249, 263
Koo, Aiko, 217

Krenwinkel, Patricia, 177-179
Ku Klux Klan, 194

L

LaBianca, Leno, 175, 178-179
LaBianca, Rosemary, 179
Lake Berryessa, 229-232
Lake Herman Road, 227-228
Lauria, Donna, 157, 161
Leach, Kimberly Diane, 206
Laetrile, 194, 197
Lennon, John, 190
Levy, Lisa, 205
Lincoln, Abraham, 247
Liu, Alice, 218
Lomino, Joanne, 158
LSD, 164
Luchessa, Anita, 217
Lupo, Sal, 161
Lust killer, 14
Lyons, Emily, 192

M

Maddox, Kathleen, 180
Mageau, Michael, 228, 232
Main, Mary, 30
Major depression, 139
Malcolm X, 248
Manson, Charles, 174-187, 201, 262-263
Manson, Charles Jr., 181
Manson, Donna Gail, 201
Manson, William, 180
Marcia, James, 124-125, 264
Marijuana, 70, 116, 164, 194-195
Marx, Karl, 246
Melcher, Terry, 176-177
Mentoring, 244-246
Mexico, 229
McQueen, Steve, 180
Mikado (the), 231
Missionary killer, 13
Mixed killer, 10
Modus operandi, 12, 18
Moral deterrence mechanism, 51-52, 54, 84, 142, 146, 253, 257
Moral development, 23-24, 31, 50-51, 65, 67-69, 72-74, 85, 87-88, 92, 120, 134, 136-141, 240, 246-248, 253, 257, 263
Moskowitz, Stacy, 161-162, 168
Mullin, Herbert, 218, 222
Multiple sclerosis, 32
Murrah Federal Building, 108, 192, 197
Myelination, 31-32

N

Nantahala National Forest, 194
Napa County Sheriff, 230
Narcissistic Personality Disorder, 142-143
Naslund, Denise, 201
National Training School for Boys, 181
McNeil Island, 182, 185
Neglectful parenting, 43, 46, 115, 126, 132, 137, 140-141, 144, 186
Neurocognitive organization, 31-33
Neuron, 31-32
New Woman All Women Healthcare Clinic, 192
New York City Fire Department, 171
Nietzsche, Friedrich, 246
Nihilist, 116
NYPD, 155, 157, 159

O

Object permanence, 33
Obligation-oriented, 92
Oliverson, Denise, 203
Opportunistic offender, 136, 139, 140, 142, 168, 171, 209, 224
Oregon State University, 201
Organized killer, 10, 20
Otherside Lounge, 191-192, 265
Ott, Janice Ann, 201

P

Parent, Steven, 178
Parks, Roberta, 201
Pelham Bay, 157
Perceived self, 123, 129-132, 145
Permissive parenting, 69, 115, 137
Pesce, Mary Ann, 217
Philosophical ideology, 103, 113
Placido, Judy, 161
Polanski, Roman, 176-177

Political ideology, 103, 107-108, 109-112, 117-118
Pornography, 207, 212-214
Postconventional morality, 72
Power and control killer, 14
Preconventional morality, 66
Presidio of San Francisco, 230
Prestige-oriented, 91
Profiling, 5, 8-9, 15-17, 22, 262, 264, 266
Project SOAR, 256
Psychological moratorium, 124, 126
Purpose-oriented, 91

Q

Queens (NYC), 157-158, 160-161

R

Rancourt, Susan Elaine, 201
Religious ideology, 103-104, 107, 196
Ridgeway, Gary, 223
Rockefeller, Nelson, 208
Rudolph, Deborah, 194
Rudolph, Eric, 17, 188-195, 198-199, 265-266
Rudolph, Patricia, 193
Rudolph, Robert, 17, 188, 192
Rule, Ann, 202, 205-208, 265

S

Sanderson, Robert, 192
Sandy Springs (GA), 191-196
San Francisco, 182, 219, 227-228, 230-231, 262-263
San Francisco Chronicle, 228, 230-231, 262
San Francisco Examiner, 228
Schall, Cindy, 217-218
Schizophrenia, 13, 19, 139
Scott, Walker (Col.), 180
Seattle Police Department, 201
Sebring, Jay, 177-178
Secure attachment, 26, 28, 38-39, 43, 45-48, 86-87, 91, 93, 124, 127, 187, 240, 243
Self-deterrence mechanism, 52, 103, 129-130, 142, 254, 257
Self-efficacy, 25, 41, 91, 128, 139, 141-142, 150, 170, 198, 238-240, 244, 250, 252, 254, 257-258

Self-esteem, 41, 45, 89-90, 97, 110, 116, 118, 123, 129, 132, 146, 150, 184, 250, 254, 256-257
Sexual efficacy, 95-101
Sexual expression, 94-101
Sexual image, 95, 99
Sexual portrayal, 95, 99-101
Sexual sadism, 222
Sexual self, 4, 87-88, 122, 155, 170, 172
Sexuality, 6, 94-95, 99-102, 122, 128, 130-131, 133, 173, 185, 222, 234, 256
Shepard, Cecilia, 229-230
Slow-to-warm, 37
Smith, Melissa, 202
Snowmass Village (CO), 203
Social deterrence mechanism, 47-50, 52
Social self, 4, 87-90, 122, 170, 174, 185
Spahn Ranch, 175, 177, 179
Sparks, Karen, 200, 209
Stiltz, Jack, 228
Stine, Paul, 230-231
Stoic, 114, 117
Stone, Charles (Sp. Agent), 194
Strange situations experiment, 27
SUPEREGO, 186-187
Suriani, Valentina, 159
Swango, Michael, 6
Symbolic offender, 136-137, 145-147, 149-152, 167, 169, 171, 196, 209, 210, 222, 225, 232
Sympathetic arousal, 53, 60-61, 79, 82-85, 87, 115, 143, 146, 211

T

Tate, Sharon, 174, 176-179, 182-184, 186
Taylor, Elizabeth, 180
Taylor Mountain, 201, 210
Teamsters, 157
Temperament, 31-41, 151, 169-170, 172, 243, 266
Terminal Island, 181
Thomas, Alexander, 34
Thomas, Cheryl, 205
Thorpe, Rosalind, 218
Threshold of responsiveness, 34
Thrill killer, 13
Topanga Canyon (CA), 175

U

Unconditioned response, 61
Unconditioned stimulus, 61
University of California at Santa Cruz, 216
University of Puget Sound, 207
University of Utah, 203
University of Washington, 200, 207
U.S. Supreme Court, 180
Utilitarian, 117-118, 122
Utopian, 117-118

V

Valenti, Jody, 157-159
Values, 66, 69-71, 73, 86, 93, 107, 116, 132, 185-186, 190, 216, 247-254, 257, 266
Van Houten, Leslie, 179-180
Violante, Robert, 161-162, 168
Visionary killer, 13
Voskerichian, Virginia, 158-159

W

Washington, George, 247
Washington State Institute for Public Policy, 138, 266
Watson, Tex, 176-177, 180
Wilcox, Nancy, 202
Wilson, Dennis, 176, 184
Wuornos, Aileen, 15, 102

Y

Yellow Submarine (Beatles), 233
Yonkers Police Department, 162

Z

Zodiac killer, 7, 154, 226-235, 263
Zygote, 250

CHARLES C THOMAS • PUBLISHER, LTD.

INTRODUCTION TO PRIVATE INVESTIGATION *(3rd Ed.)*
By Joseph Anthony Travers &
Joshua M. Travers
2014, 308 pp. (7 x 10)
$48.95 (paper), $48.95 (ebook)

INTELLIGENCE AND PRIVATE INVESTIGATION
By Hank Prunckun
2013, 240 pp. (7 x 10), 7 il., 18 tables
$35.95 (paper), $35.95 (ebook)

A STUDY GUIDE FOR COMMON SENSE POLICE SUPERVISION *(5th Ed.)*
By Gerald W. Garner
2014, 122 pp. (7 x 10)
$26.95 (spiral), $26.95 (ebook)

HISPANICS IN THE U.S. CRIMINAL JUSTICE SYSTEM
By Martin Guevara Urbina
2012, 442 pp. (7 x 10), 3 il., 6 tables.
$79.95 (hard), $59.95 (paper), $59.95 (ebook)

COMMON SENSE POLICE SUPERVISION *(5th Ed.)*
By Gerald W. Garner
2014, 366 pp. (7 x 10)
$49.95 (paper), $49.95 (ebook)

MANAGING THE INVESTIGATIVE UNIT *(2nd Ed.)*
By Daniel S. McDevitt
2012, 236 pp. (7 x 10), 2 tables
$54.95 (hard), $34.95 (paper), $34.95 (ebook)

INTRODUCTION TO CRIMINAL JUSTICE RESEARCH METHODS *(3rd Ed.)*
By Gennaro F. Vito, Julie C. Kunselman &
Richard Tewksbury
2014, 276 pp. (7 x 10), 12 il., 6 tables.
$44.95 (paper), $44.95 (ebook)

THE QUIET THREAT *(2nd Ed.)*
By Ronald L. Mendell
2010, 272 pp. (7 x 10), 4 il., 6 tables
$63.95 (hard), $43.95 (paper), $43.95 (ebook)

CRISIS INTERVENTION IN CRIMINAL JUSTICE/ SOCIAL SERVICE *(5th Ed.)*
By James E. Hendricks & Cindy S. Hendricks
2014, 472 pp. (7 x 10), 5 tables.
$59.95 (paper), $59.95 (ebook)

DISASTER RESILIENCE
By Douglas Paton & David Johnston
2006, 344 pp. (7 x 10), 22 il., 9 tables.
$73.95 (hard), $53.95 (paper), $53.95 (ebook)

FUNDAMENTALS OF CIVIL AND PRIVATE INVESTIGATION *(3rd Ed.)*
By Raymond P. Siljander &
Darin D. Fredrickson
2014, 318 pp. (7 x 10), 89 il., 3 tables.
$49.95 (paper), $49.95 (ebook)

CRIMINAL JUSTICE TECHNOLOGY IN THE 21st CENTURY *(2nd Ed.)*
By Laura J. Moriarty
2005, 334 pp. (7 x 10), 5 il., 15 tables.
$48.95 (paper), $48.95 (ebook)

O'HARA'S FUNDAMENTALS OF CRIMINAL INVESTIGATION *(8th Ed.)*
By DeVere D. Woods, Jr.
2013, 620 pp. (6 x 9), 67 il., 41 tables.
$44.95 (hard), $44.95 (ebook)

HOMELAND SECURITY LAW AND POLICY
By William C. Nicholson
2005, 410 pp. (7 x 10), 9 il., 7 tables.
$65.95 (paper), $65.95 (ebook)

Find us on Facebook
FACEBOOK.COM/CCTPUBLISHER

TO ORDER: 1-800-258-8980 • books@ccthomas.com • www.ccthomas.com